positions asia critique

T0335133

encountering violence:
media and memory in asia

volume 31   number 4   november 2023

A Dedication

This issue's cover image, a kaleidoscope of past *positions* covers, marks the thirty-year anniversary of the journal. In addition, the collage gestures toward the Korean traditional patchwork called *jogakpo*, a kind of Korean-style quilt. Taking inspiration from the folk art that salvages discarded materials to create something anew, contemporary artists and activists have adopted its aesthetic form as a method of healing from past and ongoing traumas and divisions. Artist Shine Shin-Kim, for example, has created interactive quilt projects with survivors of trauma in a symbolic act of healing by stitching disparate pieces of cloth. Likewise, an organization called Jogakpo brings together diasporic Koreans, including those from the North and South, to open dialogue toward reconciliation amid the ongoing Korean division. In the spirit of healing and renewal, the cover image is dedicated to the thirty years of the journal's stewardship under founding editor Tani Barlow, and to honor the fearless "encountering of violence" in this special issue of *positions*.

—Suzy Kim, Senior Editor

Contents

**encountering violence:
media and memory in asia**

Han Sang Kim and Sandeep Ray
Encountering Violence: Media and Memory in Asia   733

Peter J. Bloom
Voicing the Malayan Emergency: Ventriloquizing Subjectivity in British
Colonial Film and Radio   741

Sandeep Ray
Frenemies on Film: Rescreening the Sino-Indian War of 1962   769

Han Sang Kim
Can the "Comfort Women" Footage Speak? The Afterlives of Camera Images
as Document and the Flow of Life   803

Juyeon Bae

Mnemonic Politics around the Japanese Colonial Era in Post–Cold War Taiwan:
Wei Te-sheng's Colonial Trilogy and Post–New Cinema   839

Chung-kang Kim

Animating the Trauma: Colonial Atrocities and the Use of New Media
in Contemporary South Korean Museums   863

Sudarat Musikawong and Malinee Khumsupa

Archiving Facts and Documentary Films: Sites of Memorial Struggle
for the October 6, 1976, Massacre in Thailand   893

Contributors   919

Encountering Violence: Media and Memory in Asia

Han Sang Kim and Sandeep Ray

One may say that violence and the emergence of modernity were significantly interrelated at both the macro and micro levels. Establishing modern political systems and defining the borderlines of modern polities inevitably accompanied large-scale confrontations, which were reconfigured into a modern type. Various forms of violence—colonial, interstate, and internecine— necessarily paralleled the restructuring of time, space, and human mobility in the emerging capitalist system. Why does studying violence in Asia matter? What insights can the region's violent past and present bring into our discussion of the modern world?

This special issue of *positions: asia critique* originated during a collective endeavor in response to the Rohingya crisis in Myanmar's Rakhine State. Scholars, mostly from the region, gathered at a workshop titled "Sight and Sound: Challenges and Ethics of Visual Representations of War and Con-

positions 31:4   DOI 10.1215/10679847-10714233
Copyright 2023 by Duke University Press

flict in Asia," hosted by Singapore University of Technology and Design, to present their ongoing research into the still evolving lineages, forms, and discussions of violence in the media. The editors believe that the ongoing Rohingya crisis continues to share the entangled structures stemming from Asia's violent trajectories, and its media representation can be interpreted with careful reference to past cases from Asia. The "Rohingya war," if we may call it that, is a long-twentieth-century conflict embedded in postcolonial obsessions of race, ethnicity, religion, and nationhood. At the time of the gathering in Singapore in 2018, investigations into the Rohingya crisis and analyzing its relationship with the media had not been fully developed by academics. The studies are still evolving—now compounded further by the forcible seizure of the nation's administration by the junta. To welcome developing voices and ideas, to have some basis for discussion based on ground realities, and to provide a theory/practice balance to academic studies of war, we had invited journalists who were in the middle of covering the atrocities to join the forum. Drew Ambrose (Al Jazeera) discussed how shifting ground realities affected the tone and depth of media reports emerging from Myanmar. Taimor Sobhan (Fortify Rights, Bangkok) delved into the ever-increasing state of "compassion fatigue," positing that the public today is so inundated with gory news reports that our ability to react, sympathize, and politically galvanize has receded in recent years, especially with the overexposure and commodification of news and social media. Soren Kittel (Funke Media Group, Berlin) discussed the disturbing issue of the somewhat arbitrary standards held by journalist in their reporting in Rakhine, especially in situations where it becomes almost impossible to corroborate many of the stories being narrated by individuals. According to Kittel, the invariable errors made in the process of instantaneously relaying such stories in the era of social media may have grave consequences. The startling proximity of the ongoing killings, even as we somberly gathered around to read our papers in a safe environment, created a sense of futility as to what academics can do to help in such situations. The presenters did agree, however, that studying the visual and aural representation of violence in Asia will provide us, in the long run, with some insight into ways in which we can gauge the interaction, complicity, and mutual anchoring effect between the violent past in the media and the violent present.

This special issue explores the ways in which the violent experiences in Asia's past and present—including colonial rule, imperial expansion and mobilization, wartime massacres and exploitation, cold war conflicts and divisions, and state violence and oppression—are remembered, represented, and reproduced in the media. Discussing violence in Asia might have certain distinctive qualities or properties. Most explorations we found, typically involved some level of engagement with two considerations: the way various legacies of external and indigenous colonialisms have shaped power structures, and how the relatively late arrival of several forms of mass media to Asia (with the notable eruption of social media in the early twenty-first century) make it possible to track some of their effects in engendering conflict and violence. Is this sufficient to merit a case for looking at violence and its relationship with the media in Asia, as different from how its manifests in the Global North? The editors argue that it might help us understand the relationship between violence and modern political systems and its intersections with media in a way that is more relevant to Asian societies that embraced widespread visual and aural media around the same time they plunged into processes of state formation, whether colonial or postcolonial, and started developing certain social identities. (Yet, as we prepare this volume, breaking news of the Russian invasion of Ukraine reminds us that problems of identity and border delineation remain incomplete, even in Europe, and the conflict of reportage over propaganda is being fought zealously across a larger mediascape than ever before. While these articles focus on Asia, we concede that modern war tests the limits of the efforts to create, disseminate, and intercept narratives in the media, regardless of location.)

These "entangled structures" of imperialization, colonization, and the cold war (Chen 2010: 212) have made the mediascapes in Asia a specter for recurring confrontations with the past in distorted ways. Unresolved traumatic conflicts repeatedly return from the colonial past to haunt the visual and auditory imaginations of current audiences, their effects lingering in current postcolonial states' national imaginary. The sensory practices utilized by imperial regimes reconstitute themselves to be compatible with seemingly benign postimperial states in the control of friends and foes. Asia's cold war, which, in fact, is still ongoing despite the "idea of the end" from the Western perspectives (Kwon 2010: 15–36), and other sources of conflicts have made the region continuously draw and redraw the border lines. These lingering cold war conflicts as well as various other dissensions resulted in an incubation of physical and psychological geographies which "emerged as a national trauma" to the audiences of many postcolonial states (Sarkar 2009: 2). Many parts of Asia encountered the modern world order and modern ways of life by being occupied, colonized, and segmented in close association with external forces. Chen Kuan-Hsing (2010: 212) draws attention to the "tripartite problematic" in the region—namely, "decolonization, deimperialization, and de–cold war." His point is that these three processes have become mutually entangled structures, so that the historical experiences in the regions are not fully explained by the knowledge produced outside Asia—specifically, Europe and America (211–16).

Violence in post–World War II Asia was born out of a system of complex divisions. This system refers not only to geographical divisions but also to those of ethnicity, religion, and/or ideology in the concurrent, superimposed procedures of decolonization/recolonization and the emergence/continuation of the cold war order. For Asians situated in postcolonial state formation, the new conditions fostered through the emergence of the cold war system were crucial to their identity formation, adding to their derivative identity as the formerly colonized. The formation of a division system made it necessary and possible to blend colonial systems with the new objectives of the cold war in Asia. Violence in Asia, in this sense, defined the leverage of the emerging dominant political entities on state levels and the supranational system that ruled the region. As Kim Min-hwan puts it, a series of mass killings at the edge of World War II and the late 1940s in Okinawa, Taiwan, and Korea—the Battle of Okinawa in 1945, the February 28 incident in Taiwan in 1947, and the April Uprising in Cheju, South Korea, between 1948 and 1954—can be described as the "lawmaking violence" (G. *rechtsetzend Gewalt*) that constituted a new legitimate order in East Asia (Kim 2012: 32–35; Benjamin 1986: 283–88). Similar, but more entangled with the reactionary waves of recolonization in a cold war setting, circumstances lasted in former French Indochina, British Malaya, and Dutch East Indies, through such continued armed conflicts as the First Indochina War from 1946 through 1954, the Malayan Emergency from 1948 until 1960, and the Indonesian War of Independence from 1945 to 1949. These series of lawmaking violence drew the boundary between the legitimate same and the disorderly other, dividing population by ethnic, religious, and/or ideological differences. With such events in the region, the postwar system of division was established and has been still lingering nearly three decades after the end of the Cold War in the West. Violence in Asia, however, demonstrates its sociohistorical specificity at more than just the macro level. Divisions have manifested in hearts and minds, political identities, and everyday social and cultural practices—notably through audiovisual mediascapes. Violence stays extant in various forms of microaggression, such as institutional racism, guilt-by-association systems, and stigmatization of certain minority groups. The media in Asia have been the locus of such banal but sophisticated micro-victimization, as well as countering the tactics thereof.

But are the analyses of violence documented by visual and aural media, whether macro or micro, unique to situations occurring only in the colonized worlds? Or are they merely reiterations of episodes that have been observed and unpacked elsewhere? Christopher Pinney has lamented that any study of photography in a non-European setting (in his case, often India) is typically considered to be "belated," as it would almost always be classified as "commentary" rather than as theory—a footnote pointing to an original observation made in Europe. He hankers for an original "paradigm-changing" study would emerge from the "periphery" (Pinney 2012: 141–42). We believe that some of the arguments made in this issue may be instrumental in providing us with those tools. Han Sang Kim's persuasive contention after examining recent controversies over the evidentiality of camera images, that an archival camera image's indexical informative capability is limited and vulnerable to distortion as an effect of the archive's positionality in the global hierarchy, is revelatory about the peculiarities of camera images as "qualitative data" when studying violence. Of course, this is not an entirely new observation, as Tessa Morris-Suzuki (2005: 156) argues that what defines the "pursuit of historical truthfulness" in both photography and film is the "relationship between past events, the people who record those events on film, and the viewer who sees, interprets and remembers the recorded images." However, the fact that Kim's study took the layered, investigative reading of colonial and postcolonial era events, of still and moving images, to abet the argument seven decades after the atrocities suggests that we are still grappling with basic theories about the documentary value of camera images. Emerging information from World War II that had remained somewhat opaque due to cold war optics helps us better situate images and their uses. Both the recovery of images lost in archives and their disentaglement from decades of swift, limited analyses that relegated them to certain ahistorical categories constitute scholarship that has come alive in the research of academics focusing on Asia.

The contributors of this special issue cover a wide swath of time—from the late colonial period to the present day—exploring theatrical and nontheatrical film and radio, many of which are recent findings from audiovisual archives in Asia and beyond, and museum exhibitions showing the reconstruction and proliferation of narratives enabled by new digital technologies. Rather than focusing on a specific sociopolitical moment, this issue considers a variety of approaches to the histories of violence and confrontation in Asia through the long twentieth century. Nonetheless, there are three broad time frames that the reader will encounter: the late colonial period, the bottleneck years of Asian decolonization, and the emergence of postcolonial nation-states in a cold war framework. Much of the critique hovers on the reimagination of those periods, the past refracted through debate and contextualization of a wide array of visual data.

Peter Bloom brings the reader to the Malayan Emergency in the late 1940s, when colonial propaganda had become far more sophisticated than the early efforts evidenced in numerous empire outreach campaigns. Rather than narrate entire films or radio programs produced by British media agencies, the British counterinsurgency plan subtly introduced voice-over commentaries in their radio and documentary programs produced by the newly expanded Malayan Film Unit and Radio Malaya. English was used as a lure of narrative staging, giving the broadcasts authority and a veneer of legitimacy. The phenomenon of the emergence of new nation-states and the various political bodies jockeying for internal power is explored over several articles. Juyeon Bae discusses entangled histories depicted in Wei Te-Sheng's films that focus on the contestation of Taiwanese citizenship through Indigenous Taiwanese people's cinematic memory of events in the Japanese colonial era. The last vestige of this period is discussed in Han Sang Kim's exploration of the newly discovered archival footage of Korean "comfort women" in the Japanese Imperial Army in China. What is the use of film when photographs of these horrors already exist? With this baiting question, Kim delves into the rationalizations of Siegfried Kracauer to help us contextualize camera images as something beyond evidence. If photographs have often been the mainstay in depicting colonial-era excesses, Chung-Kang Kim goes against the grain of this trend by tracing the gradual rise of other nonphotographic "marketing of memory" via virtual reality and other digital media in newer trends in sensory history. She argues that these approaches have produced a generalized and reductive representation of past traumas and yet have the potential to be much more nuanced and personal. Sandeep Ray's exposition of the propaganda film *An Unavoidable Internment* made by the Films Division of India to justify the Indian government's internment of Chinese Indians in reaction to the Indo-China War of 1962 establishes, through evidence provided by more recent, independently produced films, that the measure was draconian and avoidable. Drawing on research in the last decade that has seen a resurgence on the part of survivors, journalists, activists, and filmmakers in reinvestigating that harrowing history, the article attempts to raise questions about the roles of the state and civic society in the "othering" of a marginalized group during wartime. Malinee Khumsupa and Sudarat Musikawong take this approach in a contemporary time frame by examining the Thai government's current impunity in silencing dissent among scholars and researchers who have been providing counternarratives to the state's authoritarian excesses by curating and researching independently made films. Taking a cue from James Scott and categorizing these records as a weapon of the weak, their work highlights both the meticulous and perilous nature of activist-based research aiming to substantiate a counternarrative in a top-down dominated state.

By focusing on audiovisual mediascapes, this special issue underpins new scholarship generated in Asia and foregrounds the imaginative and sensory specificities of such encounters with violence, which have long been regarded subservient to the reading of formal and written records. All the articles in this issue encounter the depictions of violence in Asia through varied critiques made by historians, media scholars, activists, and filmmakers. The Thai scholarship looks at representational politics in contemporary society, Bloom observes subtle syntax in 1940s Malayan radio broadcasts, Han Sang

Kim justifies why it is worthwhile to obsess over a few fleeting seconds of film footage, Ray calls to account the Films Division to task for being a propagandistic mouthpiece for the Indian government in the fallout from the Indo-China War, Chung-Kang Kim discusses the pitfalls of high-tech yet simplified museological productions of past atrocities, and Bae's article looks at Japan's imperial legacy in Taiwan through the reception and perception of nationalisms created through fiction. Collectively these articles aim to impress upon the reader that encountering the visualization of violence in Asia can be manifold in form, intent and interpretation, and lends itself to multidisciplinary scholarship across numerous archives and sites of memory, mostly located in Asia.

References

Benjamin, Walter. 1986. *Reflections: Essays, Aphorisms, Autobiographical Writings*. New York: Shocken Books.

Chen, Kuan-Hsing. 2010. *Asia as Method: Toward Deimperialization*. Durham, NC: Duke University Press.

Kim, Min-hwan. 2012. "Tongasia ŭi p'yŏnghwa kinyŏm kongwŏn hyŏngsŏng kwajŏng pigyo yŏn'gu: ok'inawa, t'aip'ei, cheju ŭi sarye rŭl chungsim ŭro" 동아시아의 평화 기념 공원 형성 과정 비교 연구: 오키나와, 타이페이, 제주의 사례를 중심으로 ("Comparative Research on the Formation of Peace Memorial Parks in East Asia: Focusing on the Cases of Okinawa, Taipei, and Cheju Islands"). PhD diss., Seoul National University.

Kwon, Heonik. 2010. *The Other Cold War*. New York: Columbia University Press.

Morris-Suzuki, Tessa. 2005. *The Past within Us: Media, Memory, History*. London: Verso.

Pinney, Christopher. 2012. "Seven Theses on Photography." *Thesis Eleven* 113, no. 1: 141–56.

Sarkar, Bhaskar. 2009. *Mourning the Nation: Indian Cinema in the Wake of Partition*. Durham, NC: Duke University Press.

Voicing the Malayan Emergency:

Ventriloquizing Subjectivity in British Colonial Film and Radio

Peter J. Bloom

Introduction

The Malayan Emergency (1948–60) was an early site for Anglo-American Cold War politics in Southeast Asia that relied upon film and radio as a means of shaping its reception. In the case of Malaya (consisting of present-day peninsular Malaysia and Singapore), the Straits Settlement territories of Melaka, Penang, and Singapore became integral to an evolving Cold War media complex.[1] The Emergency, which was officially declared by the British Administration on July 16, 1948, has come to be understood as the staging of an archetypal counterinsurgency campaign that crystalized as a tactics of radio-cinema propaganda that initially emerged during the final phases of World War II. However, the Emergency can be understood as a constellation of media tactics focused on amplifying a cluster of drama-

positions 31:4   DOI 10.1215/10679847-10714246

tized incidents that contributed to shaping a population-centered strategy of anti-Communism.

Whereas the prevailing historical approach to the Emergency has pointed to its role as a basis for Cold War propaganda in the years to come, this article emphasizes an approach to governmentality that examines its reliance upon media production and its projection. In particular, it addresses the role of the voice and a ventriloquizing function of subjectivity conveyed through the mechanically iterative nature of narrative media. It is within these terms that a biopolitics of security came to emerge in the name of identifying residents and containing them as ethnically defined populations. The Emergency came to emphasize acts of mediation that sought to reshape Malaya as vehicle of modernity and nationhood. In the process of this transformation, the multiethnic body of Malaya was recast during the postwar era under the cloak of counterinsurgency politics.

With the return of the British Malayan Administration in 1945, the consolidation of governance drew on a renewed conception of film and radio that created a context for mediated amplification that Philip Auslander (2008) has described as *liveness*. In addition, and more significantly, it established a form of "disciplinary realism" that the film historian Ashish Rajadhyaksha (2013) has invoked to describe how film narratives assert control on behalf of state structures. I suggest that the self-assured voice of Radio Malaya along with voice-over narration of the industrial films produced by the Malayan Film Unit sought to assert a new political project of governance that involved a shift to a model of population control and modalities of circulation.

This discussion considers an unfolding structure of institutional intentionality within the framework of a political strategy that relies upon a "biopolitics of security." This theme is adapted from Michel Foucault's writings about governmentality and subsequent commentary on its capacity for adaptation and change.[2] The underlying political strategy of the Emergency may be said to embody what Mick Dillon and Luis Lobo-Guerrero (2008: 275) describe as "the logos of war expressed as peace." While they are pointing to how political modernity may be understood as the extension of war by other means, this insight is directly relevant to describing how the bundling of policing and security relies upon anti-Communist Cold War media propaganda techniques that were closely related to the advent of Malayan independence in 1957.

Political Context for the Emergency

The immediate postwar political atmosphere in Malaya has been widely commented upon. While the fall of Singapore in 1942 has been described as a defining moment in the precipitous decline of the British Empire (Bayly and Harper 2005; Mishra 2012), the Japanese occupation to follow has been chronicled as an episode of authoritarian repression (Onn [1946] 1977). In fact, the anti-colonial resonance of the fall of Singapore was marked by Walter Lippman in the *Washington Post* (February 21, 1942), who wrote that "[Western nations] must identify their cause with freedom and security . . . , putting away the 'white man's burden' and purging themselves of the taint of an obsolete and obviously unworkable white man's imperialism" (quoted in Wolton 2000: 47). And yet, it was the Malayan Communist Party (MCP) that became the backbone of the resistance to the Japanese occupation, forming the Malayan People's Anti-Japanese Army (MPAJA), which received British weapons and training through Force 136, the Southeast Asian division of the British Special Operations Executive (Short 1975: 21). Chin Peng (a.k.a. Ong Boon Hua, 1924–2013), who later became the chief Communist antagonist during the Emergency as secretary general of the MCP, was decorated and awarded an Officer of the Order of the British Empire (OBE) medal by the British government for his heroism against the Japanese occupation (Stockwell 1993: 69; 1999: 479).

The British Malayan Administration (BMA) faced a complex series of problems upon returning. After the armistice was signed, British and Indian troops landed in Penang (Malaysia) and Singapore, respectively, from September 3 to 5, 1945. Famine along with a general state of lawlessness prevailed. A. J. Stockwell (1993: 68) has described the return of Britain within the terms of a "second colonial occupation" that was mired in overrule and the imperatives of economic production. Crucially, rubber and tin, the twin pillars of the Malayan economy, which had already been an important source of income prior to the war, were primed for export to the United States. As Nicholas White explains, not only did Malaya resume its position as the leading US dollar-earning economy in the sterling area after the war, but rubber production alone earned more hard currency than all of metropolitan Britain's combined exports to the United States. By 1952, the value of these commodities only increased with the needs associated with the Korean War, which was an adjacent and overlapping theater of active Anglo-American military operations (White 2010: 151–53).

The role and intent of the MCP in ongoing disturbances from the return of the British Administration until the declaration of the Malayan Emergency in 1948 was never conclusively determined at the time. As a result, it was difficult to parse acts of retaliation from a concerted effort to overthrow the British administration. Nonetheless, the MCP was banned by the BMA in 1948 not because they were considered a significant threat but due to concerns about the instability of the colonial government itself. Stockwell (1993: 85) has persuasively argued that it was, in fact, pressure exercised by European businessmen and Malay politicians who influenced the Governor General's decision to "identify an enemy and take action against it." This was in spite of the fact that the British Labor government under Clement Attlee (as prime minister from 1945 to 1951) was not especially convinced by this course of action. Nonetheless, Winston Churchill (1874–1965), as prime minister and leader of the Conservative Party in the period prior (1940–45) and after (1951–55), actively endorsed the fundaments of anti-Communism. Attlee's Labor government was compelled to support the policies recommended by the government's "men on the spot." The declaration of the Emergency itself, along with aggressive policies of resettlement, set in motion a more significant quality of social unrest and context for MCP grievances in the years to come. Chin Peng's (2003) autobiography, along with subsequent interviews conducted by Karl Hack (Hack 2005; Chin and Hack 2004), counter many of the misconceptions about the dominant narrative of events. Nonetheless, official Malayan Film Unit productions and Radio Malaya broadcasting demonstrate how the character and context of these events were cast as propaganda campaigns.

The trigger for the declaration of the Emergency was the murder of three rubber plantation managers on June 16, 1948. This incident has been memorialized in Noel Barber's (1971) *The War of the Running Dogs* as part of the dominant anti-Communist counterinsurgency narrative but has been conclusively challenged and specified by Karl Hack (2009), Tim Harper (1999), Kumar Ramakrishna (2002), A. J. Stockwell (1999), Souchou Yao (2016), among others. Harper has explained that the second attack at the Phin Soon estate in the town of Sungei Siput (located in the Kuala Kangsar District of the northwestern state of Perak), occurred within the context of labor unrest over wage cuts at a time of declining rubber prices. A year earlier, Harper (1999: 113–14) explains, Chinese laborers had gone on strike, and there were rumors that John Allison and his young assistant Ian Christian had mistreated their workers and connived with police to break the strike. The context of events quickly became absorbed into a developing story as symptom of a looming Communist insurgency precipitating a declaration of the Emergency. However, it was the directive issued on December 15, 1950, by the British high commissioner Henry Gurney (1898–1951) that put the Emergency on war footing, carefully avoiding a declaration of war. Instead, it became defined as "policing," which may be understood as a continuum between counterinsurgency and war that implies the internal management of populations within an imperial relationship of force.[3] It was within these terms that the government now had the power "to direct any man between the age of 17 and 45 to perform military or police service" (Short 1975: 252).

In the months prior to this declaration, General Harold R. Briggs (1894–1952) was appointed as director of operations in April 1950. Five months later, Hugh Carelton Greene (1910–1987), the younger brother of the renowned writer Graham, was appointed as head of Emergency Information Services in September 1950. The combined efforts of Briggs and Greene among others took shape as the Briggs Plan, which called for a large-scale population resettlement program.[4] It sought to reverse demographic shifts that occurred during the Japanese occupation and in the years that followed. More crucially, however, it reconfigured the productive landscape inside the country with a resettled labor force.

It has been estimated that 573,000 people were resettled from 1950 to 1960, along with the construction of 480 resettlement areas. The vast majority of those resettled were Chinese Malay and part of long-standing ethnic and linguistic communities in Malaya (Sandhu 1964: 159). Between 1954 and 1960, the British administration had resettled almost 600,000 Chinese and another 100,000 Indians and undertook an expansive estate regrouping program that Maureen Sioh estimates to have affected approximately 25 percent of the population at the time. The system of resettlement relied on a finger-printing and identification system imposed on everyone over twelve years of age (Sioh 2004: 738). The implications of these demographic shifts transformed the ecology of the interior as a new spatial regime of disciplinary power. In spite of efforts to realign these "New Villages" to create intensive contexts for production, chronic land shortages undermined these efforts. In fact, the government only had a precarious grip on the management of the New Villages at the beginning of the Emergency given the lack of social services, such as schools and medical care. These significant demographic changes may be said to have even contributed to reinforcing a basis for the "insurgency" itself as a population-centric strategy that underscores ethnic and subnational differences. The majority of the anti-government contingent emerged from the Malayan People's Anti-Japanese Army, who were partially reassembled as the Malayan National Liberation Army (MNLA) in 1949 and the *min yeun* (the people's movement that supported the MCP) in more populated areas. Estimates vary widely regarding the number of MNLA combatants and the much larger *min yeun* constituency at any given point. While Karl Hack (2008: 214) estimates that the MNLA peaked at around 7,000 men in 1950–51, Leon Comber (2008: 70) claims that there were 10,000 MNLA "communist guerillas" in the jungle and as many as 50,000 *min yeun* plainclothes MCP members in populated areas at its peak based on government statistics from the Special Branch. Needless to say, the insurgents were not only significantly outnumbered but lacked significant supplies of weapons, equipment, and, even more significantly, food. Comber writes that British Malayan forces consisted of as many as 40,000 regular troops, supported by no fewer than 67,000 regular police and approximately 350,000 home guards, which would be an advantage of more than 457,000 to 60,000 (or 7.6 to 1) if official estimates were correct. Needless to say, the number of MNLA and *min yeun* members only declined from 1951 onward, whereas British and allied forces were increasingly fortified, if not in troop and police numbers then through their logistic extensions.

Organizing Media as a Strategic Asset

While the intentions and effects of the Emergency have been addressed and contested from a wide variety of perspectives, the official narrative is worthy of further consideration. Film production undertaken by the Malayan Film Unit (MFU) and radio broadcasting on Radio Malaya were instrumental to propaganda directives. Although film and radio were in place prior to 1948, it was only by 1950 that a significant mobilization of media in the service of political objectives emerged. In the case of the MFU, the 1950 Hawes Report proved to be an influential document which led to a significant restructuring of the service in support of the Emergency (Aitken 2016: 96–100). Hugh Carelton Greene, along with his deputy C. C. Too (a.k.a. Too Chee Chew, 1920–1992) facilitated an emphasis on strategic directives within a series of broadcasting periods that were organized as campaigns.[5]

With Greene's appointment, the role of the Information Services Department expanded to include both propaganda and psychological warfare. Although mention of "psychological warfare" by radio is mentioned in confidential government documents as early as 1940, Radio Malaya was only established as a government department of the Straits Settlement government on March 2, 1940, with only limited equipment, and was only fully constituted in 1945. Nonetheless, Radio Malaya continued to broadcast programs during the occupation from Jakarta on the same wavelength while the staff was evacuated to Java as part of the propaganda war against the Japanese occupation.[6]

Radio broadcasting was considered to be such an essential form of propaganda during the war and such an instrument of governance by its end that Radio Malaya began broadcasting within a few hours of the first troop arrivals in Singapore on September 5, 1945. It was then approved as a new government Broadcasting Department for the Malayan Union and Singapore, and shortwave coverage for the entire country was established.[7] The reestablishment of radio in Malaya came to serve as the communication infrastructure for the returning British administration that continued to expand its listenership with the use of wired radio receivers and communal listening centers throughout the country.

The advent of the Emergency allowed for the expansion of media production and projection with new equipment that allowed for an even more molecular quality of on-the-spot reporting. With the adoption of lightweight, high-quality mobile recording equipment, such as the introduction of portable audio recorders, a more compelling quality of immediacy and control over the scripting of news events emerged. It was, however, the presentation and staging of events such as ambushes or attacks that pointed to a consolidation of the British military command structure, or a "new war executive system" that bypassed the decentralized Malayan state administrations. In fact, Greene's five-month commission marked the centralization of operations that used media as an extension of war, given his experience with psychological warfare during World War II as member of the Political Warfare Executive German Section. As part of a propaganda strategy that featured media projection, Greene doubled the number of cinema projectors available for public screenings and installed many public address systems that sought to enhance and amplify word-of-mouth propaganda. In addition, five hundred community listening stations were installed and another seven hundred radio sets were distributed to Chinese resettlement areas, which amplified the role and function of radio.

Given that shortwave radios were not widespread during this period, in the era prior to portable transistors, wired radio broadcasting for group listening were especially popular throughout the 1950s. A variety of formats were used to make the work of propaganda more popular and effective. It ranged from concert parties with mouth organists, dramatic organists, and dramas performed by ex-guerrillas to well-produced news programs along with films by the MFU (Short 1975: 420–21). The performances, in particular, were part of an extended spectrum of popular attractions in the Shaw Brothers's theme parks and *bangsawan* popular theaters.[8] The five- to twenty-minute-long one-reel films of the MFU were often preceded by the circulating feature films on the Malayan theatrical circuit. They were screened by a government-sponsored nontheatrical circuit in which 16mm prints were shown in schools, factories, village halls, and building sites (Aitken 2016: 62).

In addition to a locally established context for propaganda that supported the development of British military operations, directives from the Foreign Office in London were also incorporated into the flow of radio programs and films produced in support of the Emergency. This was particularly the case regarding broadcasts about China, given the regional context for Communism. Toward this end, an array of thematic directives were deployed during two-week or monthly cycles. Radio Malaya and the Malayan Film Unit were often charged with producing programs and films that supported the relevant campaigns as part of larger set of political and regional objectives. Special radio programs such as "Ambush at Windy Corner" (presented by Stewart Wavell, aired on April 2, 1953) proved to be nimbler and more reactive than industrial films addressing topical events, such as *Proudly Presenting Yong Peng (New Village)* (1953), because they could be presented with greater immediacy and topicality. It also provided a malleable structure of intermittent informational public service announcements that formed a context for mediating behavior among listeners.

Anti-bandit Directives

One example of this system of relay from London to Malaya was the establishment of directives associated with Anti-bandit Month. The Foreign Office sent a telegram on April 14, 1950, explaining that the goal of Anti-bandit Month was not expected to produce any spectacular results with regard to the actual stated goals of apprehending Communist insurgents.[9] The terms *banditry* and *emergency* were strategically used to avoid declaring a colonial war, thus allowing planters and mining firms to claim losses of stock and equipment from the London-based insurance companies (Deery 2003: 237). The role of this anti-banditry campaign sought to mobilize the population of Malaya behind the government itself. According to documents from the Foreign Office, this effort led to an array of broadcasts that succeeded in achieving this goal. In a recorded segment excavated from the tape-to-tape collection at Radio Television Malaysia in Kuala Lumpur, a former unnamed and reformed Tamil "bandit" describes his treatment as a member of the Communist Insurgency and how he suffered ill treatment by MCP leaders.

This recording was staged as a "confession" and conducted as a dialogue with a Radio Malaya British commentator. It should also be noted that some essential Radio Malaya commentators, such as Tufton "Tony" Beamish and

David Kennard, actively participated in the MI6 British counterintelligence operation in Malaya. In a brief interview that was later broadcast, an anonymous ex-Communist Tamil Singaporean describes how he learned about Communism as a trade unionist and became trained in insurgency methods. He was then turned into an operative who was given "clothes and a revolver" to serve on an outside contact squad. After leaving his job in Singapore, he was stationed deep in the jungle, where, he explains, the leaders were "arrogant and very strict." Furthermore, almost all of the recruits were demoralized because the Chinese Communist leaders were "greedy and did not take care of the squadron." He explains that he was not able to see his own family, and upon realizing his "unhappiness," he tried to surrender to British authorities, to no avail. Fortunately, he explains, he was recently captured. In conclusion, he says that he would have been happy if this "revolution brought peace to the Malayan people," but unfortunately "the Reds" are not concerned with the interests of the people. He continues by saying that the Communists have done more harm to the movement and advises Indian workers sympathetic to the MCP to "seek a negotiated settlement."[10]

This staged confessional recording repeats talking points and key phrases that were emphasized in news reports and other documentary formats that deployed a mnemonic phraseology of suggestion to listening audiences. It may also be understood as a logomachy of spoken words authorizing oppositions between truth and falsehood that protects itself by annihilating opposing speech (Goodrich 1990: 280). These programs not only were broadcast in English but often were translated into Malay, Tamil, and various Chinese vernacular dialects. The interview format creates a quality of intimacy with the listener and in this case not only served as a preamble to offering a substantial bounty for the capture of Communist leaders and guerrillas to prospective listeners but also demonstrated a willingness to offer fair treatment to Surrendered Enemy Personnel (SEP). Upon Greene's urging, SEPs were featured on lecture tours and used to demonstrate how they were well treated in government hands. There was, in fact, a script that they were required to follow. It was intended to create an "impression of policy" directed toward "bandits," who later became known as Communist terrorists. Kumar Ramakrishna has explained that the operative language was very specific about what the SEPs were authorized to say. For example, they were not allowed to say "It is the generous policy of the government to free men like me" but were authorized to say "I am a free man." In other words, any implication that SEPs would not be prosecuted was carefully removed from official communication, and yet upholding the theme of fairness in their treatment was frequently reaffirmed (Ramakrishna 1999: 249).[11]

Collective Punishment

A 1952 Radio Malaya recording demonstrates yet another facet of a more controversial tactic that was widely debated. It involved staging collective punishment and took the form of a speech delivered to a group of Chinese Malay villagers by Gerald Templer, the newly appointed governor general of Malaya from 1952 to 1954. Churchill appointed Templer while granting him extraordinary powers of authority as supreme commander, or "Supremo," following Gurney's assassination in an ambush on October 6, 1951. Templer's speech was delivered a few months after his arrival on Thursday, August 21, 1952, to seventy-nine villagers in Permatang Tinggi, a village located in the Bukit Mertajam district of Wellesley province.[12] The policy sought to hold the collective shop house responsible for the murder of an assistant resettlement officer, Teoh Boon Hoe, on August 15, 1952. News of the event, along with Templer's speech, was widely reported in newspapers of the period but did not prove effective in convincing villagers to identify the perpetrators (see *Straits Times* 1952b, 1952c; *Singapore Free Press* 1952).

This incident has been described as part of a strategy of mass detention codified as Regulation 17 D-A (1949), which was first significantly applied following the assassination of Henry Gurney on October 6, 1951. The punishment was enacted in the village of Tras and involved detaining two thousand people because of the suspected involvement of five women and fifteen men in the ambush. Other incidents of mass detention in Malaya were also widely reported and commented upon in greater detail. However, the best-known incident took place in the Selangor village of Tanjong Malim, whose five thousand inhabitants were punished with reduced rations, a twenty-two-hour curfew, and the closure of schools. It was conceived as a response to the murder of an assistant district officer and eleven others on the outskirts of the village on March 25, 1952, and became widely known in the international press. It has been described as a "publicity stunt" that exaggerated Templer's purported ruthlessness in order to achieve a degree of deterrence with a minimum use of force (Ramakrishna 2002: 137). It also served to project Templer's authority as a charismatic leader and figurehead of an emerging counterinsurgency paradigm.

The incident was reported in the *Times* of London and debated in both houses of Parliament, for which a motion against it was signed by more than one hundred British Labor MPs.[13] In spite of Templer's own awareness of its limited effect, mass punishment still continued until 1953, when it became synonymous with a strategy of colonial policing throughout the empire, particularly against the Mau Mau in Kenya.[14] Though less well known, the incident in Permatang Tinggi is of interest because Templer's recorded speech serves as a staging of policy about which Maureen Sioh's (2004: 741) discussion of the written transcript provides some guidance regarding its underlying context.

The speech was delivered in person with the assistance of an interpreter, who briefly translates sections into Hokkien, which was the most widely spoken Fujian Chinese dialect in the region. Its delivery may be likened to an ethics lesson in a silent assembly hall. By the end of the fifteen-minute speech recorded for broadcast, he asks if there are any questions or if anyone would like to talk with him privately. He then asks whether they understood him, to which there is no reply. He finally says, "Nobody?" An echo chamber effect resonates, and Templer's voice enacts a rhetorical strategy rather than an address to the audience itself. The implied audience of the villagers stands in for an intended radio audience, and the Hokkien interpreter's voice functions as a sound effect for non-Sinophone listeners that marks its location. If a secondary audience was in fact the *min yeun* in the populated areas or the MNLA in the jungle, they were unlikely to have heard this unbending approach to discipline, culminating in a series of initiatives that sought to constrict contact with insurgents. The broadcast becomes a context for the assertion of authority and a strategy of contact tracing, which was one of the most significant claims of Templer's purported "intelligence gathering" approach to the Emergency.

In the speech itself, he describes the details under which a curfew will be imposed and asserts that none of the members of the shop houses will be allowed to leave for the next four days. He establishes a deadline, saying that unless they "come forward with information about the murder of the officer by the coming Monday, August 25, they will be removed from the village, placed in detention, and resettled elsewhere in the country, never to return to their home ever again." None of the villagers provided information about the incident, and they were forcibly removed at 9:00 a.m. on August 25, 1952. Accordingly, sixty-two villagers were sent to a detention camp, and twenty-one others were deported. This "New Village" consisted of eighteen shop and dwelling houses. It was located a half mile from Matang Tinggi, which was a center for the pineapple industry in the region. As part of the Emergency regulation, they were required to pay a fine of $250 per shop house and $150 per dwelling house, totaling $4,650, and their belongings were confiscated and auctioned (*Straits Times* 1952a). The village itself was destroyed and, as Maureen Sioh (2004: 741) explains, six months later the villagers were moved back to the site of the village, which had been rebuilt and transformed into a fenced area. Although the mass punishment regulation, known as 17 D-A, was disbanded a year later, in 1953, and largely was considered an unsuccessful propaganda campaign, it was then adapted into a larger narrative regarding the expansion of "white" or safe areas. It is the graphic quality of whiteness as safety that marked a renewed cartography of normalcy, which also stands in as its own profilmic spatial imaginary.[15]

While intermittent ambushes continued, the expansion of free white zones expanded as a more effective strategy than calls for collective punishment. It became increasingly clear that a return to normalcy was a more effective technique to quell unrest than the forced imagination of counterinsurgency. Colonel Arthur Young (1907–1979), who was appointed as the Malayan police commissioner in 1952, suggested the white zone concept in order to demonstrate that the administration cared for the people, and on September 3, 1953, Templer declared one-third of the state of Melaka along the coast to be safe for freedom of movement. As the number of areas that were declared white continued apace with Templer's imminent departure in 1954, the advance of "white area freedom" pronouncements became a means of attracting public support for the government's role in winning the war against the Communist terrorists (Ramakrishna 2002: 138). However, the underlying context for counterinsurgency leads to a further interrogation of the construction of a national imaginary as defined by a series of oppositions.

The Test of Nationhood

The graphic conceit of whiteness in documentary films produced by the Malayan Film Unit after 1953 became a demonstration of a nation-form newly inoculated against the threat of the Communist insurgency. With the appointment of Donald MacGillivray as high commissioner upon Templer's departure in 1954, a transitional period in political leadership culminated with the elevation of Tunku Abdul Rahman (1903–1990), who later became the first prime minister in 1957. Nonetheless, it was Lieutenant General Geoffrey Bourne (1902–1982), the newly installed director of operations upon Templer's departure in 1954, who ensured continuity with the ongoing emphasis on active policing and additional security operations. He sought to establish his presence through frequent appearances on Radio Malaya as well as frequent meetings with Chinese community leaders, who were among the most important economic stakeholders. As Ramakrishna has explained, it was less a matter of ideology, or "hearts and minds," than of convincing the Chinese population in the New Villages that the political alliances in the newly independent Malaya to come would be organized within the terms of a decidedly anti-Communist Cold War order.

Once Tunku Abdul Rahman was elected as chief minister in 1955, an avowed policy of Malayanization became part of the public discourse for which several founding figures were conscripted into government service including Dato Abdul Razak (1922–1976), Tan Cheng Lock (1883–1960), Colonel H. S. Lee (1900–1988), and V. T. Sambanthan (1919–1979). The path toward independence was already established as an inevitability by the Foreign Office as early as 1948, but the maintenance of the British-controlled export economy and its political structure within the Commonwealth was to take the form of Malayan responsibility and British operational control that continued well beyond independence. It may even be argued, as suggested by Nicholas White, that the plantation and extraction economies in particular remained largely in the hands of foreign investors, especially British companies, until 1970 (Yacob and White 2010: 923, 925).

The "unfinished business of *merdeka*," or independence, as they describe it, still remained under wraps. Nonetheless, it still leads us to consider the parasitic relationship between the Emergency as a counterinsurgency campaign and the modernity of independence, which relied upon the staging of nationhood in the radio-cinema imagination that was at once a claim to modernity and form of governmentality. *Test of Nationhood* (Ow 1960) presents significant plot points of this narrative as it was released to coincide with Tunku's declaration of the end of the Emergency on July 12, 1960.[16]

Test of Nationhood is compilation film with a voice-over narration that relies on footage assembled from a series of films produced by the MFU.[17] This particular film is worthy of close analysis because it is a synoptic portrayal of the history of the Emergency that is positioned as the "test of nationhood." The film begins with the printed phrase, "For twelve long years we fought the enemy in our midst . . . we fought against an alien ideology . . . against terror and intimidation, against militant communism. This is the story of our STRUGGLE and our VICTORY."

In the English-language version of this film, the voice-over begins with an assertion that Malaya is one of the richest countries in Southeast Asia, which is intercut with images of rice cultivation, rubber plantations that covers four million acres, and tin mining claimed to draw upon the largest reserves in the world. These resources of wealth are then associated with the multiracial makeup of its population, pictured as tending to these important raw materials. The underlying threat to Malaya's wealth is then asserted, which is none other than "the grim specter of Communism."

With the declaration of the Emergency on June 16, 1948, the narrator continues, industrial infrastructure was under attack. Trains and trucks are shown to be capsized, villages razed to the ground, and acts of murder are invoked for those who defy the Communist guerrillas. However, we are then told that help is on its way with the recruitment of twenty-four thousand special constables taught to handle weapons and guard the outposts of industry. In addition, a national registration is set up, checkpoints on roads and highways are instituted, and contraband is confiscated. These themes are illustrated with a series of cutaways as part of a sequencing in which the security forces are now on the offensive. This segment of the film then transitions to the resettlement campaign that is primarily described as a humanitarian approach to the squatter problem, and those living on state land who are defenseless against the encroaching Communist insurgents.

The Briggs Plan is then described as resettlement in the name of security against terrorists and for its generosity in providing compensation for those moving into a new protected community. As the narrative voice proclaims, "A half million people were shifted to new villages by road and rail, while others have been moved by water." This narrative segment then sets up the effectiveness of Operation Starvation, which was launched in June 1951, seeking to starve out the terrorists. As the narrator explains, under this plan, food-restricted areas were created, food lodges were guarded, and in some areas, central kitchens were created. In addition, security forces have supported the operation by destroying terrorist plots of land and uncovering bandit supply depots with great success. The effectiveness of the "starve them out" campaign has been corroborated by Chin Peng in later interviews.

The next narrative cue, based on the success of Operation Starvation, is Anti-bandit Month, which five hundred thousand Malayans endorsed as a sign of "their sincerity." As part of this initiative, a series of tactical military bombings are then featured that include the deployment of platoons in the swamps, the use of helicopters, and the fair treatment of captured prisoners. The recourse to military violence is justified in the name of the 1951 ambush against Sir Henry Gurney, the British high commissioner, and with the appointment of Gerald Templer in the year to follow, who "streamlined the forces of war, and established intensive training for jungle combat." Templer is featured as savior and avatar of a strategy who has restored confidence and propels the narrative forward. By the third reel, we are informed that Templer's methods have achieved remarkable success, beginning with a mass surrender within the first few months after his arrival. The militarization of the conflict relied on a genre of World War II battleground footage depicting a multinational volunteer army of soldiers from Africa, Australia, Fiji, India, and the United Kingdom. The so-called vigor of the anti-Communist campaign is on display, along with an array of statistics demonstrating its purported success. The claim is that by 1952, three thousand terrorists were eliminated and paratroopers were sent in to "flush them out."

In addition, and as a sideline, the narrator explains that British Commonwealth anti-Communist forces are winning the confidence of the Orang Asli "Aborigines," whose help is essential, and they are rewarded with schools for their children. The narrator then states that "winning over the Aborigines contributed to the collapse of the enemy." The ability of the government to work with them is then contrasted with the sacrifices of professional soldiers, as the aerial images in one particular segment depicting an Orang Asli village were in fact rescued from a crash in which the two Malayan Film Unit cameramen perished. Just as this segment depicting an aerial view is complete, a diagram of the first white area, consisting of 221 square miles off the coast of Melaka, is shown. This becomes the basis for Templer's success after two years of service.

With Templer's send-off in 1954, Malaya is now said to be recovering and reassembled with the establishment of new schools, as depicted in segments about the Yong Peng New Village, and the Rural Industrial Development Authority for Rubber, where latex is collectively processed. The narrator then pronounces without irony, "Resettlement is a blessing." With the revival of industry, local elections are introduced as the dawning of a new era that culminates in the merger of three major parties and establishment of the majority Alliance Party, which wins the majority of federal seats, by which time Tunku Abdul Rahman is elected as chief minister in 1955.

The fourth and final reel then opposes the rising national stature of the Tunku, who initially attempts to broker an amnesty agreement with Chin Peng, in his declining fortunes as secretary general of the Communist Party and leader of the MNLA. The newsreel-like quality of this segment was drawn from an earlier MFU film in which their encounter was documented as part of the failed 1956 Bailing Amnesty talks, and blame is cast upon Ching Peng for "hollow promises" of putting down arms upon independence. Instead, the film asserts that the conflict intensified and joint operations against the terrorists continued on the northern Thai border, where the remaining insurgents eventually took refuge. Tunku's confidence as the new leader of Malaya is foregrounded in this final section of the film. This is then followed by Tunku's flight to London in order to negotiate the full independence of Malaya within eighteen months. This is asserted to be two years ahead of schedule, "achieving," in the words of the narrator, "the impossible!" Furthermore, it is claimed that the Tunku has indeed "stirred the people's imagination," and we then are transported to Melaka as the site for the declaration of Merdeka, or independence, on August 31, 1957.

Finally, in the aftermath of independence, another Merdeka Amnesty is offered along with the surrender of 646 terrorists. It is from this point on in the film that the white areas spread in a series of graphic illustrations and a final victory is in sight. A series of nation-building accomplishments are then proclaimed including social and economic concerns, the establishment of Malay as the national language of the Malayan Union, social and health services, as well as an economic program. In addition, it is claimed that more land is opened up for rubber plantations. Furthermore, we are told that the tin-mining economy is back on track and rural development is on the horizon. New housing is being built; the first parliamentary elections are held in August 1959, through which citizens may decide their own destiny; and, most importantly, all Emergency restrictions were repealed. We are told that the end of the Emergency is imminent thanks to the security forces of the Commonwealth along with "Malayan fortitude and courage." The final intertitles at the end of the film proclaim, "[For the] price of our VICTORY, we salute our glorious dead . . . Lest we Forget."

I have described this film in some detail because it not only embodies an official narrative of the Emergency itself but also demonstrates how it functioned as a proxy for counterinsurgency politics that continued in the years following independence. Rather than merely providing supplemental information as a means of correcting the misleading statements that *Test of Nationhood* asserts, it is of greater interest to consider its role as a genre of propaganda that deploys a "voice" of authority, illustrating how a biopolitics of security becomes an expression of sovereign law. Toward this end, the carefully scripted voice-over narration is grounded in the ventriloquist's art of governance (Hill 2010), whose source, once revealed, becomes cloaked once again in a renewed construct of citizenship and identity. The rhetorical staging of independence within the register of "disciplinary" documentary realism revives many of the same rhetorical devices deployed at the end of World War II within the tradition of British documentary cinema. The question of who speaks for whom might, in fact, demonstrate how a form of internal colonization was achieved in the production of biopolitical bodies subject to a new arrangement of sovereignty. The symbolic handoff by the British colonial administration to the newly appointed Malayan parliamentary order involved a well-rehearsed act of "ventriloquism" within the conceit of independence as popular spectacle.

Voice, Ventriloquism, and Media

Film and radio broadcast throughout the British Empire was partially conceived as a long-range plan in which colonial broadcasting was envisaged as an instrument of "advanced administration." It was derived from a series of initiatives developed under the aegis of the Empire Marketing Board starting in 1926—which included the impetus behind the BBC Empire Service, later renamed the BBC World Service. Most prominently, perhaps, it also served as a mandate for a series of government-sponsored documentary film initiatives closely associated with John Grierson. The multifaceted basis of the campaign in Malaya may be understood by reference to themes developed as part of the Projection of Britain campaign developed by Stephen Tallents and is part of the long tail of British documentary media more generally. Nonetheless, the use of media in Malaya was deployed as an extension of British counterinsurgency techniques modeled on militarized containment and a vast campaign of resettlement in the New Villages.

There was considerable discussion by the Colonial Office regarding the emerging context for "advanced administration." The shifting parameters for indirect rule allowing for maximum economic advantage meant that colonial officers were trained to develop a set of new adaptive techniques. Indirect rule was replaced by local government along with self-rule during the postwar period. In a passing remark, Rajadhyaksha (2010) has referred to the notion of radio-cinema governmentality as a critical facet of an enduring legacy, and, I would add, it can be further defined as a critical feature that enabled a graduated approach to indirect and self-rule.[18] Within the terms described in Foucault's writing on apparatuses of security, radio-cinema governmentality anchors postcolonial strategies of neoliberalism in the contemporary digital media economy. The containment of populations by means of counterinsurgency techniques points to the shaping of a political narrative and the uses of military "equipment" in the name of a biopolitics of security in a neoimperial order.

The emergence of British colonial film and radio in the postwar era may be understood as a means of enacting and administering colonial authority through a shifting context for "state spatiality" through strategies of verticality and encompassment. The emphasis on "governmentality" throughout this discussion serves as source and vehicle for mediation that also functions as a "sovereignty machine" (Hardt and Negri 2000: 78–79) in that it stamps postcolonial governance within a parallel logic of population control as an empire within and beyond colonial administration. The voice may then be said to activate an affective power in the reinvention of a "tactics of government which makes possible the continual definition and redefinition of what is within the competence of the state and [that] which is not" (Burchell 1991: 103).

The thematic of governmentality (Pinkerton and Dodd 2008; Scott 1995) that has been invoked throughout is crucially instantiated by the power of the mediated voice of authority, which hails to the legibility of the English-speaking voice itself. Even though British Overseas Radio broadcast programs in Malay, Mandarin, Tamil, among other regional languages, it was English, particularly BBC English, that gained currency as the trusted voice of authority capable of commanding the power of assertion, suggestion, and judgment. The close relationship between film and radio in the late colonial context was a means by which cultural authority was assessed and asserted at a moment when colonial hierarchies could no longer be sustained, but repositioned as a dialectical play of politics and language. Finally, "radio-cinema governmentality" relies on a series of tactical techniques as a means by which to model citizenship and defer popular manifestations of self-determination.

The tactical quality of warfare techniques has been described in a series of declassified military studies,[19] along with literature about counterinsurgency as paradigm (Hack 2009; Nagl 2005). Most relevant to this discussion is the psychological construct of the Emergency that has engaged the role of the propaganda war (e.g., Carruthers 1995; Ramakrishna 2002; Stubbs 1989). In these earlier works, the role of film and radio has been largely described from a policy-making perspective, and yet it is the quality of a voice that may be said to have emerged. The question of the voice is a speculative one, and its effects function beyond the context of pragmatic usage. Instead, it becomes an internalized site of bodily awareness. On the one hand, the projection of the voice marks its detachment from the body. And yet, precisely because of the act of projection, it is the imprint of the voice that resides in the same position as sovereignty. This means that the voice can suspend the validity of law and "inaugurate a state of emergency" as Mladen Dolar (2006) has written. Through the conveyance of film and radio as symbols of modernity, a quality of authority and governance emerged within the terms of nationhood, which is yet again another vexed category, or "retrospective illusion," as Étienne Balibar (1992) has suggested. Radio-cinema modernity leads us to consider how it has been refashioned as a digital media discourse with new types of state and corporate controls as well as narrative conventions that remain within a neoliberal space of imperial sovereignty.

Notes

1   The Straits Settlements (Melaka, Penang, and Singapore) were derived from the British East India Company as free ports and came under direct rule as British Crown Colonies in 1867. Their structure dissolved in the aftermath of World War II. For further discussion of the historical context for Malay Peninsula, see the website with historical maps maintained by the University of Malaya (*Economic History of Malaya* 2022).

2   The most significant source for this direction in Foucault's thinking can be found in Foucault 2007. Foucault's earlier references to governmentality have become actively commented upon in a wide range of texts, including those developed by Stuart Elden (2007), Michael Dillon (2007), and Dillon and Luis Lobo-Guerrero (2008).

3   See, in particular, the discussion of policing by Ruth Streicher (2020: 5) in which she describes a larger context for "policing the imperial formation" in colonial Siam, with an emphasis on Southern Thailand that borders on present-day Malaysia.

4   The Briggs plan was in fact developed by Robert Thompson and Henry Gurney. Robert Thompson served in government positions from 1948 to 1960 in Malaya and served as head of the British Advisory Mission in South Vietnam from September 1961 to March 1965. He is known to be a key figure in developing the tactics and propaganda associated with counterinsurgency. For further discussion, see Thompson 1966.

5   C. C. Too became an integral member of Emergency Information Services up until March 1952, when he quit over friction with Greene's replacement, Alec Peterson. Nonetheless, Too was well regarded and asked to return in 1955 by O. W. Wolters, the new Head of the Psychological War Section, and become head of the section upon Wolters's departure. Notably, Too played a critical role in drafting the wording of the 1957 Merdeka Amnesty, which encouraged

MCP combatants to lay down their arms and become loyal to the newly independent government; furthermore, the amnesty asserted that MCP combatants would not be prosecuted for any offence connected with the Emergency (Ramakrishna 2002: 198). His significant role also demonstrated that the counterinsurgency efforts were as much a part of Malayan interest groups as they were a reaffirmation of British colonial prerogative (Lim 2000).

6 Report of the Department of Broadcasting for the years 1946–52, Singapore: Acting Government Printer, 1953: 2. Central Library, National University of Singapore Library.

7 Notes on Department of Broadcasting, December 5, 1947, to December 31, 1946, 1–2/11, British National Archives-Kew FCO141/17090: Governor-General, Malaya, 120/47: Joint Broadcasting Affairs Committee: Radio Malaya.

8 Yunn Chii Wong and Kar Lin Tan (2004) have described the nature of the New World Amusement Park–Singapore during the interwar period, but this park, among other venues, continued into the late 1960s.

9 Joint Intelligence and Propaganda Committee, April 28, 1950, "Directives from London," 2/2, Telegram number 97, National Archives-Kew: FCO141/4490: "Instructions to Radio Malaya, re: Broadcasts on Situation in China."

10 Radio Television Malaya, Kuala Lumpur, Interview with ex-Communist Indian bandit, ca. 1950, reference no. B2004, July 2016. Thanks to Sheela Gangadharan, then the archivist at RTM, for facilitating access to this material.

11 Ramakrishna cites the following inward telegram for this discussion: National Archives-Kew: PRO CO 1022/49, inward tel. 593 from Gerald Templer to Arthur Lyttelton, May 12, 1952. Furthermore, he explains that SEPs were defined as "enemy personnel who willingly surrender to the forces of law and order at a time when they could otherwise willingly have made good their escape." See "Commissioner's Instruction No. 3: The Treatment of Surrendered Enemy Personnel (SEP) and Captured Enemy Personnel (CEP)," NA-Kew: PRO CO 1022/49.

12 Radio Television Malaya, Kuala Lumpur, "Templer talking to people in Matang Tinggi," September 5, 1952 (16:32), reference no. B1665. Wellesley Province was renamed Seberang Perai and is part of Greater Penang, the second-largest urban area in Malaysia.

13 *Times* of London, March 28, April 7, and April 8, 1952, as described in Mannheim 1955: 48–49.

14 Discussion about the role of colonial policing in Kenya has returned recently thanks to the declassification of a large number of records known as FCO 141 (the migrated archives) of Hanslope Park in Buckinghamshire. These records can now be accessed at the National Archives at Kew. For a brief survey of the debates about these archives in relation to Borneo and Malaya, see Phillips 2013: 86–92; Hack 2012.

15 Priya Jaikumar (2019) evokes the quality of profilmic space as a basis for her remarkable address to a more capacious address to the role of space and place in her recent work about the Films Division of India and a series of midcentury films in relation to India.

16 The film is held at the Imperial War Museum and screened on site. Ref. COI 626. 3776 ft., 42 min., 3 reels. Hassan Muthalib, the former head of the animation section of the Malayan Film Unit (MFU) who has actively published his research about the history of the MFU, interviewed Peh Kim Pew, an assistant who worked on this film. In their discussion, Pew describes the final seventy-two-hour period to complete the film by the deadline for its public presentation, and notes that the popular singer and performer Zainal Alam serves as the voice-over narrator. Interview conducted by Hassan Muthalib with Peh Kim Pew, unpublished interview notes, April 17, 1992.

17 Hassan Muthalib, in particular, has been a pioneer in advocating for the significance of films produced by the MFU, along with his ongoing research and interviews with many of the surviving members. In addition, the Imperial War Museum in London retains accessible copies of several of these films. A collection of the MFU films are held by FINAS in Kuala Lumpur. For further discussion of the MFU and related films, see Aitken 2016; Bloom 2017, 2018; Chan 2016; Hee 2017, 2019; Muthalib 2011, 2013; Rice 2019.

18 See also Rajadhyaksha 2020, which points to the relevance of Michael Hardt and Antonio Negri's (2000) *Empire*.

19 L. T. Dunnett, *The Malayan Emergency, 1948–1960* (restricted), commissioned by the [British] Royal Air Force and published by the Ministry of Defence AP 3410, June 1970, British National Archives-Kew (BNA-Kew), AIR 10/8584.

References

Aitken, Ian. 2016. *The British Official Film in South-East Asia: Malaya/Malaysia, Singapore, and Hong Kong*. London: Palgrave Macmillan.

Auslander, Philip. 2008. *Liveness: Performance in a Mediatized Culture*. 2nd ed. New York: Routledge.

Balibar, Étienne. 1992. "The Nation Form: History and Ideology." In *Race, Nation, Class: Ambiguous Identities*, by Étienne Balibar and Immanuel Wallerstein, 86–106. London: Verso Books.

Barber, Noel. 1971. *The War of Running Dogs: How Malaya Defeated the Communist Guerillas, 1948–60*. London: Collins.

Bayly, Christopher, and Tim Harper. 2005. *Forgotten Armies: The Fall of British Asia, 1941–1945*. Cambridge, MA: Belknap Press of Harvard University Press.

Bloom, Peter J. 2017. "The Language of Counterinsurgency in Malaya: Dialectical Soundscapes of Salvage and Warfare." In *The Colonial Documentary Film in South and Southeast Asia*, edited by Ian Aitken and Camille Deprez, 63–78. Edinburgh: Edinburgh University Press.

Bloom, Peter J. 2018. "Global Asia and the Legacy of Counterinsurgency: Malaya Speaks and the Malayan Film Unit." *Social Text Online*, May 9. https://socialtextjournal.org/periscope _article/global-asia-and-the-legacy-of-counterinsurgency-malaya-speaks-and-the-malayan -film-unit/.

Burchell, Graham. 1991. "Peculiar Interests: Civil Society and Governing 'The System of Natural Liberty.'" In *The Foucault Effect: Studies in Governmentality*, edited by Graham Burchell, Colin Gordon, and Peter Miller, 119–50. Chicago: University of Chicago Press.

Carruthers, Susan L. 1995. *Winning Hearts and Minds: British Governments, the Media, and Colonial Counter-insurgency, 1944–1960*. London: Leicester University Press.

Chan, Nadine. 2016. "Making Ahmad 'Problem Conscious': Educational Film and the Rural Lecture Caravan in 1930s British Malaya." *Cinema Journal* 55, no. 4: 84–107.

Chin, C. C., and Karl Hack, eds. 2004. *Dialogues with Chin Peng: New Light on the Malayan Communist Party*. Singapore: Singapore University Press.

Chin, Peng. 2003. *Alias Chin Peng: My Side of History*. With Ian Ward and Norma Miraflow. Singapore: Media Masters.

Comber, Leon. 2008. *Malaya's Secret Police, 1945-1960: The Role of the Special Branch in the Malayan Emergency*. Singapore: Institute of South East Asian Studies.

Deery, Phillip. 2003. "The Terminology of Terrorism: Malaya, 1948–52." *Journal of Southeast Asian Studies* 34, no. 2: 231–47.

Dillon, Michael. 2007. "Governing through Contingency: The Security of Biopolitical Governance." *Political Geography* 26, no. 1: 41–47.

Dillon, Michael, and Luis Lobo-Guerrero. 2008. "Biopolitics of Security in the Twenty-First Century: An Introduction." *Review of International Studies* 34, no. 2: 265–92.

Dolar, Mladen. 2006. *A Voice and Nothing More*. Cambridge, MA: MIT Press.

Economic History of Malaya. 2022. "Evolution to Malaysia." https://www.ehm.my/about /history-of-malaysia (accessed October 2).

Elden, Stuart. 2007. "Rethinking Governmentality." *Political Geography* 26, no. 1: 29–33.

Foucault, Michel. 2007. "18 January 1978: General Features of the Apparatuses of Security (II)." In *Security, Territory, Population: Lectures at the Collège de France, 1977–1978*, edited by Michel Senellart, 29–53. New York: Palgrave Macmillan.

Goodrich, Peter. 1990. *Languages of Law: From Logics of Memory to Nomadic Masks*. London: Weidenfeld and Nicolson.

Hack, Karl. 2005. *Dialogues with Chin Peng: New Light on the Malayan Emergency*. Singapore: Singapore University Press.

Hack, Karl. 2008. "Corpses, Prisoners of War, and Captured Documents: British and Communist Narratives of the Malayan Emergency, and the Dynamics of Intelligence Transformation." *Intelligence and National Security* 14, no. 4: 211–41.

Hack, Karl. 2009. "The Malayan Emergency as Counter-insurgency Paradigm." *Journal of Strategic Studies* 32, no. 3: 383–414.

Hack, Karl. 2012. "Everyone Lived in Fear: Malaya and the British Way of Counter-insurgency." *Small Wars and Insurgencies* 23, no. 4–5: 671–99.

Hardt, Michael, and Antonio Negri. 2000. *Empire*. Cambridge, MA: Harvard University Press.

Harper, T. N. 1999. *The End of Empire and the Making of Malaya*. Cambridge: Cambridge University Press.

Hee, Wia Siam. 2017. "Anti-Communist Moving Images and Cold War Ideology: On the Malayan Film Unit." *Inter-Asia Cultural Studies* 18, no. 4: 593–609.

Hee, Wia Siam. 2019. *Remapping the Sinophone: The Cultural Production of Chinese-Language Cinema in Singapore and Malaya before and during the Cold War*. Hong Kong: Hong Kong University Press.

Hill, Andrew. 2010. "The BBC Empire Service: The Voice, the Discourse of the Master, and Ventriloquism." *South Asian Diaspora* 2, no. 1: 25–38.

Jaikumar, Priya. 2019. *Where Histories Reside: India as Filmed Space*. Durham, NC: Duke University Press.

Lim, Cheng Leng. 2000. *The Story of a Psy-Warrior: Tan Sri C. C. Too*. Batu Caves, Selangor Darul Ehsan, Malaysia: Lim Cheng Leng.

Mannheim, Hermann. 1955. *Group Problems in Crime and Punishment*. London: Routledge and Kegan Paul.

Mishra, Pankaj. 2012. *From the Ruins of Empire: The Revolt against the West and the Remaking of Asia*. New York: Farrar, Straus and Giroux.

Muthalib, Hassan. 2011. "The End of Empire: The Films of the Malayan Film Unit in 1950s British Malaya." In *Film and the End of Empire*, edited by Lee Grieveson and Colin MacCabe, 177–98. London: British Film Institute.

Muthalib, Hassan. 2013. *Malaysian Cinema in a Bottle: A Century (and a bit more) of Wayang*. Petaling Jaya, Selangor, Malaysia: Merpati Jingga.

Nagl, John. 2005. *Learning to Eat Soup with a Knife: Counterinsurgency Lessons from Malaya and Vietnam*. Chicago: University of Chicago Press.

Onn, Chin Kee. (1946) 1977. *Malaya Upside Down*. 3rd ed. Kuala Lumpur: Federal Publications.

Ow, Kheng Law, dir. 1960. *Test of Nationhood*. Kuala Lumpur: Malayan Film Unit. 42 min.

Phillips, David. 2013. "Research Notes: The 'Migrated Archives'; The Underbelly of Colonial Rule in Borneo." *Borneo Research Bulletin*, no. 44: 40–92.

Pinkerton, Alasdair, and Klaus Dodd. 2008. "Radio Geopolitics: Broadcasting, Listening, and the Struggle for Acoustic Spaces." *Progress in Human Geography* 33, no. 1: 10–27.

Rajadhyaksha, Ashish. 2010. "Colonial Film Policy after the 1925 Imperial Conference." Keynote address presented at the conference "Colonial Cinema: Moving Images of the British Empire," Birkbeck College, London, July 7–9, 2010.

Rajadhyaksha, Ashish. 2013. "Why Film Narratives Exist." *Inter-Asia Cultural Studies* 14, no. 1: 62–75.

Rajadhyaksha, Ashish. 2020. "The Great Transition: Our Battles over History." *Inter-Asia Cultural Studies* 21, no. 1: 57–89.

Ramakrishna, Kumar. 1999. "Content, Credibility, and Context: Propaganda Government Surrender Policy and the Malayan Communist Terrorist Mass Surrenders of 1958." *Intelligence and National Security* 14, no. 4: 242–66.

Ramakrishna, Kumar. 2002. *Emergency Propaganda: The Winning of Malayan Hearts and Minds, 1948–1958*. Surrey, UK: Curzon.

Ramakrishna, Kumar. 2003. "Making Malaya Safe for Decolonization: The Rural Chinese Factor in the Counterinsurgency Campaign." In *The Transformation of Southeast Asia: International Perspectives on Decolonization*, edited by Marc Frey, Ronald W. Pruessen, and Tai Yong Tan, 161–79. Armonk, NY: M. E. Sharpe.

Rice, Tom. 2019. *Films for the Colonies: Cinema and the Preservation of the British Empire*. Oakland: University of California Press.

Sandhu, Kernial Singh. 1964. "The Saga of the 'Squatter' in Malaya: A Preliminary Survey of the Causes, Characteristics and Consequences of the Resettlement of Rural Dwellers during the Emergency between 1948 and 1960." *Journal of Southeast Asian History* 5, no. 1: 143–77.

Scott, David. 1995. "Colonial Governmentality." *Social Text*, no. 43: 191–220.

Short, Anthony. 1975. *The Communist Insurrection in Malaya, 1948–1960*. London: Frederick Muller.

Singapore Free Press. 1952. "Death Village Gets Detention: Troops Round Up Silent Men at Nine a.m." August 25.

Sioh, Maureen. 2004. "An Ecology of Postcoloniality: Disciplining Nature and Society in Malaya, 1948–1957." *Journal of Historical Geography* 30, no. 4: 729–46.

Stockwell, A. J. 1993. "'A Widespread and Long-Concocted Plot to Overthrow Government in Malaya'? The Origins of the Malayan Emergency." In "Emergencies and Disorder in the European Empires after 1945," edited by Robert Holland. Special issue, *Journal of Imperial and Commonwealth History* 21, no. 3: 66–88.

Stockwell, A. J. 1999. "Imperialism and Nationalism in South-East Asia." In *The Twentieth Century*, edited by Judith Brown and William Roger Louis, vol. 4 of *The Oxford History of the British Empire*, 465–89. Oxford: Oxford University Press.

Straits Times. 1952a. "$4,650 Fine for Murder Village: Death at the Coffee-Shop." August 16.

Straits Times. 1952b. "Seventy-Nine Silent People Get Four Days to Name the Killer Gang: Detention Camp after Monday—if They Still Don't Talk." August 22.

Straits Times. 1952c. "The Not-One-Whisper Villagers Are Punished: Six Trucks Take Sixty-Six to Detention." August 26.

Streicher, Ruth. 2020. "Introduction: Policing the Imperial Formation." In *Uneasy Military Encounters: The Imperial Politics of Counterinsurgency in Southern Thailand*, 1–15. New York: Cornell University Press.

Stubbs, Richard. 1989. *Hearts and Minds in Guerrilla Warfare: The Malayan Emergency, 1948–1960*. Singapore: Oxford University Press.

Thompson, Robert. 1966. *Defeating Communist Insurgency: The Lesson of Malaya and Vietnam*. New York: Frederick A. Praeger.

White, Nicholas J. 2010. "Malaya and the Sterling Area Reconsidered: Continuity and Change in the 1950s." In *The International Order of Asia in the 1930s and 1950s*, edited by Sigeru Akita and Nicholas J. White, 151–76. Surrey, UK: Ashgate.

Wolton, Suke. 2000. *Lord Hailey, the Colonial Office, and the Politics of Race and Empire in the Second World War: The Loss of White Prestige*. New York: St. Martin's.

Wong, Yunn Chii, and Kar Lin Tan. 2004. "Emergence of a Cosmopolitan Space for Culture and Consumption: The New World Amusement Park-Singapore (1923–70) in the Inter-war Years." *Inter-Asia Cultural Studies* 5, no. 2: 279–304.

Yacob, Shakila, and Nicholas J. White. 2010. "The 'Unfinished Business' of Malaysia's Decolonisation: The Origins of the Guthrie 'Dawn Raid.'" *Modern Asian Studies* 44, no. 5: 919–60.

Yao, Souchou. 2016. *The Malayan Emergency: Essays on a Small, Distant War*. Copenhagen: NIAS Press.

Frenemies on Film: Rescreening the Sino-Indian War of 1962

Sandeep Ray

> I looked at our neighbors who were watching us carted off like common crimi-
> nals: a grandmother...her thirteen-year-old granddaughter and eight-year-old
> grandson. They didn't look at us as friends or neighbors. It was a different look,
> one of astonishment. It also seemed to say were outsiders. A flood of simultaneous
> emotions overwhelmed me: bewilderment, fear of the unknown, and a feeling of
> shame: shame for being Chinese.
> —Yin Marsh

In 1963, a film titled *The Unavoidable Internment*, made by the Films Division of India, a government agency tasked with the production and distribution of documentaries addressing national issues, was screened in movie
theaters across the country. The film showed scenes from a camp in Deoli,
Rajasthan, where Chinese residents of India (some of whom were Indian

positions 31:4   DOI 10.1215/10679847-10714259
Copyright 2023 by Duke University Press

citizens) were interned in 1962 after the two nations went to war over border disputes. The film portrayed the environment in the camp to be safe, the food nutritious, and the conditions humane. The act of interning Chinese civilians was explained as "unavoidable"—arranged for their own safety. The circumstances resonate with the internment of Japanese Americans after Pearl Harbor was bombed in 1941. Journalist Dilip D'Souza notes that although there is an obvious parallel to these events, the Japanese American internment is not a forgotten history—whereas people in India seem to have largely overlooked what happened in Deoli (D'Souza and Ma 2020: 138–40).

While the period of the internment will be the focus of this article, I take a longer view, detailing how various motion picture media in India saw the relations between the countries until 1962, when there was an abrupt change in narrative—from friend to enemy. I will then discuss how in recent years there have been several responses to this statist version of the events of 1962. Of special note, an independently produced "rebuttal" category has emerged in recent decades. Two films made by Rafeeq Elias and one by Taiwanese filmmaker Chung Shefong have directly challenged the portrayal of the internment of 1962. This article will review fiction films, Films Division documentaries, and this set of newer documentaries by independent filmmakers made in collaboration with survivors of the internment. I will explore how these films both reflect as well as influence the production of relations in the relevant communities.

While the "war" (some describe it as a skirmish) remains in popular memory, surfacing in the Indian media sporadically, discussions about the internment mostly draw blanks both at the state and civilian domains. Absent from textbooks used in secondary schools is this historical event where over two thousand men, women, and children from the eastern Indian states of West Bengal and Assam were forcibly moved to the arid desert of Rajasthan. Many remained in captivity for almost five years as a security measure for a war that had lasted just a month. While this article cannot detail the complex geopolitical layers of the long-standing and continuing military escalations between India and China, a skeletal overview out the outset would be useful to contextualize the films I discuss later.

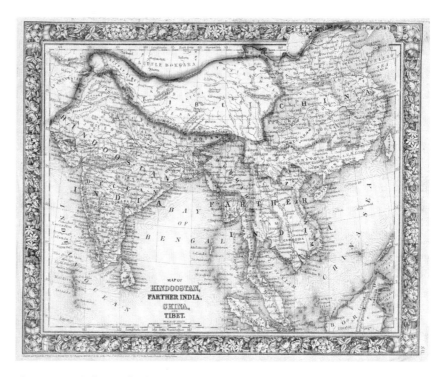

Figure 1 Mitchell Map of India, Tibet, China, and Southeast Asia, 1864.

Against Porosity

The story of how Cyril Radcliffe, a British lawyer who had never been to Asia, hastily and haphazardly drew up the borders for India and Pakistan in 1947 is well known. But the marking of boundaries of territories in the subcontinent began much earlier, long before talks of decolonization. Historian Payel Banerjee (2007: 437–63) explains that British entanglements in regional politics involving India, Afghanistan, Russia, China, and Tibet, and their interest in maintaining a hegemonic stronghold in the area, led to an acute push for mapmaking and border defining as early as the mid-1800s. Of particular interest was to demarcate Tibet (see fig. 1) and to create a buffer with Russia. A series of contradicting lines drawn between 1865 and 1914 by various British colonial servants in meetings inconsistently attended by Indian, Chinese, and Tibetan officials led to convoluted reinterpretations. The problem lingers. Along the vast territory flanked by India and China, there are two main zones of contention: one along the border of Ladakh in the North—called Aksai Chin—and in the other in the Northeast, right above Assam and Arunachal Pradesh, called the North East Frontier Agency (NEFA).

In 1951 India annexed a small area called Tawang in the NEFA, creating resentment in the new Maoist Chinese government. From 1956 to 1958 China paved a 204-kilometer highway through land that India claimed to be within its territory in the Aksai Chin area. An Indian patrol was sent to the region to investigate matters, and China deemed this an act of intrusion. In 1959 Chinese premier Zhou Enlai openly declared dissatisfaction over both the Aksai Chin and NEFA borders. It was not easy to categorically challenge China's claim in an open-and-shut way based on the tenuous documents with their various interpretations. Zhou Enlai declared that China was the rightful owner of land that India claimed to be in its jurisdiction. Diplomatic barbs between the two nations began to be traded regularly in the newspapers and in international summits. In this tense political climate, the decision of the Dalai Lama to seek asylum in India resulted in open hostility between the two countries. Both deployed troops in the Aksai Chin and in the NEFA between 1960 and 1962. War broke out on October 20, 1962, and a cease-fire was declared just one month later, on November 21. While acute acrimony over the border issue has receded, tensions remain high, keeping both governments on tenterhooks. The problem remains unsolved, and periodic charges of incursion continue, occasionally leading to the deaths of border patrollers on both sides.

It is noteworthy that at that time these contested areas were not assessed to be particularly lucrative in minerals and resources, nor were they densely inhabited.[1] The impetus of nations to go to war cannot always be explained through economic motivation or nationalism driven by local populations. Rather—as Prasenjit Duara (1995: 477–79) elaborates in his review of *Siam Mapped* (1994), Thongchai Winichakul's influential monograph on politically motivated cartography—it is a "fetishistic power of geo-body" that gradually develops because of the modern introduction of lines and maps, and "this history renders all those who have been at the peripheries, the margins, or, simply, outside the ambit of historical states in the region as the historical property of the nation-state and so to be directly controlled by it." What in the past was considered somewhat shifting and amorphous changed with these newly contested lines. British security interests from the nineteenth century and the resulting imperialist cartography created the precedent for postcolonial territorial politics. This lingering ambiguity would become central to the discourse of nation building and nationalism during the Sino-Indian War. The idea of a porous border based on traditional understandings was unacceptable under new imaginations of the nation-state. Thongchai Winichakul (1994: 100–1) elaborates on this modern political reasoning:

> In the indigenous interstate relations, the overlapping margins of two power fields was not necessarily considered a problem.... Multiple sovereignty was well considered by the parties involved as the status quo.... For modern polities, however, the overlapping frontier is not permissible. The division of territorial sovereignty between states must be clear-cut at the point where both power fields interface.

The 1950s saw narratives swiftly created along jingoistic lines, sidelining the wishes of the actual inhabitants of these frontier areas, plotting them within the geopolitical drama of two very large countries, India and China. They would go to war over these convictions.

Hindi-Chini Bhai Bhai (India and China Are Brothers)

Relations between India and China had been remarkably strong till the downhill spiral over the border problem. Some of this is reflected in the early cinema form the region. After the invasion of Manchuria in 1931, followed by the horrifying "Rape of Nanking" in 1937, Indian nationalist leaders declared solidarity with China as Japan continued its invasions. Allied sorties originating from Assam in northeastern India would later fly over the dangerous eastern "hump" of the Himalayas, providing ammunition and supplies to Chiang Kai-shek's holdouts in southern China. The support was bipartisan. There are popular tales of heroic camaraderie, some real, others embellished. In 1938, at the request of Mao Zedong, medical missions from

Figure 2 *Dr. Kotnis ki amar kahani*
(*The Eternal Tale of Dr. Kotnis*, 1946).

India were authorized and galvanized by Jawaharlal Nehru, then the head of the Indian National Congress. One Dr. Dwarkanath Kotnis joined Mao's famous Eighth Route Army and provided medical services on the frontlines of the Sino-Japanese War. He died in Yunan in his fifth year of service and posthumously received tributes from both Mao and Soon Ching-ling, popularly known as Madame Sun Yat-sen. In 1946, Bollywood produced *The Eternal Tale of Dr. Kotnis*, a biographical account of his selfless deeds starring V. Shantaram as Kotnis and Jayashree as Ching Lan, his Chinese love interest, whom he married in 1942 (fig. 2).

Perhaps in response to the faltering diplomatic relationship between the two nations, Mrinal Sen directed *Neel akasher nichey* (*Under a Blue Sky*) in 1958. Set in the early 1930s, the film revolves around Wang Lu (Kali Banerjee), a Chinese hawker in Calcutta, and Basanti (Manju Dey), a Bengali housewife and outspoken anti-imperialist (see fig. 3). Wang Lu meets Basanti by chance while hawking his wares and sees a kindred soul. Inspired by her tale of courage and defiance, he eventually returns to China to fight the Japanese after the invasion of Manchuria. The initial meeting between Wang Lu and Basanti when he comes to her home to hawk goods is revealing of the director's vision of an idealist panethnic identity, surmounting the obvious ethnic difference:

Basanti: I don't use foreign stuff.

Wang Lu: What? Foreign? Me foreign? No, no, I no foreign. I am a Chinaman. Chinese, Chinese, do you know what a Chinese is? No foreigner, no foreigner. Here, look (*he shows her his arm*), no white, no English. Chinaman. (*He points to his eyes.*) No blue.[2]

Basanti is charmed by his theatrics and can't help laughing, signaling the start of a friendship. The film was generally received well in India.[3] Mrinal Sen (2004: 50), the film's director, writes in his memoirs, "Even Nehru liked the film and remembered it for quite some time. Most possibly he liked the film for its content, which unequivocally espoused that our struggle against colonial rule was inseparably linked with democratic world's fight against fascism." Predictably, just as the military operations between the two countries started, the film was banned. The Information and Broadcast Ministry seemed to have confused the period the film was set in. Or perhaps a sympathetic portrayal of the Chinese was against the grain of wartime jingoism in the country. The ban, however, was short-lived, lasting a couple of months.

As Sen suggested, the cue to portray China as India's compatriot in a long struggle against oppression (under different rulers) would have been taken from highest level of the Indian political sphere—from Jawaharlal Nehru. The first Indian prime minister's love and possibly inflated sense of a personal role as "big brother" toward China is well known and documented. The phrase "Hindi-Chini Bhai Bhai" gained popularity in 1954 when Nehru visited China, calling it "the most important foreign mission of my life." The photographs and films of that trip documented extensively by the Indian government show Chinese civilians cheering in rapt adulation as he walks among them (fig. 4). In a crowded hallway a schoolgirl puts a scarf on him as his daughter Indira watches. The narrator reads:

> For more than thirty years he [Nehru] had dreamed of the day when India and China, breaking through the barriers that foreign rule had set up, would renew their ancient ties. And from across the peaks of the Himalayas they would clasp each other's hands in friendship again. "Greetings to you, young friends of India and Asia, resurgent Asia's promise and hope!"

It is said that the reversal of India's relations with China broke Nehru's heart, contributing to his early demise. While it would be pointless to try to ascertain the truth of this claim, Nehru did feature in numerous films, presenting himself as a great ally and champion for the Chinese people. A department within the government of India's many public relations agencies—the Films Division—produced these documentaries. I will discuss these films in some detail to highlight the transition from ally to foe, from depict-

Figure 3 Basanti (Manju Dey) and Wang Lu (Kali Banerjee) meet in *Neel akasher nichey* (*Under a Blue Sky, 1958*).

Figure 4 Jawaharlal Nehru and his daughter Indira visit China in 1954.

ing China as a compatriot jockeying for power in the postcolonial era to depicting it as a duplicitous, untrustworthy nation.

The Films Division of India

Much academic research has been done on the institution called the Films Division of India—one that has produced a staggering corpus of eight-thousand-odd documentary films. These government funded productions allowed audiences across the large country to "see the state" and the concrete activities that it was undertaking with the aim of improving the newly independent nation. The Films Division had an assured funding model: 1 percent of all revenue from commercial movie houses was used to produce the documentaries (Roy 2007: 41). The distribution was straightforward: till 1994 all movie theaters had to screen a Films Division–produced documentary before the start of the main attraction. It created a distinctive genre of documentary in which both state and nonstate actors collaborated; well-known filmmakers were often asked to produce on behalf of the government, to promote the cause of national integrity and showcase its development agenda.

When Indian authorities took over the mantle of production from the British in 1948, anti-fascist war propaganda, the driving rationale behind the large output of films in the 1940s was no longer relevant. A new agenda was installed: showcasing development. As film historian Camille Deprez

(2017: 64–80) observes, "[Indian] documentaries, mainly short films, had to play a significant role in terms of political and social cohesion and socioeconomic development by circulating official information, spreading a sense of national belonging, educating the vast illiterate sections of the population on various topics ranging from agriculture to hygiene, and reporting on the progress of the young independent nation."

This drive to produce short, nonfiction films about the country's aspirations to become a self-supporting, diverse, postcolonial democracy saw a high volume of productions for several years, the majority made under the banner of the Films Division. Though there were exceptions, the films were often self-congratulatory of India's bold forays into Nehruvian models of development and were typically heavily narrated with a booming, paternal voice that represented the state. They were dubbed into several Indian languages for wider reach. It must be noted here that this model of nonfiction filmmaking, often bordering on statist propaganda, has seen considerable disruption in recent years. In 2012, a new initiative called the FD Zone began curating and screening both films produced by the Films Division as well as external producers, a program that spread to nine cities. Films Division funds were also made available for collaborative projects with creative independent filmmakers (Kishore 2021).[4] In 2013, the Films Division, with external curators, organized "A Hundred Years of Experimentation: A Retrospective of Indian Cinema and Video." Unfortunately, these newer models of debate, expression, and documentary construction, screened in varied venues, are now faced with extinction, as per the recent announcement by the Ministry of Information and Broadcasting of the Government of India (PTI 2021). While the efforts currently underway to dismantle the organization face considerable opposition from members of India's artistic community, it is unlikely that the Films Division will exist long as a relatively autonomous entity, one that had begun to evolve and reinvent itself. The fate of its considerable archive, including the films discussed in this article, hangs in the balance.

In 1962, Nehru asked the Films Division to produce two films a week covering the Chinese "aggression" and the threat of a possible invasion. It was a drastic shift both in the mandate of the Films Division (it typically focused internally and not on foreign policy) as well as in India's portrayal of

China on screen. Some of these films are worth scrutiny. *The Chinese Threat* (1962) was narrated by none other than the famous voice-over talent Melville de Mellow. Mellow was anything but. His baritone was immediately recognizable. The film starts with a pastiche of scenes from World War II— Hitler giving a speech, Jews being driven out of their homes, bombs dropping in Europe, the attack on Pearl Harbor, and a man rescuing a baby from an inferno. Mellow reads stirringly: "These are scenes of horror and tragedy from the Second World War, when fascist aggression posed a grave threat to mankind. Our program this evening is about a threat to world peace which is as grave. Commentator Melville de Mellow brings to you the facts about this new menace to peace and freedom—the Chinese aggression." The film uses a remarkable number of maps and charts. It presents itself almost as the opening argument of a legal case. Text quotations of Zhou Enlai's own words are highlighted, establishing their duplicitous content. Border areas are clearly demarcated, showing what are allegedly the areas of intrusion, and signatures on documents are filmed in close-up. The evidence is compelling. Nehru is the star of this movie; excerpts of him speaking movingly at the United Nations and scenes from his efforts to shore up the Non-aligned Movement are edited deftly. The main takeaway from this film was that it was not just India's borders that were being challenged—the very ideal of world peace was under threat due to China's rabid militancy. Given the timing of the film, what rings somewhat hollow is the insistence that India maintained a commitment to seeking harmony in ethnic diversity. The Indian government soon passed the Foreigners Law Act in 1962, which in essence allowed them to apprehend and incarcerate anyone (including citizens), without showing reason, "who, or either of whose parents, or any of whose grandparents was at any time a citizen or subject of any country at war with, or committing external aggression against, India" (Cohen and Chiu 2017: 845). The target was, of course, the local Chinese.

United We Stand begins on a petulant tone—the accusation that Zhou Enlai had deviously charmed India into his confidence and had then played a duplicitous game by abruptly turning hostile. Indeed, there is even a shot of him at an unspecified masquerade party (fig. 5), donning the "mask of deceit." The rest of the film shows a nation rallying under one banner, chal-

Figure 5 Zhou Enlai's "mask of deceit." Still from *United We Stand* (1962).

Figure 6 Anti-Chinese demonstrations in 1962. Still from *United We Stand* (1962).

lenging the Chinese aggression (fig. 6) through volunteer efforts: blood banks, exhibition sport matches, buying government-issued wartime treasury bonds, donating money and jewelry, women knitting sweaters for soldiers, movie stars hosting fund raisers, and even women training with weapons. Images not seen in the documentary include civilians who looked remotely Chinese. Given that the incursion was happening in the northeastern part of the country, the omission was deliberate.

Perhaps the most compelling and detailed film made during this period—*The Great Betrayal*—continues with the theme of Zhou Enlai and Mao's "duping" of India. Like *The Chinese Threat*, the film is full of "evidence" of Chinese diplomatic disingenuousness, including a repeated typewritten excerpt that floats on the screen quoting Zhou Enlai in 1954: "The recognized boundary between India and Tibet should remain inviolate." He is then seen being driven through the streets of India, hands folded amicably, practicing deliberate deception relative to the plan he is hatching. The friend had not merely turned into an enemy; the transformation had occurred in a backstabbing manner, taking advantage of a trusting Nehru and the Indian Republic.

The film has two other components that make it a bit different from the typical Films Division production. First, many actors were hired to reenact a battle with Chinese soldiers. The scenes are filmed in rugged, mountainous terrain and are not wholly unrealistic. Special sound effects, music, and some competent acting help the narrative. Second, by evoking images of

Tagore, Gandhi, and Sun Yat-sen, we are provided with a sense of the *past-ness* of a great pan-Asian bond between India and China. Ancient India, after all, the narrator informs us, had always upheld the will to maintain friendly relations with its neighbor. Once again Nehru becomes central to this quasi-historical piece. He is seen in Bandung, Indonesia, hugging delegates from all over Asia and Africa. He works hard to convince the many international delegations that China ought to be included in the new, trusting fraternity of the Non-aligned Movement. Over a scene of Zhou Enlai moving through a crowd, the narrator says: "And when Mr. Zhou Enlai walked to the historic gathering it was as if the task of Asian unity to which India had given herself was being fulfilled. It was a happy time, this joyous meeting of age-old friends whom centuries of foreign rule had torn apart. A new era in the history of the Asian people was about to begin." The theme of India's championing of China, its "age-old friend," continues with clips of Nehru at the United Nations in New York asking delegates from around the world to "give China her rightful place." China reciprocates this grand gesture with written eulogies to Nehru, several of which flash on the screen. Soon after, we see Nehru using his diplomatic credibility to successfully dissuade Mao from encroaching on Burmese territory. Next the film contends that in 1956, Mao betrayed India by demanding a reassessment of the borders between the two countries. Like *The Chinese Threat* but in more detail, the film too builds a quasi-legal case by showing maps and documents ratified with official signatures. The producers of the film locate Chinese texts, mostly in books by scholars and travelers, and a map drawn up at the University of Peking that clearly shows the McMahon line as being official and accepted by both countries. Indigenous people in the disputed areas are displayed like ornaments, with the narrator insisting that they identify as citizens of India.

The film builds up to a final dramatic crescendo, with the world waiting for the Cuban missile crisis to implode in October of 1962 while China invades Indian territory. What follows is an astonishing two-minute sequence of Nehru's face superimposed over various images from the 1950s. It begins with the "good old days"—his visits to China, garlanded and paraded by Asian leaders, surrounded with Nasser's followers, Mao's peaceful trips in India—and ends with corpses in the battlefield. Indians are seen rising up

Figure 7 A woman donates her jewelry. Still from *A Nation Stirs* (1962).

Figure 8 Men enlist at army recruiting centers. Still from *A Nation Stirs* (1962).

in protest all over the country against the Chinese aggression. The music moves from elegiac to triumphant. China is friend no more; the people have decided.

Shorter, reedited, punchier versions of these films described above were distributed widely. *A Nation Stirs* is a two-minute film that repurposes some of the scenes from *United We Stand* as an effective campaign tool for raising money. Scenes from politicians in a parliamentary session discussing war matters is followed by a bejeweled woman taking off her ornaments as donation for the war (fig. 7). This is followed by scenes of more women handing over personal artifacts, the wealthy present checks (ostensibly covering large amounts) to the government, and the poor from slum areas drop coins into a small tin can. "People donated according to their means. More than one crore [10 million] rupees have been raised," reads the narrator. The film is dubbed in Hindi, presumably to include non-English speaking sections of society. The war effort is portrayed along gender lines—women giving up jewelry and donating their time to knit clothes for the troops; men donating money and labor and enlisting in volunteer military forces (see fig. 8).

Collectively, these films signal an abrupt departure from the early style of the Films Division projects. As Sirupa Roy (2007: 50–51) summarizes, the situation with China shifted the priority: "Martial strength was the defining attribute of the state; vulnerability the distinguishing characteristic of the nation; and sacrifice and bravery the constituting features of the ideal citizen." In a glaring oversight, not one of the films above had included or considered the position of the most vulnerable group of people in this episode—the local Chinese who had made India their home. They are absent from the footage, the analysis, and the many elaborately produced scenes of the turmoil enveloping the nation. Considering that they were a sizable portion of the roughly 20,000 people living in the northeastern area near the NEFA lines, it would seem as though they were deliberately omitted. In 1962, *after* the internment of approximately 2,300 individuals, the Films Division did produce a documentary called *The Unavoidable Internment* highlighting the story of the local, displaced Chinese.

Filming like the State

The Unavoidable Internment, produced in 1963, is structurally akin to a Griersonian style of wall-to-wall narration, B-roll footage, some reenacted footage, and heavy, polemical voice-over. This time, however, the makers did not make Nehru an integral part of the narrative. This was unfortunate because Nehru himself had been imprisoned in Deoli, Rajasthan, where the internment camp was located. The camp had been used by the British to imprison Italian and German POWs during World War II; the Panditji served time there when he was deemed a threat as an anti-colonial. This irony—that the free Indian state was using the same location to intern civilians where the oppressive colonial apparatus had once imprisoned dissidents—is bitterly pointed out by Yin Marsh (2016) in the classic autobiography of her years in Deoli, titled "Doing Time with Nehru."

The film presents basic "facts" upfront recapping the betrayal that led to war: Zhou Enlai arrived in Delhi in 1955 promising peace but reneged on his word and attacked India in 1962. Next, and for the first time since the tensions started, we see Chinese Indians on screen. They are depicted as "security risks." Calling the internment "unavoidable" and evidently acting in full compliance with international convention, we are shown various scenes of the internment site where the rounded up Chinese Indians are forced to live. Over footage of children running around, the narrator reads, "Acts of subversion and sabotage have to be guarded against, and potential fifth column activities nipped in the bud." The roughly 2,300 people interned, the voice-over continues, had to be protected from "the wrath of

Figure 9 An internee plays tennis in Deoli. Still from *An Unavoidable Internment* (1963).

Figure 10 Mr. Lee being interviewed. Still from *An Unavoidable Internment* (1963).

the Indian people angered by the invasion of their land." The government is shown to have provided electricity, water, and sanitation, and even to have installed a democratic system of electing camp leaders. Food distribution is depicted in detail—fish, vegetables, pork, eggs, mutton, and milk. The narrator claims that each adult is assured a healthy, well-balanced diet of 2,500 calories. These claims were all later vociferously challenged by survivors. Other considerations and amenities include slates and books for children, a fifty-bed hospital, access to medicine, and a state-of-the-art health care facility. Graffiti on a canteen wall reads "20/11/1962 Remember" (this is the date the war officially ended) and some undecipherable scribbles on a common area wall indicate the year to be 1963, dating the film. Over a scene of men playing tennis in clean, bright sportswear (fig. 9), the narrator explains that an officer of the Red Cross had visited the camp in December 1962 and had expressed his strong approval.[5] The narration adds that internees had been given "free choice" either to remain in India (in the camp) or to be repatriated to China. A Mr. Lee is interviewed in his modest but clean quarters (the only time we hear any internee speak) and asked his thoughts on the matter (fig. 10). His response is polite and positive (as one would expect of a person speaking with the authorities of an internment camp). He is approving of the government's efforts. He says, "I am born in India and there is no question that I should go back because my family and everything is settled in Darjeeling. And another thing is that I do not like the communistic method of ruling or living. I have acquired the method of democracy of India." A formally dressed Mr. Lee providing such soundbites, saying next that "the constitution also suits me well," is ironic because it was precisely the recent ratification of the Foreigners Law Ordinance (which subsumed all previous laws about foreigners, stripping them of their legal rights) that enabled the government to incarcerate him with no direct charges. The narrator summarizes the interview, concluding that "for people like Mr. and Mrs. Lee, India was their home," underscoring the tragedy of the situation.

The last episode of the film follows internees being repatriated. The narrator claims that the process was entirely voluntary, as it was the "inalienable right" of an ethnic Chinese to leave India. About 10 percent of the detainees leave India on a ship sent by the government of Taiwan. They are shown being provided with funds for the journey, new clothes, and even medical assistance on the way to the harbor in Madras before their long voyage home. The film ends with the following proclamation, "Those who have left the country have India's good wishes. Those who have elected to remain are honored guests." What is not clear is how long those who were still in the camp (the honored guests) would remain interned.

Let us now look at the more recent filmic discourse that challenges this 1963 state-produced account of life and events in the Deoli internment camp and the claim of Chinese Indians being treated as "honored guests" in their country of domicile.

Rebuttal to the Narrative

Fifty-three years after the arrests and subsequent internments, Rafeeq Ellias, a Mumbai-based photographer and filmmaker, produced *The Legend of Fat Mama*, the first film to highlight scars of those who were imprisoned in Deoli. The twenty-four-minute documentary revolves around the search for a mythical lady who prepared delectable dishes and presumably ran an eatery in Calcutta's Chinatown in the 1950s or 1960s (it is unclear). With this premise, Rafeeq travels in the city's Chinese neighborhoods to seek answers. The film begins as an ethnographic record of a dwindling community holding on to its fragile traditions through New Year celebrations, mah-jongg clubs, hand-calligraphed publications, and, of course, street food. But a couple of unexpected interviews with survivors of the Deoli camp bring to the surface a tragedy not discussed much—the irreparable damage that the internment did to this community. Barely 10 percent of the Chinese population from the 1960s had remained in the country. "As the two giant neighbors and one-time friends battled it out in the mountains, an unspoken human tragedy unfolded in Calcutta," reads the narrator over newspaper headlines from that tumultuous period. Liu Yew Shen, an Indian citizen of Chinese origin, owner of an eatery, tells us in perfect Hindi how his entire family was suddenly and forcibly transported to Rajasthan with little to eat during the journey. The film shifts its focus from the search for the legendary chef to the issue of forcible incarceration in Deoli (though the interviewees on occasion dwell upon the mythical Fat Mama). Several residents of Chinatown discuss the horrors, indignation, and humility of being members of a community that was racially targeted and sent across the country. Ellias then moves the film's setting to Toronto, where a number of Indian Chinese people fled to in the late 1960s, and asks them about the sudden abductions, the relocation to Rajasthan, and its devastating effects on the morale of the Chinese diaspora in India. The occupations of the interviewees vary—supermarket owner, lawyer, technician, acupuncturist—and all are members of the Indian-Chinese Association of Toronto. The collective ethos is similar; they had made India their home, but the government of India mistreated them with no legal basis over a war that had absolutely nothing to do with them.

Ellias's second documentary on the subject, *Beyond Barbed Wires: A Distant Dream* directly confronts the history of the internment. It begins with a poem written by Japanese American woman named Ann Muto who was born in a war camp after the bombing of Pearl Harbor, when Japanese people living in America were incarcerated. Ellias draws the parallel between the two situations: Japanese American war camps in Hawaii and the Chinese Indian internment camp in Deoli. The analogy is clear: in each case, individuals from an ethnic group, most of whom were citizens in their country of residence, were forcibly removed from their homes to a distant location, causing great indignity, an irreparable rupture of social life, and a massive loss of both individual and communal wealth. Filmed in Canada and in Northern California, we are privy to interviews with Chinese people of Indian origin and their descendants. Acting as a therapeutic catalyst for discussion, the film becomes an intergenerational dialogue where several members who spent time in Deoli talk about their experiences with their children. Yin Marsh explains that the very act of remembering began when her daughter decided to interview her as part of an oral history project for college. That experience opened a floodgate of emotions that had welled up for decades and finally found expression in her autobiography. Siblings Liu Chin Wong and Ying Shen Wong tell Ellias how their father had died of medical negligence in Deoli. Effa Ma recounts how her elderly grandmother, who was from a generation where women still had their feet bound, was not spared and was roughly transported to the camp. Many of the individuals interviewed make it a point to inform viewers that they identify with being Indian despite the experience. Yin Marsh says that when faced with a large group of Indians or a large group of Chinese, she feels more comfortable among Indians. Joy Ma, who was born in the Deoli camp says, "Ironically, my dad never lost his love for India.... He has hypertension, but he eats jalebis, he eats samosas, when he is here in the Bay Area, he listens to Oakland's Hindi station." Thus, they were never able to shut out their Indianness from their lives and continue to hanker for a sense of home, even if symbolic. It is in relation to this need to connect with their pasts that raises the most pressing point in the film: many of the former detainees and their children say that they would like an apology from the Indian government. In the words of Ming-Tung Hsieh who was born in Calcutta: "Now looking back more than fifty years ago . . . everybody makes mistakes. I think we deserve to be told that the authority of that time was doing wrongly and apologize to us. That will clear a lot of pent-up fear and anger inside." The idea that an official apology, no matter how late in coming, can help heal emotional wounds, has been accepted in the post–World War II era. Ellias ends the film with a title card emphasizing President Ronald Reagan's signing of the Civil Liberties Act of 1988, which formally apologized for the wartime imprisonment of Japanese Americans. It is noteworthy that several Japanese civilians who were in India during World War II were incarcerated in the same camp in Deoli, Rajasthan (Sutton 2016).

One other project to take note of in this "rebuttal through film" effort is the 107-minute documentary by Taiwanese director Chung Shefong titled *From Border to Border: Chinese in India* (2015). While this narrative takes on a much longer time frame, locating the immigrant story all the way to 1780,

Figure 11 Still from *From Border to Border: Chinese in India*. Internees being taken to Deoli.

when Chinese arrived in India in considerable numbers, there is a substantial section on the internment in Deoli and its aftermath. In fact, the story of Chinese immigrants in India, according to Shefong, appears to have a distinct crack: before and after 1962. It was the year that forever altered their history of being settlers in India. Like Ellias, Shefong uses interviews to get personal narratives across, but he intercuts them with archival photographs (fig. 11), film footage, and even animation to recreate the train journey from eastern India to Rajasthan.

The harrowing plight of the Deoli experience is reinforced through additional accounts in *From Border to Border*. Shefong establishes that families that had even one member with a Chinese passport were taken away. Chang Kuo Tsai, a newspaper publisher, says, "I had a passport from Communist China, my father had a Kuomintang passport, and my brother had an Indian one." But they were all incarcerated. He also informs us, contrary to what is seen in *The Unavoidable Internment*, that the food was quite awful, the bread "as hard as stone." One additional aspect that Shefong's film covers is the sense of public life in India as a person of Chinese origin once the troubles began. Paul Chung, president of the Indian Chinese Association, says:

> In 1962 when this happened, they thought we Chinese were the enemy. The government took a patriotic stance, encouraging Indians to feel patriotic about India. That effort turned into pointing fingers at Chinese here.... When we'd walk down the street, the children would ridicule us and call to us, "Chinese thieves! Chinese thieves!" Some of the elderly would even say, "Go back to China! What are you doing here?" Some

would speak in Hindi or Bengali. They thought we didn't understand what we were saying.

Many were in Deoli for up to five years, and upon their return they found their lives decimated in several ways. First, their businesses were lost, shops and stores gutted; second, the government of India put severe restrictions on their movements, even within the state. And finally, all requests for citizenships, even for those born in India, were put on hold. It was not till the late 1990s that Chinese born in India were granted citizenship, normalizing their civilian status.

In his essay on the recently discovered footage of Korean comfort women, published in this issue, Han Sang Kim (2023: 804) refers to Bill Nichols's (2016) observation that because no uniform ethical baseline exists among documentary film producers, they can easily fall short of established standards expected from formal disciplines like history or journalism. The Films Division created a film where an omnipresent narrator stood in for the government's voice to educate citizens about the purported facts of the Chinese internment. It was a situation in which subjects, in Nichols's (2016: 151) words, "relinquish any and all rights to how what is recorded of their lives gets used." In contrast, Ellias and Shefong interview survivors, decades later, in a more back-and-forth conversational setting. But while they appear to participate in the making of the film and have some agency in how their narrative is shaped, they still fall under that tenuous, expansive category of "documentary film," where the boundaries between "ethical" reportage and personal agenda are often blurred. What criteria then can we apply to argue for or against aspects of historicity in these films? Indeed, Kim posits that even in "established" academic fields there is no consensus of a methodology on how film should be interpreted. Thus, the academic researcher involved (described by Kim as "excavator-interpreter") takes on the "task of decoding or analyzing documentary films based on their own choice of approaches." Accordingly, in this article I take it upon myself to interrogate whether the government produced film violated basic ethical standards of reportage.

There are limited precedents in academic research on propaganda films of internment camps.[6] The most well known of these is Karel Margry's (1992: 145–64) article on the Nazi-produced film called *Theresienstadt* (also known as *The Führer Gives the Jews a City*), made in 1944 in Theresienstadt, now Terezin, in the Czech Republic. There are similarities between this film and *The Unavoidable Internment*. The objective in both cases was to make a positive film depicting good, healthy camp life, to be showcased for the world outside that had little access to the area. Both productions show healthy inmates partaking in relaxed pastimes (see fig. 12) and enjoying robust outdoor activities. Not a single guard or soldier is present in either. And, as expected, the narrators describe aspects of "good conditions in the camp" as the internees reenact their own lives, producing an unnatural impression of an environment where they were forcibly interned. In an additional strange parallel, the idea for the Theresienstadt film first surfaced when the camp was asked to clean up its image in preparation for the arrival of the International Red Cross. A Jewish actor-director residing in the camp, Kurt Gerron, was initially given the task of making the film by using inmates as the cast. Prisoners gave carefully scripted performances to express how content they were. The historian Rudolf Mrazek goes so far as to suggest that this film is possibly much better known than the camp itself. He mentions the long sequence of a soccer match (fig. 13), calling it "a fake, like everything in the camps." But he calls the staging of the match fake, conceding that primary sources do mention many soccer matches being played "irrespective of the film" (Mrazek 2020: 74). Like *Theresienstadt*, *An Unavoidable Internment*, too, was meant to delude the outside world about the actual conditions of the camp. But the flaw in categorically denouncing propaganda films as being untruthful and duplicitous is that they often depict *some* truths. Even Margry (1992: 155) warns us against imagining that the environment in Theresienstadt was completely fabricated and the film an outright lie:

> The film's visual authenticity is much greater than most people think. Many of the things shown in it actually existed in Theresienstadt or formed part of the prisoners' daily life. . . . A number of scenes were filmed on locations that had not been "beautified." Even the narration—the main truth-distorting element in the film—contained elements of factual truth. In the final analysis, the film's blatant dishonesty turns on what it did not show: the hunger, the misery, the overcrowding, the slave work for the

Figure 12 Women in relaxing in the common space. Scene from *Theresienstadt* (*The Führer Gives the Jews a City*, 1944) in the Theresienstadt camp.

Figure 13 Men playing soccer. Scene from *Theresienstadt* (*The Führer Gives the Jews a City*, 1944) in the Theresienstadt camp.

German war economy, the high death rate, and, most of all, the transports leaving for the East.

There can easily exist coverage in a propaganda film that is somewhat accurate, containing those "elements of factual truth." Producers may choose to show those scenes or interviews and yet skew the larger narrative. In the case of Deoli, at the time of the filming, the quarters were actually habitable and the environment mostly unthreatening, possibly as it happened in conjunction with a Red Cross visit. It was later that conditions would deteriorate (Griffiths 2013). What we are not shown is the sense of despondency among the inmates. How long would they remain there? What was happening to their livelihoods back home? There was never a follow-up to this film as the years in internment rolled on. Despite this alarming lack in depth of coverage, it is not easy to challenge the Films Division on the grounds that it was an entirely "made-up" film. At the same time, to let it slide as partially accurate would be unconscionable.

The structural similarities notwithstanding, comparing the nature of events at the Chinese Indian camp at Deoli with the Nazi camp north of Prague would be erroneous. As far as we know, while some died due to malnutrition and medical ailments, no one was sent to their death from Deoli, although there is a horrifying account of a young girl who was allegedly buried alive by mistake (*Deoli Diaries*, 2013), and many instances of gross medical neglect leading to death.

But unlike *Theresienstadt*, which is now in the public domain and has been meticulously researched by historians, there has been little exposure of *An Unavoidable Internment*, and, to the best of my knowledge, no critique exists of it.[7] There are documents in the public domain about the details of most Nazi camps and of the Japanese internment in the United States. There are hardly any on Deoli, and thus there is a need to locate models of analysis that have some parity with the film discussed. A new book authored by Joy Ma, who was born in Deoli, and the journalist Dilip D'Souza, titled *The Deoli Wallahs: The True Story of the 1962 Chinese-Indian Internment*, is the first major interview-based analysis and exploration of what happened in Deoli, but it was released as recently as 2020. Both authors were influenced by Ellias's documentary attempts to capture reflections on this difficult past. If we were to look for sources, the only ones available are these testimonials of survivors recorded in recent years. Thus, the "rebuttal" films take on the dual role of being documents that both establish a clearer picture of the years at Deoli as well as act as a critique of the 1963 production of *An Unavoidable Internment*.

Even with minimal referencing and conjecture, it is apparent that *An Unavoidable Internment*, while not containing outright lies, is full of misleading information. The film gives us the impression that people were arrested for two primary reasons: (1) to protect them from patriotic Indians angered by China's incursion; and (2) to incarcerate those who may have been involved in fifth column activities of subterfuge. In the government's own words, as narrated over the film, "Amongst the security measures taken was the internment of persons of Chinese origin resident in the sensitive border areas and persons of Chinese origin who were known to be security risks." This cannot justify the internment of the many elderly people who were transported to Rajasthan. Were Indian mobs really going to attack them, years after the brief military engagement was over? Why could they not have been released after a few weeks? We are given the impression that the members in the camp were there for as long as there existed a security risk. This, again, does not explain why some people were incarcerated for as many as five years for a war that ended in a month. Most tellingly, not a single person sent to Deoli was ever formally prosecuted for crimes against the government of India. The film gives us the impression that only those who wished to leave the camp and go back to China or Taiwan were permitted to leave as a matter of personal choice. And yet there are records of ethnic Chinese from all over India being arrested in their homes and directly deported. The film does not address arrests and events happening outside the Deoli camp. Banerjee's (2007: 437–63) meticulous research extrapolates the following from the government's own data sets: "Forced deportation of Chinese residents in India (in the name of national security) continued to occur as late as in December of 1967, five years after the outbreak of the war. The government of India repatriated about 1,665 Chinese internees along with their 730 dependents to China by September of 1963." In 1964, the inmates were told that they would all be deported. Interviews with survivors reveal that the process was arbitrary and not all were deported. Some families were split up and some sent to Calcutta, from where they were deported to collective farms in China (Mazumder 2010).

If deportations by the government accounted for a few thousand, the voluntary exodus from India in the years after the war would be phenomenal. About a tenth of the original numbers of Chinese Indians from 1962 remain in the country now. These figures do not suggest an environment that was habitable for the small minority—as declared in the last moments of the film, "those who have elected to remain are honored guests." Having no reassurance a normal life in India again, Chinese Indians scrambled to emigrate. The limited individual accounts of survivors of Deoli now available are of tales of indignity and humiliation of a people ripped away from their normal lives, and of their loss of money and property. Most families saw their savings, homes, and businesses entirely wiped out.

The New Collectivity and a Quest for an Apology

In the introduction to this essay, I suggest that the films discussed herein both reflect the shifting relationships between India and China and contribute to producing these relationships. The conditions for the first conjecture are easier to establish. Commercially released films like *The Eternal Tale of Dr. Kotnis* and *Under a Blue Sky* demonstrably reflect a period when efforts were made to showcase political camaraderie between the two countries—

overthrowing fascism was held up as a common cause for both Indians and Chinese.

Documentary footage of Nehru in China, moving slowly among throngs of admiring people, and then in Bandung, Indonesia, clearly showcase his desire to be seen as the leader of the Non-aligned Movement and a great ally and supporter of China. The subsequent films produced by the Films Division—*The Chinese Threat, United We Stand, A Nation Stirs*—are clearly a result of the Indian government's new position in calling out China for its territorial threats and to galvanize the Indian population in preparation for war. *An Unavoidable Internment* is unabashedly straightforward in its effort to present the violent act of interning Chinese Indians as justified and necessary. The government of India had a multipronged approach to propaganda and the dissemination of information, film being just one prong. The others included official annual Government of India (GOI) reports made available to Indian citizens and to the international community, ongoing public discussions in parliament, publications by the Ministry of External Affairs (MEA), and the Ministry of Information and Broadcasting Publications Division (MIBPD), which included the Films Division. Thus, while we cannot determine the extent of the *influence* of any of these efforts without implementing a stochastic process with many variables, what can be established is *intention*. It was clearly in the interest of the Indian government to create their version of the incarceration at Deoli with minimal opposition. It was a war they had not fared very well in, and it was important to create a version of history that displayed they had the upper hand over the Chinese. What was lacking in battle was compensated with manufactured morality. The films produced by the Films Division were intended to build the sociopolitical case for interning Chinese in India by depicting decent, livable conditions at the camp at Deoli. In the case of the films made in recent years with members of the Deoli community, the intention has been to chronicle survivor accounts and to insert into historical discourse the events of 1962 and its tragic aftermath. It may be argued that this later "rebuttal" category of films are also a sort of propaganda, films possibly exaggerating the plight of the camp survivors. Apart from being a false equivalence (the government of India's film wing arriving in Deoli compared to independent filmmakers interviewing elderly, dispossessed civilians), a couple of factors weaken this view. The accounts in these films have been corroborated by a number of survivors. The main method of bringing us this documentation are direct interviews, unlike the mostly narrated film made by the Films Division. Second, the survivors seem to have little to gain from the exposure; they are not demanding compensation or filing a lawsuit against the government of India.

One of the most significant aspects in recent years within the fraternity of Deoli camp survivors was the creation of the Association of the India Deoli Camp Internees (hereafter AIDCI) in 2009. Based in Canada, it now functions as a body working with the Indian Chinese Association to push for an apology from the Indian government. Ellias's filming can be identified as an early contributor of this grassroots effort; most accounts by members of the AIDCI refer to his work. Whether this was Ellias's intention or an inadvertent by-product of his project is hard to determine. *The Legend of Fat Mama*, made in 2005, was possibly the first chronicle of this discussion with survivors that went public after being screened in many film festivals and receiving some acclaim (including an award for Best Ethnographic Film in India at the National Film Awards). In the bibliography generated since, the film is referred to by several in the Chinese Indian survivor community as a document that formed an initial basis of pursuing oral histories. Ellias (2014) is well aware of the influence of his work.

> The film, broadcast in over 200 countries in 2006, generated a groundswell of interest in the community and its history. It triggered serious academic interest (two students, one in Montreal and the other in London, both began a study of the diaspora for their PhDs); two major symposia on the subject; a website of the Indian Chinese; and at least three more documentary films being independently produced.

In 2012, possibly in response to the wide release of his film, he began recording the voices of ex-detainees who had settled in the United States and Canada; producing a second documentary, *Beyond Barbed Wires: A Distant Dawn*. The two films have gained considerable exposure. The director's own YouTube uploads have received about seventy thousand views. Additionally, there have been hundreds of screenings in auditoriums and via shared social media links. In 2015 NDTV, a premier television network in India, broadcast a fifteen-minute special called "Untold Stories of a Forgotten War," in which several ex-detainees (including Yin Marsh, author of *Doing Time with Nehru*) were interviewed about their experiences in Deoli and their determination to make people more aware about the events of that internment. The newscaster opened the studio section by reading out, "The catalyst for this journey was a documentary by Rafeeq Ellias on the prisoners of Deoli. Through him and the film the group came together on what they call a pilgrimage." It is unlikely that in 2005 Rafeeq, who is not Chinese, would have imagined that his film would generate the platform for a very marginalized community in coming together. But it has undoubtedly been instrumental in creating a survivors fraternity and has given them a modicum of agency, a letterhead from which to conduct business.

Indeed, in the last decade, since the grassroots efforts began, several major publications have featured stories about this initiative including *Open*, the *Wire*, *Scroll.in*, the *Atlantic*, *Caravan*, and BBC Radio. Considering that it has been over five decades years since the Sino-Indian War, one can made a reasonable conjecture that these short films, along with the activism that they generated, contributed to a quick uptick in public interest in the matter. The driving force to create an awareness about the incidents in Deoli has not emerged from universities. As Marc Ferro (1974) has argued, history has many hearths, and academics are not the sole history teachers. Film can indeed be a historical product that both shapes and reflects the world around. But it has not been easy going. Ellias's attempts to get information from the government of India proved futile. Unlike Karel Margry, whose bibliographic research points to a host of archives containing accessible documents, Ellias hit a wall. In a publicly available document Ellias requested the government for information under the Rights to Information Act (2005). These were his questions, requesting basic facts:

1. How many people of Chinese ancestry (Indian and Chinese) were arrested during and after the 1962 India-China war[?]
2. How many of them held Indian nationality[?]
3. How many were sent to Deoli camp in Rajasthan[?]
4. How many were adults, how many children[?]

5. How many adult males and how many adult females[?]

6. How many of them died in prison and reason for their death[?]

7. Please list number of families who properties were attached[?]

8. How many of them recovered their property after they were released[?]

9. How many Chinese were repatriated by ship[?]

10. How many were released[?]

11. What was the longest period of detention[?]

The response from the Ministry of External Affairs New Delhi read, "The information sought by you is not available with the CPIO. The application has been forwarded to the Ministry of Home Affairs since it appears that the information sought is maybe available with MHA."[8] The word *is* is struck through and replaced with *may be*. The follow-up was futile. Ellias writes, "They just bounced me around from Home Ministry to Ext. Affairs to Defence and back to Home" (pers. comm., February 2, 2017). The archives and records on Deoli have been silenced.

It has been harder to track the influence of Taiwanese director Shefong's *From Border to Border: Chinese in India*, as she has not been directly connected to the grassroots efforts connected with the AIDCI.[9] However, information found online shows that it has had over thirty-three thousand views on YouTube and several international screenings, including in India. In addition, the AIDCI website and Facebook page, meeting points for action and dialogue, posted the film, resulting in online discussions.[10]

Unlike *An Unavoidable Internment*, which currently does not come up with a single Google search result other than the Films Division website where a DVD of the film can be bought for a hundred rupees, the recent documentaries continue to be referenced and watched.[11] *The Legend of Fat Mama* is still actively screened and discussed in forums and in print, sixteen years after its release. This leads one to surmise that in the current social media climate, the effective reach of films produced by private citizens can be enduring. They continue to remain in circulation as long as the topic is valid. Educational institutions and grassroots organizations can use them to create dialogue around the government's silence over the internment of 1962. But there appears to be no indication that the government of India is likely to issue an apology to the internees of Deoli in the near future. In 2010, soon after its inception, the AIDCI sent a letter to then prime minister Manmohan Singh requesting permission to erect a commemorative plaque in Deoli. Receiving no reply, they sent a letter again in 2011, which said, in part, "To mark the 50th anniversary of the Deoli incident, the survivors of the camp, their descendants and families wish to erect a monument to honour those who lost their lives at the camp."[12] The AIDCI never received a reply. In subsequent years, in 2017 and in 2021, similar attempts to communicate with the prime minister's office received no acknowledgment. With a population of Chinese Indians currently hovering just around two thousand in a country of 1.3 billion, and with the border still in active dispute (Gamble 2018), it is unlikely that the Indian government, regardless of political party, will acknowledge Deoli in the foreseeable future. But their crusade, undertaken along with members of the Indian Chinese Association, in educating the public and collecting oral histories has galvanized the academic community to some extent. The record of what happened in Deoli matters to a small group. To use a term frequented by the late anthropologist Michel-Rolph Trouillot, they may be referred to as the "collectivity," those who have the most invested in setting the narrative straight. In his words, "Collectivities experience the need to impose a test of credibility on certain and events and narratives because it matters to them whether these events are true or false, whether these stories are fact or fiction" (Trouillot 1995: 11). And it is the effort of this Deoli collectivity, years after events that occurred, that might lead to exhuming of facts, creating an interest in the larger community. The question of what happened in 1962 has broad implications and affects the present day. D'Souza posits that the events of that time, when the government actively facilitated the othering of a group within the country without real basis, cheered on by Indians convinced that they were being patriotic, is what makes it possible for people today to express their "deepest prejudices" against minorities inside the country adjudged to be anti-national. Deoli is the precedent for contemporary internecine troubles (D'Souza and Ma 2020: 184).

Perhaps these accounts, the recent films discussed in this article, and the emerging academic literature will help irrefutably establish, albeit unofficially, that the internment was avoidable. And for posterity, perhaps as important as that long-awaited apology is the ongoing collection of information that makes publicly accessible, an alternate view to the Indian government's account of what happened to the Chinese Indians in the 1960s and thereafter. History is often limited to what archives can point to. The growing archive of accounts of this episode records and preserves both events and memories. Independently produced film has played a significant role.

Notes

1 This assessment has changed dramatically in the last decade. In 2021, Xie Chao, an Indian studies scholar at Tsinghua University, chided the Indian government after the Atomic Minerals Directorate for Exploration and Research announced a positive outcome after preliminary exploration for uranium in Arunachal, a contested area in the NEFA region. Conversely, the Indian media has been steadily reporting on the enormous investments being made by China for gold and mineral mining along the extremities of the Chinese-controlled area of Arunachal.

2 Unless otherwise indicated, all translations are my own.

3 In Dilip D'Souza and Joy Ma's book *The Deoli Wallahs: The True Story of the 1962 Chinese-Indian Internment*, Ma, who was born in the camp in Deoli, writes about a family friend named E. Sau Wan who was a cointernee. E. Sau Wan, a *feriwala* (peddler) in real life, had a small role in the film—he was cast as a "cruel, lascivious landlord" who took advantage of the main protagonist's (Kali Banerjee, playing a Chinese *feriwala*) sister. See D'Souza and Mas 2020: 118–19.

4 The author was fortunate to have one of his independently produced documentaries screened as part of this initiative.

5 According to Joy Ma, it was the only time the International Red Cross had visited the camp and had delivered some aid. There was an instance a few years later when the Red Cross was turned away from the camp gates by the camp commander. Ma's mother was one of the women sent to reason with the camp commander and plead their case to the Red Cross. The internees were refused. See D'Souza and Ma 2020: 123–24.

6 While it is beyond the scope of this article, two other propaganda films from the 1960s that could be explored and discussed for a comparative study on films about internment are *The Island of Hope* (1961/62) about an offshore penal colony established by the Singaporean government in Pulau Senang. It is available online courtesy of the National Archives of Singapore, and *The Island of Buru*, about the internment of communists and suspected communists produced in the late 1960s by the Ministry of Information and the Ministry of Foreign Affairs of the Republic of Indonesia in collaboration with the Operational Command for the Restoration of Security and Order—a military body established after the 1965 coup attempt by Suharto's New Order regime. This film, recently located by Indonesian film archive scholar Lisabona Rahman, is not publicly available yet.

7 The surviving twenty minutes of *Theresienstadt* can be accessed online at the Internet Archive (among other websites). See https://archive.org/details/19064theguidegivesthecitya reportonapropagandafilmgermanfilmvwr (accessed July 3, 2023). It recently circulated in the public domain again after the 2008 film *The Boy in Striped Pajamas* used an excerpt of it.

8 Ministry of External Affairs communication with Rafeeq Ellias No. E/55l/ 22 /2016-RTI, Subject: Information sought under Right to Information Act, 2005, July 1, 2016.

9 At the time of writing this article, I was unable to contact the filmmaker to get a personal perspective of her project and its aftermath.

10 While *From Border to Border* was viewable on YouTube during the research phase of this article, at the time of publication, it can only be viewed in its entirety at Culture Unplugged (website), https://www.cultureunplugged.com/documentary/watch-online/play/52496/from -border-to-border (accessed July 3, 2023).

11 *The Unavoidable Internment*, Films Division, Ministry of Information and Broadcasting, Government of India, https://filmsdivision.org/shop/the-unavoidable-internment (accessed July 10, 2023).

12 Letter dated January 24, 2011, published online in *India Today*, https://www.indiatoday.in /india/story/53-years-of-indo-china-war-indian-chinese-prisoners-recount-horror-behind -barbed-wires-269077-2015-10-20 (accessed July 10, 2023).

References

Banerjee, Payel. 2007. "Chinese Indians in Fire: Refractions of Ethnicity, Gender, Sexuality, and Citizenship in Post-colonial India's Memories of the Sino-Indian War." *China Report* 43, no. 4: 437–63.

Chuen Chen, Liu. 2015. "53 Years of Indo-China War: Indian-Chinese Prisoners Recount Horror Behind Barbed Wires." *India Today*, April 15. https://www.indiatoday.in/india/story /53-years-of-indo-china-war-indian-chinese-prisoners-recount-horror-behind-barbed-wires -269077-2015-10-20.

Cohen, Jerome Adam, and Hungdah Chiu. 2017. *A Documentary Study*. Vol. 2 of *People's China and International Law*. Princeton, NJ: Princeton University Press.

Deprez, Camille. 2017. "The Documentary Film in India (1948–1975): Independence and the Challenges of National Integration." *Studies in Documentary Film* 11, no. 2: 64–80.

D'Souza, Dilip, and Joy Ma. 2020. *The Deoli Wallahs: The True Story of the 1962 Chinese-Indian Internment*. New Delhi: Pan Macmillan.

Duara, Prasenjit. 1995. Review of *Siam Mapped: A History of the Geo-body of a Nation*, by Thongchai Winichakul. *American Historical Review* 100, no. 2: 477–79.

Ellias, Rafeeq. 2014. "A Photographic Journey through Kolkata's Shrinking Chinatown." *Scroll*, September 19. https://scroll.in/article/679044/a-photographic-journey-through-kolkatas -shrinking-chinatown.

Ferro, Marc. 19734. "Le film, une contre-analyse de la société?" In *Annales: Économies, Sociétés, Civilisations* 28, no. 1: 109–24.

Gamble, Ruth. 2018. "China and India's Border Dispute Is a Slow-Moving Environmental Disaster." *Conversation*, June 17. https://theconversation.com/china-and-indias-border-dispute-is -a-slow-moving-environmental-disaster-97173.

Griffiths, James. 2013. "India's Forgotten Chinese Internment Camp." *Atlantic*, August 9. https://theatlantic.com/china/archive/2013/08/indias-forgotten-chinese-internment-camp /278519/.

Kim, Han Sang. 2023. "Can the 'Comfort Women' Footage Speak? The Afterlives of Camera Images as Document and the Flow of Life." *positions: asia critique* 31, no. 4: 803–38.

Kishore, Avijit Mukul. 2021. "Why Films Division Matters: It's the Largest Moving-Image Repository of Indian History." *Scroll*, December 29. https://scroll.in/reel/1013895/why-films -division-matters-its-the-largest-moving-image-repository-of-indian-history.

Margry, Karel. 1992. "Theresienstadt (1944–1945): The Nazi Propaganda Film Depicting the Concentration Camp as Paradise." *Historical Journal of Film, Radio, and Television* 12, no. 2: 145–62.

Marsh, Yin. 2016. *Doing Time with Nehru: The Story of an Indian-Chinese Family*. New Delhi: Zubaan Books.

Mazumder, Jaideep. 2010. "The 1962 Jailing of Chinese Indians." *Open*, November 21. https://openthemagazine.com/article/india/the-1962-jailing-of-chinese-indians.

Mrazek, Rudolf. 2020. *The Complete Lives of Camp People: Colonialism, Fascism, Concentrated Modernity*. Durham, NC: Duke University Press.

Nichols, Bill. 2016. *Speaking Truths with Film: Evidence, Ethics, Politics in Documentary*. Berkeley: University of California Press.

PTI. 2021. "Actors, Filmmakers Write to I&B Ministry against Merger of Films Division, NFAI with NFDC." *Wire*, December 22. https://thewire.in/film/actors-filmmakers -write-to-ib-ministry-against-merger-of-films-division-nfai-with-nfdc.

Roy, Srirupa. 2007. *Beyond Belief: India and the Politics of Postcolonial Nationalism*. Durham, NC: Duke University Press.

Sen, Mrinal. 2004. *Always Being Born*. New Delhi: Stellar.

Sutton, Hedley. 2016. "Forgotten Stories from the Second World War." *Untold Stories Blog*, British Library, August 4. https://blogs.bl.uk/untoldlives/2016/08/a-forgotten-story-from-the-second-world-war.html.

Trouillot, Michel-Rolph. 1995. *Silencing The Past: Power and the Production of History*. Boston: Beacon.

Winichakul, Thongchai. 1994. *Siam Mapped: A History of the Geo-Body of a Nation*. Honolulu: University of Hawaii Press.

Can the "Comfort Women" Footage Speak?

The Afterlives of Camera Images as Document and the Flow of Life

Han Sang Kim

Introduction

Following the summer 2017 discovery and public release of US Army Signal Corps footage documenting Korean victims of wartime sex slavery under the Imperial Japanese Army in China, some South Korean academics questioned whether it should be understood as new evidence, since some of the subjects in the moving images had already been identified in photographs discovered in the 1990s. This view of the footage seemed diametrically opposed to the agitated reports circulating in the mainstream media and social media praising the discovery of new, documentary evidence depicting those *moving* women. This article originally grew out of my personal interest in untangling what had driven me to join the project's research team[1] as a researcher in charge of locating those moving images: Why did I feel

positions 31:4   DOI 10.1215/10679847-10714272

obligated to provide this specific form of records documenting the victims? Was it a means of proving something that the world did not have enough evidence to conclusively establish? Additionally, in response to those other academics' skepticism: What can a piece of film footage bring to our time that a photograph cannot? Since the showcase, however, the afterlife of the film footage, which had originally been made for US Army wartime intelligence, has become self-regenerating and extended to problematic issues, including the endemic question of how to represent the victims. Along this line of development, my own questions have evolved into a more complex one: If we assume the film, as qualitative data, can speak for a party other than the creator, does it do so on behalf of the victimized subjects in it, or of the researcher who tries to interpret it? If we take the latter to be the case, or at least adopt the view that the former is possible only through the latter, then what would be the degree of truth the film as a document can contain and deliver, and how can a researcher access it?

The film's afterlife, especially if implicated in the real-life documentation of violence and victimization, also poses a question of ethics. In his book on documentary ethics, Bill Nichols (2016: 151) states that "there is no code of conduct, no set of ethical standards that governs all documentary filmmaking," and this definition justifies his view that the field of documentary filmmaking falls short of the standards of other disciplines such as journalism, sociology, and anthropology. For historians and historical sociologists who deal with film as an archival document, there is a comparable shortcoming, at a similar degree, in the ethical consensus on how to interpret film. Nichols discusses certain conflicts of interest between filmmakers and their subjects, particularly in circumstances where the subjects are supposed to "relinquish any and all rights to how what is recorded of their lives gets used": while the subjects may claim the right to intervene in how their actual lives are represented, the filmmaker's prerogative to "make the work they envision, with due regard for ethical considerations," not "the one their subjects expect from them," also carries significant weight (151). When considering the relationship between the academic interpreter and the subject, these conflicts of interest are resituated similarly in the realm of ethics, especially when the subjects are not physically existent or have less capacity to speak for themselves. What are the limits to the interpreter's discretion to infer the subjects' actual lives from the way they are represented in the film? If there is probable cause to believe that the subjects' representation testifies to atrocities in the past, is the excavator-interpreter liable for the (possibly posthumous) exhibition and circulation of the subjects' filmic representation? Or, conversely, does the excavator-interpreter even have the right to instigate that chain of events?

This article delves for the seemingly ungeneralizable answers to these thorny questions, specifically by tracing back over the very process of archival excavation, traversing recent issues around camera image documents and memory, and theorizing film's capacity to speak. That is, this article seeks to explore film as a medium that embodies the reality of the subaltern and, if circumstances allow, speaks on their behalf in a period distinct from that of the film's original production, even after a long lapse of time.

Collecting Post/Colonial Images from the Archives of a Visualizing Power

Seoul-based Sinologist Paek Wŏn-dam once pointed out that "the heterotaxis of modern Asian historical documents"—by which she meant to suggest that the best place for Asian studies was Asia-related institutes and libraries in the United States—had long deferred the proper representation of Asia's multiple temporalities (IEAS 2009: 91). The location of the "comfort women"[2] footage, the US National Archives and Records Administration (hereafter NARA), is indeed testament to the heterotaxis of Asian historical documents. Since the late 1970s, NARA has been the site of hidden archives that yielded secret records about unspoken atrocities, such as the US massacre of Korean civilians during the Korean War, and that have dramatically upended important historical narratives. Over the last two decades, South Korea's government-sponsored institutions and libraries, including the National Institute of Korean History, the National Archives of Korea, and the National Library of Korea, have invested in locating, collecting, and cataloging Korea-related documents in NARA, and as a result, the sight of Korean scholars busily photocopying documents in NARA's reference room in College Park, Maryland, over their summer or winter recess has not been an unfamiliar one until recently, before the COVID-19 outbreak.

This disconnect between the loci of past events and their archives—that is, the heterotaxis—is due not only to the fact that the United States was one of the key actors in these same events, but also to the fact that the United States was and is the foremost power for collecting knowledge from and gazing at other parts of the world. NARA, the federal archive that collects and preserves all records and manuscripts created by the US government, can therefore be called an archive that visualizes each and every unseen and invisible bit of knowledge from other parts of the world within the United States' reach.

However, this archive of visualizing power is not a voracious whirlpool of information but rather a generous benefactor providing information to many. Upon visiting NARA, you are required to verify your identity with a government-issued picture ID, after which they issue you a researcher card enabling you to pull their holdings out from the stacks. If you follow their rules and regulations for dealing with their documents, such as not bringing scanners with automatic feeders and not touching celluloid or photographic documents with your bare fingers, then you are free to photocopy or scan as many unclassified or declassified, public-domain US government documents as you like, at no cost. As a result, not a few researchers from South Korea and Japan complain about their own national libraries and archives' bureaucracy and secretiveness in providing access, particularly when compared to NARA. The discrepancy between the level of autonomy for Asian researchers accessing NARA's data and the more restricted access to their own national archives' data is, in a way, due to the respective managing principles of those archives. In the discipline of archival studies, NARA actualizes one of the two major theoretical traditions in modern Western archives—the one espoused by American archivist Theodore R. Schellenberg (1903–1970). Schellenberg, who began his career at NARA in 1935 and later became the program adviser to the Archivist of the United States in 1948, challenged the other major tradition upheld by British archivist Sir Hilary Jenkinson (1892–1961), who emphasized the archivist's "duty to serve the record by continuing the line of [the creator's] unbroken custody" (Stapleton 1983–84: 77). That is, their key difference lay in their respective views of who was most important at each and every stage of archival management, including collection, appraisal, selection, cataloging, preservation, and providing access. While Jenkinson saw the creator's original intention as the most important, Schellenberg prioritized the future "reference and research use" value, or "useability," of archival collections (78). From Schellenberg's point of view, the stages of appraisal and selection held much more importance than they did under Jenkinson's archival principles (Kim S. 2016: 77), and the archivist had more freedom in evaluating which data should remain in the archives. According to Stapleton, this emphasis on the data's potential for future use sprung from "the American attitude—and [Schellenberg's] own strong feeling—that public records are, indeed, public property" (Stapleton 1983–84: 78). This usability-oriented style of archival management has become NARA's defining principle for managing its holdings.

It is worth noting, however, that the relatively greater freedoms for research at NARA is given to the researcher as an *individual*. The "Research Room Rules" on NARA's official website state, "Researcher cards can only be issued to *individuals* if the records they are researching are physically located within the National Archives" (emphasis added).[3] At NARA's reference rooms, researchers do not officially represent their nations or institutions but only themselves as individuals. Though a considerable number of foreign government- or institution-affiliated researchers visit every day, each researcher is regarded an individual researcher, undefined by nationality, occupation, or affiliation. This stance on individuality tells us a lot about the structuring logic of the archive itself. As individuals, researchers gradually adjust themselves to the hierarchy that structures archival data, a hierarchy that echoes the US federal government's own structure. According to Schellenberg, at NARA, "record groups were established for records of administrative units of varying status and authority in the government hierarchy" (Stapleton 1983–84: 79). More importantly, researchers as individuals naturalize the hierarchy that structured how data creators and archivists looked into what happened in other parts of the world, where the data were originally created. I call this gradual internalization process that the individual researcher experiences at NARA a facet of liberal governmentality. That is to say, the heterotaxis of Asian documents does not simply mean the collecting power of Western archives. It also signifies the politics of those archives' geographical locations, which affect the archivist's appraisal, selection, and structuring of archival data. It entails the subsequent naturalization of that geopolitically driven, structural understanding of records of the past and considerably affects the episteme of Asian academia. The "comfort women" documents housed in NARA, therefore, need to be considered in the contexts of archival management, along with that of original creation.

The Positionality of Archives and the Problems of Cataloging

The documents, whether textual or not, collected by Asian scholars from NARA are conveyed to their country of origin and supplement local archives there to remedy the shortage of primary sources in the historiography of modern Asia. In the process, the question whether the documents are the exact records of pertinent historical events occasionally comes under dispute. More often than not, the undeniably excessive reach of US intelligence works to convince people of the documents' admissibility as information, or possibly as evidence. However, the structural logic of the original archives, parts of which housed those documents in NARA's catalog, is our major concern here. NARA's identification procedures for Korean "comfort women" in US Army film footage show how archival management and the positionality of archives affect the ways excavated documents can or cannot serve the aim of providing relevant information or evidence.

The two pieces of "comfort women" footage released in 2017 were cinematographed by the US Army, and the unit in charge of making that footage was the US Army Signal Corps. Since its establishment just before the outbreak of the American Civil War, the Signal Corps has been overseeing all communication-related activities in the US Army as a whole and has dispatched its soldiers to battle units in the field (Raines 1999: 5–8). The Signal Corps actively made use of machine-powered, visual documentation technologies, including photographs and motion pictures, and during World War II it collected a massive amount of photographic and filmic images from battlefields, former enemy territories, current and former colonies, and occupied areas (*Signal* 1953: 25). While conducting research at the textual and photographic reference rooms in NARA, the research team found that around 1944, the Signal Corps dispatched the 164th Signal Photo Company to the battlefield in the border region between China and Burma. Signal soldiers out in the field usually operated in teams of two, one for photography and

Figure 1 A clapperboard image in *Lungling Remains, China* (RG111-ADC-2738), one of the moving-image items discovered and released in the summer of 2017. Courtesy of NARA.

the other for cinematography (Pak Ŭ. 2017: 20). Some of the photographic documents and captions collected by the research team indicated that Sergeant Hatfield and Sergeant Fay were among those soldiers who took pictures in the region. Fay was the cinematographer working with Hatfield, who, in turn, left some photos depicting "comfort women." Working from this information, I started searching for film materials either shot by Fay or shot in the relevant regions, such as Tengchung, Songshan, and Lungling in China; and Myitkyina in Burma. I viewed over seventy reels of Signal Corps–produced films in Record Group 111, "Records of the Office of the Chief Signal Officer," at NARA, and found two items with several images of what are likely either "comfort women" or "comfort houses." *Lungling Remains, China* (RG111-ADC-2738) is an unedited compilation of film footage taken in the border area between China and Burma, Lungling, on November 10, 1944, and presents the image of a so-called comfort house. The footage of this hotel-turned-comfort house was shot by Fay, as evidenced by his name on the clapboard image at the beginning of the footage (see fig. 1). The other footage, depicting images of six female POWs captured at Songshan in 1944, is compiled in *World War II in China* (RG111-ADC-9706).

The identification of these women and the venue was not a simple task. Since Signal Corps soldiers sent their original negative films to the Signal Corps Photographic Center, later Army Pictorial Center, in Astoria, New York, to process and archive them (Raines 1999: 352), the films' subsequent archival descriptions seem to have been created usually by collection managers or archivists at the photographic center. Those in charge of creating descriptions were thousands of miles away from the filming locations and had most likely never visited those places. Therefore the descriptions frequently have inaccurate or incorrect information about the subjects in the films. After those films had finished serving as raw materials for secondary production, the films were then sent to NARA to be preserved as data produced by the federal government. The photographic center's descriptions of these films were some of the essential pieces of information that NARA had to collect and apply to their own cataloging. To identify specific figures, locations, or objects in those archived films, therefore, one must consider this context of archiving and these films' possible trajectories before ending up housed in a stable, governmental archive.

The description in NARA's catalog about the filmed footage compilation *World War II in China*, which the research team has confirmed as including moving images of living "comfort women," describes the women as "Chinese girls." This is a common example of racial generalization in NARA's cataloging, whereby a non-Caucasian-looking subject without relevant, personally identifying information is arbitrarily identified as a member of a specific racial or ethnic group. Keeping such instances of misinformed cataloging in mind, I entered keywords like "Chinese" and "Japanese," along with "Korean," into NARA's online catalog, and retrieved a shot list that included the term "Chinese girls" in a description of a medium shot ("MS") of female subjects in the footage (see table 1). The Signal Corps Photographic Center's description of the "comfort house" film even refers to the women at the venue as "Geisha girls," freely using the name of Japan's traditional entertainers, who have been objects of fetishism and myth, often misrecognized as prostitutes, especially through Western eyes (H. Kim 2018: 303–4). Therefore, it is highly likely that the women in the moving images were involved in sex slavery or sexual services under the Japanese Army, regardless of their actual ethnicities. We can identify such misinformation

Table 1. The catalog description for *World War II in China* (111-ADC-9706), https://catalog.archives.gov/id/23471 (accessed April 8, 2023)

Item	*WORLD WAR II IN CHINA*
NAID	23471
Local ID	111-ADC-9706
Shot List	Summary: Sequence: Chinese refugees loading belongings and household goods on RR freight trains. Trains crowded with men, women and children. MS, CUs, civilian refugees leaving burning city of Kweilin. Sequence: Coolies loading 75mm How ammo onto C-47 "Airdrop plane." AVs, dropping cargo over Tengchung. Chinese using bulldozers together with ancient methods in widening Burma Road. LS, We Tung Bridge over Salween River. Gen Wei Li-Huang, Commander Chinese Forces, with Col John Darral. MS, Gen Hsiao-I- hsu. VSs, loaded trucks travelling along winding roads. MS, Chinese girls. MCU, Gen Claire L Chennault with Red Cross workers at airport.
Dates	The creator compiled or maintained the parent series, Moving Images Relating to Military Activities, between 1947–1964.
	This item documents the time period of 1940–1949.
Edit Status	Audiovisual record(s) in this item have not been edited.
General Notes	(No Captions)
Sound	Audiovisual record(s) in this item are silent.
Access	Unrestricted
Use	Possibly Restricted
	Use of these archival materials may be restricted for the following reason: Copyright
Subjects and References	2
	■ Places: Guilin (China)
	■ Media Types: Motion pictures
Part of	Record Group 111: Records of the Office of the Chief Signal Officer 1860–1985
	>> Series: Moving Images Relating to Military Activities 1947–1964
Creator	Department of Defense
	Department of the Army
	Office of the Chief Signal Officer
	September 18, 1947–March 1, 1964

Figure 2 A photo album page with a description of "'Geisha Girls,' Jap Korean women" with the women's pictures. Courtesy of NARA.

by cross-checking with several other documents in different formats. For instance, in the research team's collection of NARA photographs, there is a photo album page with a description using the term "Geisha girls" to designate Korean "comfort women" in Okinawa, also calling them "Jap Korean women" (RG80-G 319133; RG80-G 319155; RG80-G 319156; RG80-G 319157; RG80-G 319163; see fig. 2). Based on textual documents indicating which US Army personnel took charge of photography and cinematography (Kang 2019: 151), the movements of the US-China joint forces in the region (Chŏng C. 2018: 117–288), and the fact that there were Korean "comfort women" in the territory (occupied by the Imperial Japanese Army until the joint forces defeated them) (230–84), the research team and I were able to locate these two pieces of film footage which included images of former "comfort women" believed to be Koreans, along with images of their place of residence.

Photos previously collected by the research team helped presume the ethnicities of several women in the footage. A Signal Corps photo taken from the China-Burma-India (CBI) theater of war, depicting four women who were captured there by the joint forces, has a caption on its reverse side, which seems to have been typed by the photographer at the time of printing, indicating that the women in the photo were "Korean" (RG111-SC 247386). While another photograph taken by the same unit, which was released to the public in the 1990s, has a caption identifying these four women as Japanese (RG111-SC 230147), there was a countertestimony that a pregnant-looking woman in the photo was actually Korean, one who was living in the northern part of Korea at the time. The woman, Pak Yŏng-sim, testified in 2000 that she was the pregnant-looking woman in the picture (Y. Kim 2000). By comparing the iconic proximity of facial features and clothing in these documents of different formats, compounded with supporting testimony from a survivor, the research team concluded that at least two women in the footage compilation, *World War II in China*, were Korean, with the strong possibility that one other woman was Korean as well.

The process of identifying these female Asian subjects in images held at an American government archive points to issues of racial politics and questions about postcolonial/neo-imperial topography. Who photographed or cinematographed the subjects at these specific moments in history? What was the photographer/cinematographer's racial and/or cultural background, and was it cognate with the photographer/cinematographer's position, angle, and/or capacity to provide additional information about the images? How many, and what kinds of, stages did those photographed/cinematographed images pass through before ending up in NARA, and who was in charge of appraisal and cataloging at each stage? What archival principle informed American archivists' decisions in selecting, cataloging, and providing access to these images, at least until Asian researcher-excavators eventually reached them? Were the archivists' cultural backgrounds cognate with the vocabularies, expressions, and/or omissions in the metadata they created? It may be difficult or even impossible to answer these questions for every single document; however, the act of questioning itself and the recognition of NARA's positionality will help the researcher-cataloger at local archives catch any discrepancies between the visual document's actual context of creation and the metadata subsequently created.

The Politics of Optical Evidentiality

When the research team released these two pieces of film footage to the public in July 2017, they immediately garnered immense attention, especially on the internet. Media outlets and anonymous Korean internet users circulated these moving image clips through various online media platforms, accompanied by sensational headlines and, at times, considerably angry comments about the Japanese Army's inhumanity. There were also relatively self-possessed but strategic responses requesting that the government use the footage in diplomatic maneuvers: "There have been many viewers who want this footage to be 'an ace in the hole' to get Japan to the table of renegotiation" (Pak U. 2017: 19). At the same time, in some academic groups, there were some markedly different attitudes. A number of academics raised questions about the newly excavated footage's usefulness, so to speak, asking, "What is the use of an additional discovery of film footage, when there is already photographic evidence of the same event?" (19) These academics expressed skepticism about the footage's admissibility as new evidence, largely because they believed that the existing photographic evidence of Pak Yŏng-sim, which was discovered at NARA in the 1990s and then verified by Pak in 2000, was enough to *prove* the existence of Korean "comfort women" in the Imperial Japanese Army. Alternatively, the sensational ways in which the media used the excavated footage to catch the public's attention might have given these academics a negative impression of the use of moving images.

In fact, these two stances are rooted in the same belief. Specifically, it is the belief that camera image documents, including both photography and film, are scientific evidence of the subject's existence in reality. Many see camera image documents as exact copies of the real world, since they are the products of optical technology, as well as mechanical production and reproduction. In *Kim-Gun* (2018), a documentary that traces the story of an unknown citizen soldier photographed during the Kwangju Uprising in 1980, this belief in optical evidentiality is called a "quasi-science," one that has generated ludicrous social controversy over the identity of photographed subjects. In particular, the Far Right political commentator Chi Man-wŏn claims that there was a conspiracy to stoke growing unrest against

Chun Doo-hwan's junta and cause a riot by smuggling disguised North Korean soldiers into Kwangju. He and his fellow "professionals" juxtapose reportage photographs of citizen soldiers from 1980 with recent news photos from North Korean media, each of which is matched to an old photo from Kwangju, so as to argue that the photographed citizen soldiers in Kwangju were actually soldiers from the North, who, after the Kwangju Uprising, returned to North Korea and were elevated in status as a reward. The key figure of the documentary, "Kim," is the first photographed subject that Chi identifies as one of these North Korean soldiers. The documentary crew meets with those who remember Kim, those who were assigned to the same military unit, and those who might themselves be the photographed anonymous soldier, and they try to reconstruct the memory of Kim and his unit in the citizen militia. After putting the pieces of the puzzle together, the crew comes to the conclusion that Kim was a ragpicker who used to live under a bridge in Kwangju and, during the uprising, voluntarily joined the citizen militia. In the end, the documentary confronts the audience with the possibility that Kim was shot to death by Chun Doo-hwan's martial law troops at the end of the Kwangju Uprising.[4] Over the course of the investigation, the documentary also portrays other citizen soldiers who realize that Chi has identified them as North Korean soldiers. Having resumed their previous lives as ordinary citizens after the end of the uprising, they find Chi's accusations insulting and bring a libel suit against him. Their attorney, having secured testimonies from the photographer who actually took the photos on May 22 and 23, 1980, expresses her confidence about winning the lawsuit to the documentary crew, saying, "The testimonies have concreteness and coherence that only the person who was at the scene can provide." To many, camera image documents are considered objective and scientific, as exemplified by the computer display scene, where Chi and his professionals skillfully compare the contour line points of a subject's facial shape with those of his Northern counterpart. However, the veracity of such evidential images can only be supported or refuted by coherent and concrete memories in their full contexts. One of the citizen soldiers who survived the massacre in Kwangju fires back, "Isn't the act of collecting evidence and testimonies to refute the suspicion that we were fake the same act they commit against us in presenting certain evidence?" This question is also relevant to the preference for evidentiality in discussions of the "comfort women" footage's usefulness. Why is it important to provide a "brand-new" set of evidence to prove that "comfort women" really existed in history? Isn't the act of excavating new evidence from NARA to refute Japan's denial of wartime sex slavery the same as Japan's act of denying based on the alleged nonexistence of any written evidence?

The documentary's unrepentant pursuit of truth in spite of the survivor's pessimistic question gives us a clue to the answer to these questions. *Kim-Gun* begins with an accusation and ends with its dispelling. However, the documentary does not merely focus on how to disprove an accusation's "quasi-scientific" or "fake forensic" (Kim J. 2020: 233) evidence. Rather, it gives more room for the affective contexts of the memories of Kwangju and its aftereffects on survivors' lives, including the ways that lower-class, orphaned ragpickers won their self-esteem in their fight against state violence, the reasons why so many of them remained anonymous and forgotten even after being victimized, and the ways that the survivors' agony and trauma linger on. And in the process, those photographs that previously seemed like mere phlegmatic proof of someone's existence gradually disclose the subject's affects and emotions. The subject in question, Kim, and some of his fellow citizen soldiers of similar social backgrounds seem to have collectively identified as being marginalized and unnoticed in society, so their service in the citizen militia might have been an important source of self-esteem and dignity as members of Kwangju society. Kim's sharp and wary eye in the photograph, as the photographer himself speculates in the documentary, might have been an expression of his displeasure at the photographer's unauthorized shot, which not only put Kim in jeopardy by potentially exposing him to government agents but also dethroned the power of the gaze, replacing Kim's reconnoitering gaze as a citizen guard with the camera eye mechanically recording the scene. By providing such fleshed-out descriptions of Kim throughout the whole film, the documentary successfully presents a more comprehensive picture of the photographed scene. That Kim was a real citizen of Kwangju is just a small part of the picture.

Aside from the fact that camera images have been "easily manipulated or altered" to prove the subject's existence or nonexistence (Sturken and Cartwright 2001: 17), we need to question the nature of the "truth" that a camera image can deliver to the viewer. Even in cases where photographs were "actually taken" on the very site of atrocities, to say they are *true* "tells us very little about the way in which they communicate an understanding of the devastation to those who did not experience it" (Morris-Suzuki 2005: 82). In this sense, the identification of the Korean "comfort women" victims in NARA's film footage contributes very little to our knowledge of what happened to them and how they experienced that time. The evidentiality of the seemingly scientific, mechanically produced Signal Corps film footage was confirmed only by intertextual investigation and, more importantly, with the survivor's own testimony. The iconic proximity of the subjects did not provide the scientific evidence to help this confirmation, because it does not prove the indexical relationship between the image and the subjects in reality. Similarly, Chi Man-wŏn's photographic identification based on the visual comparison of iconic signs was completely refuted by the voices of Kwangju survivors and the rich contexts they provided. In this way, the camera image document's own evidentiality is vulnerable and incomplete without contextual support. If the filmic imagery of those moving, living victims and their place of residence can contribute to a more comprehensive understanding of wartime sexual transgressions, then that contribution must be something more than the fact that they existed there, which I will discuss later in this article.

For that reason, the research team's February 2018 release of another piece of NARA footage, this time depicting dead bodies piled in a pit located among the remains of the Japanese Army in Tengchung, China (RG111-ADC-2417), was, while politically effective and headline-grabbing, contentious in terms of both the act's academic value and the ethics of representation.[5] The research team released the death pit footage, along with a US-China joint forces daily operation diary that described how in September 1944, on the "night of the 13th the Japs shot 30 Korean girls in the city."[6] Additionally, the team released the footage at an international conference commemorating the March First Independence Movement, an event cohosted by the Seoul Metropolitan Government on February 27, 2018 (Yi M. 2018). They showcased moving images of dead bodies, taken from NARA footage, before TV reporters and journalists, who were given a press release. The digital copy of the graphic scenes of corpses then began spreading at an alarming rate, first through the YouTube channels of major television news shows and, shortly after, through various social media outlets including Facebook, Instagram, Kakao TV, and Naver TV. Much like the previous NARA footage release, this wide public release seemed to generate the expected effect of reassuring people that there was concrete, visual evidence of "comfort women's" sexual slavery and mass killing committed by the Imperial Japanese Army. At least, this was the consensus among Korean-language users on the web, whereas the Japanese Far Right vehemently denied its admissibility as evidence. After the footage's release, the latter group immediately questioned the footage's capacity to prove that the incident had really happened, especially since the metadata in NARA's catalog (RG111-ADC-2417) provided a shot list identifying the bodies as "dead Japanese soldiers" and "dead civilians, women and children in open pit" (Kim P. 2018). Again, considering the racial politics of NARA's archival management, the identification of the dead bodies as Japanese does not necessarily mean that they were indeed ethnically Japanese, especially in light of the fact that the US Army Signal Corps Photographic Center's archivist very likely misidentified Koreans in the Japanese Army as Japanese in 1944, before the end of WWII. The textual document describing the killing of thirty Korean women,[7] together with the visual similarities linking the film footage's presentation of the dead and their clothes with that of other photographic documents collected from NARA (111-SC-212090; 111-SC-212091), both point to the high probability that the footage depicts a real incident against Korean "comfort women" victims. However, aside from the footage's high probability as a record of the incident, one should also consider the effect of releasing such visual documents to the public through the mass media, as these documents do not merely verify the existence of historical figures or events but rather also impact the viewer's affective experience of the visualized scenes.[8] While the research team could have easily predicted the controversy over the footage's evidentiality, particularly in light of their own experiences with NARA's cataloging errors and missing information, they also did not seem to treat these documents with any special care, such as, for example, limiting the release to an on-site exhibition or restricting the audiences with access to the graphic images. The widely circulated moving images portrayed the naked bodies of the dead, their genders unidentifiable, piled one on top of another. When we assume that those dead bodies were female, following the inference that they were mostly Korean "comfort women" killed by the Japanese Army, what is the affective impact of the footage's very public release, particularly with regard to the victims' representation?

First, the showcased and circulated images of "mutilated female bodies" worked to "urge the responsibility of men" and the nation, two parties that had failed to protect women from the cruelty of foreign forces (Y. Kim 2018: 163–64). The use and movement of these images followed a familiar pattern, recalling the 1992 crime scene photographs of Yun Kŭm-i, a victim of fatal abuse by a US Army soldier, and the 2002 graphic images of a US armored car accident that killed two Korean female students. While these images successfully posited *men* as the primary agents in the struggle against imperialism and/or neo-imperialism, they also rendered the "acute sense of pain the violated *female* bodies had experienced unspoken or marginalized," allotting women only a "mediating role" in men's fight (Kim Yŏng-hŭi 2018: 163–64). Such foreclosure of women's agency in framing national narratives reaches its dramatic peak in displaying the victims' lifeless bodies. In serving as a mediator for men's heroic fight, these spectacular camera images of mutilated female bodies function to bring another effect—"atrocity's normalization" that would generate the viewer's "narcotization" in being "overwhelmed with information" (Zelizer 1998: 212–13). That is, the exhibition of these graphic images has little educational value to prevent a recurrence of such inhumane crimes but rather familiarizes the viewer with the bodily representation of atrocities against women.

In a similar vein, the showcasing of those bodies erases victims' agency by objectifying their naked, lifeless bodies and limiting the representation of "comfort women" to a strict binary: one as a "familialized" grandmother-activist who fosters solidarity within the bounds of "the same national identity" (Hŏ 2018: 146–51) and the other as an idealized little girl, undefiled and immune to the dangers of sexualization[9] and, more importantly, whose "life after victimization" has never been represented (Kwŏn-kim 2019: 68–9). I will discuss this matter later in this article.

Last but not least, the research team's public release again reminds us of the preoccupation with the evidential capacity of camera images, which generates certain political developments disconnected from the affective or representational aspects of showing victims' images. Since the Japanese government has vehemently denied the Imperial Japanese Army's forced mobilization of Korean women into wartime sex slavery, academic discussions around this issue have long centered on how to prove the crime and what evidence can do so. Pursuing such evidence, one of the research team members claimed that the footage was effectively "the documents that [would] provide information about the circumstances and actual conditions of Korean comfort women in the last stage of WWII, while the Japanese government [was] denying the fact of mass killing" (Yi M. 2018). The same researcher, however, admitted that photographs are not "a faithful depiction of reality" and that there is "always a *blind side* to the photograph" (Kang 2019: 145). As a way of remedying this blindness, he suggests "a more accurate analysis" by cross-examining with "verified historical facts" (147). This view sums up the research team's basic understanding of camera images as documentary evidence; that is, they see camera images as containers of information, which, because of "the photographer's position," necessarily leave out or "conceal" some information (145). From this perspective, camera images can serve as evidence only by first being accurately verified. This is a revised version of the belief in optical evidentiality, or in the "truth of an indexical," to use Allan Sekula's (1986: 6) term, which prioritizes the information value of camera images. This belief entails that camera images from the past are containers of historical information and that the present-day viewer's encounter with them is a matter striving for an "accurate" understanding of the past, specifically by sorting through information from both the container itself and other "verified" sources. Therefore, for proponents of this view, both the ethical issues of representation and the foreclosed agency of women/victims are collateral and insubstantial elements in the process of historicizing the past. The fundamental meaning of camera images is their role as evidence.

Photographer and photographic historian Janina Struk (2004: 15) grimly states that the photographic representation "does not give a comprehensive account of the historical events" and that it is not possible for it to do so because photographic images are mere "fragments" of the past events. What the research team wanted to deliver through the exhibition of the death pit footage was a narrative that could be constructed by absorbing and conflating a series of information, including the facts that the Imperial Japanese Army's sex slavery in Tengchung had existed, that Korean women had been mobilized to serve as sex slaves in the region, and that there had been a mass killing of Korean "comfort women" before the shooting of this footage. However, none of these facts can be proved by the footage itself; other types of documents, such as textual records, photographic records with captions, and the surviving victim's oral testimony, proved them. What the footage delivers is only the visual "fragments" of what happened to exist right in front of the camera at the time of shooting. In other words, the camera image of the death pit cannot function as the evidence of the historical narrative of the atrocity against Korean "comfort women" by the Imperial Japanese Army. What the research team tried to fill the vacancy with was not a "blind side" of the camera image as a container but, according to Struk, a "created memory" or a "fiction" that would invite "fantasy" (213).

Camera images, despite this fundamental limit in giving a comprehensive account, are often welcomed to serve as scientific evidence of the historical events. At a general discussion of how to remember "comfort women," feminist scholar Chŏng Hŭi-jin criticized this preoccupation with evidentiality, particularly among "mainstream 'comfort women' researchers" in South Korea. These researchers have positioned themselves as "standard" experts who collect and provide materials as "objective evidence" in the "division of labor" formed around South Korea's "comfort women" studies, where "standard activists" and "standard victims" coexist with "standard experts" (Chŏng H. 2019). These "standard" roles have formed in both the government-centered, academic financing system and in the nationalization of discourses on victimhood. To help the nation-state in its diplomatic fight against Japan, these "standard" actors have continuously demanded, produced, circulated, and utilized certain types of evidence and evidence-based arguments. Interestingly, their anti-nationalist counterpart also claims to advocate objectivity, as evidenced by the recent controversy over Pak Yu-ha's book *Cheguk ŭi wianbu* (*Comfort Women of the Empire*) (Chŏng H. 2019). To counter nationalist narratives of victimization, Pak selectively collected evidence for her hypothesis from testimonies compiled by her antipode, the Korean Council for Women Drafted for Military Sexual Slavery by Japan.

This "usurping of testimonies" (Yi H. 2017: 353) has served Pak's "naïve composition of opposition" between "domestic nationalism and cosmopolitan feminism," which lacks proper consideration of the multifaceted roles of nationalism and feminism in the postcolonial world and has merely "perfected a weightless feminism" (Hŏ 2018: 144).

The emphasis on the evidentiality of camera images, as well as of other types of documents, often limits what the document represents and/or is capable of representing to what is useful for adopting or rejecting certain hypotheses, whether nationalist, anti-nationalist, or even feminist. The questions about the newly discovered footage's admissibility as evidence, the quasi-scientific belief in the photograph's optical evidentiality, and the decision to publicly release graphic images as strong factual data favoring the confirmation of a historical narrative—to some degree, all share the same attitude and ethical stance on the representation of victims in camera images. Once the representation is tried in the court of evidentiality, the most important issue becomes who has the authority to judge a camera image's capacity to deliver evidence proving a past event, and notably not how the representation interacts with the viewer in the present day.

The Camera Image Subject's Capacity to Speak

My question here centers on what a piece of footage can give us beyond the indexical information prioritized by the view of images as containers. Put differently, my question concerns the subject's capacity to speak in camera image documents. I find that there is a recurring correlation between the camera image's evidentiality and its subject; that is, the more a camera image document's nature is emphasized as scientific and measurable, the more the agency of its subject is ignored or erased.

To delve deeper into this, it is worth looking at another case notable for its camera images' evidential contribution to contemporary South Korean historiography—specifically, the photographs of the 1948 Yŏsu-Sunch'ŏn incident and its aftermath. The incident occurred on October 19, when the 14th Regiment of the South Korean Constabulary (a former branch of the Republic of Korea Army) rebelled in Yŏsu, refusing to transfer to Cheju to suppress a popular uprising on the island. The rebellion was led by leftist officers and soldiers who had opposed the establishment of a separate government in South Korea and afterward had expressed strong dissatisfaction with the newly established government's suppression of the Cheju Uprising. In response, the Syngman Rhee government and the pro-government media steadily produced and circulated "disciplinary knowledge" equating the rebellion with "violence in and of itself," largely by visualizing the rebel forces' alleged cruelties and hard-heartedness (Im C. 2005: 116). Among the materials deployed, photographs were frequently used to fill these purposes. South Korea's right-leaning artists' association, Chŏn'guk munhwa tanch'e ch'ongyŏnmaeng (National Federation of Cultural Organizations), in 1949 published the book *Pallan kwa minjok ŭi kago* (*Rebellion and the Nation's Resolution*), which included several photographs and illustrations of the mutilated bodies of civilian victims, who had allegedly been killed by "cruel insurrectionists" (117). Im Chong-myŏng defines the two strategies of visualization used in these photographs as, on one hand, the "numerical representation" that "offered seeming objectivity," specifically by visualizing the number of victims and losses in the photographs' metadata, such as their captions, and on the other, the "figurative representation" that "gave shape to gruesome scenes of the incident" and "emphasized reality by appealing to instinctive senses" (112–13). The rebel troops, most of whom had been subdued, executed, purged, or exiled from the army, were saddled with the blame and guilt for the terrible scenes in the Yŏsu-Sunch'ŏn photographs.

Interestingly, a counternarrative to this rightist historicization of the incident has also garnered public attention with the support of photographs. Documentary photographer Yi Kyŏng-mo's collection *Kyŏktonggi ŭi hyŏnjang: Yi kyŏng-mo sajinjip* (*The Scenes of the Turbulent Era: Yi Kyŏng-mo Photo Collection*), was first published in 1989 and suggested a new type of historical data for the emerging, progressive historiography that had begun to reexamine the Yŏsu-Sunch'ŏn incident. While Yi viewed the incident from a pro-government journalist's perspective (Kim Tae-sik 1990: 353), his documentary photographs did not fail to document the slaughter of civilians, who the police suspected were rebels or pro-rebel leftists (Yi K. 2010: 76–83). At the time of the book's publication, one reviewer, Kim Tae-sik (1990: 353), attributed a high value to Yi's photo collection, noting, "Whereas a historian's document is ex post facto, a camera's document is immediate on the scene."

Yi's photographs of the victims' dead bodies and the victims' family members wailing beside them were received by many, much like Kim described, as the document testifying to the real event that the authoritarian government had concealed. In the same vein, the National Archives of Korea have included his photographs in their official collections, having appraised the photographs as having "archival value" (Chǒng I. 2003). The indexicality of camera images here works to refute the one-sided historicization of the event and to lay the groundwork for a counternarrative. The issue of a camera image's indexical nature, specifically during the Yǒsu-Sunch'ǒn incident, has recently evolved into a legal matter. In March 2019, the Supreme Court approved an application submitted by the bereaved families for a retrial for the death sentence given to three Sunch'ǒn residents who were prosecuted for supporting the rebel forces and, only twenty-two days after their arrest, were executed by the military (Pae M. 2019). The plaintiff's special committee submitted photos taken by then *Life* photographer Carl Mydans, along with his own memoirs, as key pieces of evidence. A television news report interviewing the committee chief put two photographs by Mydans on air, with the reporter's voiceover narration drawing attention to the dead bodies of civilians left in the bushes, and a couple of soldiers looking at them (Yang 2018).

The mass killings of anti-government army personnel, political prisoners, and civilians before, during, and after the Korean War have been the center of attention in investigations of past atrocities, which have been undertaken as a means of democratizing historiography and overturning unjust convictions in South Korea. As with the Yǒsu-Sunch'ǒn incident, camera images have often provided circumstantial clues, sometimes legal bases, to support plaintiffs' claims in many investigations. In 1999, a series of photographs discovered in NARA by a New York–based Korean American scholar, Do-young Lee, supported the textual record written by a CIA agent, which claimed that at least two thousand political prisoners in Taejǒn were massacred by South Korean government authorities between July 2 and 6, 1950, immediately after the outbreak of the Korean War (Cumings 2002: 159–60).

However, in most historical narratives based on camera images as evidence, those who were murdered have been represented only as victims or as objectified figures visualizing the violence committed by the assailants. The disclosure of the execution photographs, many from journalists' photo collections and many others from NARA's excavated collections, have also contributed to the photographed subjects' victimization. Do-young Lee's excavated photographs offered a powerful visual narrative depicting each step of the execution procedure, including the political prisoners being forced to disembark from a truck, the prisoners lying face down and beaten in the fields, the military executioners pointing their rifles, the prisoners being shot, the executioners checking for survivors, and a right-wing youth group burying the dead bodies in a pit (Pak T. 2017). While this narrative successfully countered the rightist historiography catering to the authoritarian government, it also did not give any answers to the question of the victimized subject's agency.

Here, we need to pay attention not to the idea of these images as containers but rather to the ways they were exhibited and the context in which viewers saw them. While the images were used to support historical hypotheses, the exhibitors saw them exclusively as manifestations of objectivity. The optical machines that captured the scenes were posited as objective witnesses indexically recording the truth and therefore were seen as having transferred their authority as a witness to the excavator-exhibitors in the present day. The rightist historians of the Syngman Rhee regime, who demonized the rebel forces, and the progressive historians of the democratic era (particularly those who proved the victimization of political prisoners and pro-leftist civilians) shared this self-image of upholding objectivity. As such, even though progressive historians sought to free victims from unjust charges, they spoke for the victims only so long as they remained victims.

However, when the viewer tries to see beyond the limits of indexical and evidential information and admits that her/his own subjective position affects her/his interpretation, camera images can occasionally allow for the photographed subject to communicate with the viewer. One example is a 1949 piece of film footage depicting the execution of five Communist officers and soldiers in the Korean Constabulary, taken by an American officer, James H. Hausman. The footage, now in the Hausman Archive at the Harvard-Yenching Library, was shot in Susaek, then a suburb of Seoul, in late 1949 (Kim Tŭk-chung 2001). It opens with a scene of the officers and soldiers being transferred to an undisclosed site by truck. Over the following sequences, the faces of the young officers and soldiers do not just reveal

Figure 3 A scene from the Hausman footage, courtesy of the Harvard-Yenching Library of the Harvard College Library, Harvard University. Used with permission.

their anxiety over their looming execution but also shift from being serene and unconcerned to animated in laughter over something a Korean officer said—an officer who might have once been their colleague but is now guarding them as enemies (see fig. 3).

In the next scene, where the prisoners get out of the truck and pose for the camera, the man on the left, Lt. Kim Chong-sŏk, who was the leader of an underground Communist organization in the Korean Constabulary, even gives what might be interpreted as a confident smile. Kim shakes hands with an American officer on the right, Captain Hausman, who oversaw the execution, as well as the filming of this footage. In Hausman's own memoir, he mentions that he and Kim were close and that he had trusted Kim until the latter's secret thoughts came to light (Hausman and Chŏng 1995: 191–2). When the two shake hands, Kim is smiling widely (which Hausman seldom

Figure 4 A scene from the Hausman footage, courtesy of the Harvard-Yenching Library of the Harvard College Library, Harvard University. Used with permission.

does), and he seems to be trying to exhibit self-esteem before his former boss and now executioner (see fig. 4).

This footage gives viewers a glimpse of the already warlike atmosphere in South Korea even in peacetime, just before the outbreak of the Korean War, as well as of how and what those purged in these maneuvers tried to speak in front of the camera. When trying to interpret the men's facial expressions and gestures, it is difficult to limit their identities to that of mere victims. The montage of their scenes, therefore, provides some bits of information that does not necessarily lead to hard evidence or indexical truth. This kind of analysis may seem subjective and less important to those seeking authentic, factual information in camera images; however, as we have seen in the controversy over the ethnicity of dead bodies in the US Army's Tengchung footage, what is presumed factual and indexical still faces the question of its admissibility and still needs to be cross-referenced with other supporting data. Moreover, at this point in the analysis, the crucial element is whether and how the viewer-interpreter's active reading draws out voices from the camera image's subjects, not only through the camera images' visual data but also through the circumstantial data contextualizing the situation, thoughts and beliefs, and possibly emotions of the subject. Hausman's memoir recalls Kim Chong-sŏk's last words as "both knowable and not knowable" (Hausman and Chŏng 1995: 192), while several historical works on underground activities and the cultures of Communist organizations in colonial Korea document Communist activists' efforts to maintain their integrity (Yu 1947; Im K. 2002: 269–71). Together, sources like these sketch out the stories of the captured officers and soldiers and provide us with clues for hermeneutic interpretation.

The Flow of Life and Experience: Camera Image as Qualitative Data

The German-born sociologist Siegfried Kracauer once wrote that film has an affinity with life. The positivist framework of science in academia and beyond has been built on the idea that the camera is an "objective" machine that "captures reality" (Sturken and Cartwright 2001: 280) and that a captured moment of time can be scientific evidence. In other words, a camera image is understood as scientific material proving a thing's actual existence at a specific moment in time. Kracauer saw this indexical view as having an affinity with the historical approach championed by Leopold von Ranke, who famously described the historian's task as showing "wie es eigentlich gewesen" (how it really was) (Ranke 1874: vii). What set film apart for Kracauer (1960: 71) was its affinity with life: "One may also say that [films] have an affinity, evidently denied to photography, for the continuum of life or the 'flow of life,' which of course is identical with open-ended life. The concept 'flow of life,' then, covers the stream of material situations and happenings with all that they intimate in terms of emotions, values, thoughts." Under this notion of the flow of life, filmic imagery can be more than evidence of something's existence. It can connote the subjects' material reality, and occasionally even their inner world. The brave and confident expressions on the faces of Kim Chong-sŏk and his fellows tell us, at the very least, that even as political outlaws they did not want to appear meek before their executioner, who simply had a conflicting ideology. This potentiality of film to connote the material reality of open-ended life, with which Kracauer denied photography's affinitive ability to identify, can be related to one of my initial questions: "What can a piece of film footage bring to our time that a photograph cannot?" Film scholar Paula Amad (2010: 21) argues that film, with its *counter-archival*[10] substances of "disorder, fragmentation, and contingency," has "even more arbitrary and undisciplined style of evidence" than photography, so that it "undermines even further the archival support it inherited from photography," such as the archive's physical data management systems like "the index card, filing cabinet, and the archive" itself. As in Giorgio Agamben's (2000: 55) famous statement, "The element of cinema is gesture and not image," what makes film more arbitrary and undisciplined than photography is its gestural and movable feature. The *moving* images of bodies, although they are only fragments of a moment of time, present themselves as "gestures that have diverse latent potentialities of the bodies that would have had an infinite number of directions after the moment of time" (H. Kim 2020: 698).

Additionally, I want to draw attention to the elastic position in which Kracauer situates the viewer-interpreter of a camera image.[11] The viewer-interpreter should presuppose a wide range of possibilities where the image depicts life, because the affinitive two—film and life—are both open-ended. I argue that this approach to camera images should be seen as a qualitative method. That is, viewer-interpreters are not decoding quantifiable or objectifiable data when they interpret the camera image but rather are facing a situation comparable to that of an ethnographer conducting fieldwork. They are deconstructing and recombining the "fabrics" of image and life, making "quilts," in ways that simultaneously recall photography theorist John Tagg's (1988: 100) and qualitative methodologists Norman K. Denzin and Yvonna S. Lincoln's (2005: 4) accounts. The open-endedness of both image and life implicates "reference" that lies "behind" them—"a subtle web of discourse through which realism is enmeshed in a complex fabric of notions, representations, images, attitudes, gestures and modes of action which function as everyday know-how, 'practical ideology,' norms within and through which people live their relation to the world" (Tagg 1988: 100).

Figure 5 A captured image from the scene of *World War II in China* (RG111-ADC-9706) in which researchers assume the images of Korean "comfort women" were recorded. Courtesy of NARA.

The viewer-interpreter of the camera image, as a qualitative researcher, is "a maker of quilts" and "uses the aesthetic and material tools of his or her craft, deploying whatever strategies, methods, and empirical materials are at hand" (Denzin and Lincoln 2005: 4). The relative arbitrariness in interpreting camera images does not mean that the subsequently generated data is of lesser value but rather suggests that more "observations" and more "inscriptions" are necessary. In providing these, viewer-interpreters can turn what they see in camera images from "passing" imagery, which "exists only in its own moment of" display, into an "account, which exists in its inscriptions and can be reconsulted" (Geertz 1973: 9, 19).

Observing and inscribing the film footage of former "comfort women" also allow us to give an account of something that has thus far been left out of the discussions around the footage's evidentiality. The women's facial expressions in the footage released in 2017 can be interpreted as reflecting their nervousness and anxiety over being in front of the camera (see fig. 5). While the footage does not show all the relevant parties, it is obvious that there were American soldiers behind the camera, possibly one cause of the women's anxiety. It is also possible that these women, while under sexual slavery by Japanese soldiers, were taught that the US Army, the enemy of the Japanese Army, was evil and would not release them upon capture. Even though their oppressors had run away, these women's situation was fundamentally as prisoners of war, captured by their former enemies. Moreover, in this scene, another filmed party, the Chinese officers and soldiers—who went to the village to liberate it from Japanese military occupation and who, after this point in the footage, were going to release the women—wear expressions that seem to point to the actual situations the women encountered and would also encounter in their home village. Aware of what the women did for the Japanese Army, the soldiers' smiles can be interpreted as somehow ill-natured. These images entail a range of different contextual fabrics, among them that the women were captured as POWs and were inspected by formerly demonized enemy soldiers; that the camera was set before them as a visualizing power, with many other eyes watching them being filmed; that even for the Chinese liberators, the women could still be sexualized; and that many former "comfort women" would return to their families and speak out about their experiences only to be labeled the shame of the family or even of the nation. Considering these fabrics, the Chinese male soldiers' smiles disclose an affinity with the material realities of patriarchal, postcolonial South Korea, which the women would have had to confront first individually and then virtually in the present, as subjects of the camera image. When we think of the aforementioned, binary representation of "comfort women" in South Korean media—the "familialized" grandmother-activist and the idealized little girl—the reemergence of these young women, moving and alive in the film footage, carries a lot of weight for the South Korean mediascape. Their apparent fear and anxiety echo those of present-day women confronted by violence and cruelty as well as by the gaze of the media. Moreover, as the subject of camera images, they speak to present-day audiences through their recurring presence in exhibitions, wrenching open the "silencing structure" (Park 2005: 181), the structures that have made these women—gendered victims of violence—invisible to the postcolonial nation-state, its media, and its academia.

Returning to our initial discussion about NARA's archival principle and positionality, it is important to note that the researcher wanting to collect camera images from its archives should be aware of those images' characteristics as qualitative data. Despite the long-standing myth of camera images' indexical nature, there is plenty of room for different interpretations rooted in knowledge of the images' creators, collectors, appraisers, and archivists, as well as in the viewer-researcher's own subjective positions. The researcher wanting to discover documents and reconstruct a narrative of the past, therefore, should always question the archive's logic and structure and allow for the possibility of disproving the archive's metadata. This methodology better positions us for postcolonial approaches to Western or former imperial archives.

Notes

This work was supported by the Ministry of Education of the Republic of Korea and the National Research Foundation of Korea (NRF-2019S1A5A8040231).

1   The research project began at the Human Rights Center at Seoul National University in 2014 and has since distinguished itself from the center, following the retirement of its chief researcher as the center's director. I temporarily joined the project's archival research and collection activities from May to June 2017 as a person in charge of conducting research on film materials at the US National Archives II in College Park, Maryland, and did not get involved in the two rounds of public releases of the collected footage in July 2017 and February 2018. Hereafter, I will refer to the team in charge of the project as "the research team."

2   The term used in this article for victims of wartime sex slavery under the Imperial Japanese Army, "comfort women," is in quotation marks to indicate that it was used by the Japanese military to designate such victims, underscoring the fact that the victims' sexual service was positioned as a means of comforting soldiers and the fact that it was not a name chosen by the victims themselves but a historical title.

3   NARA (National Archives and Records Administration), "Research Room Rules," February 6, 2019, https://www.archives.gov/research/research-room-rules.

4   In 2021, the person in question publicly revealed his identity. According to him, whose real name was Ch'a Pok-hwan, he had not even known about Chi Man-wŏn's claim that the person in the image was a North Korean spy until his wife by chance watched the documentary *Kim-Gun* on television and recognized her husband's sharp eyes from the photograph. In May of the following year, the May 18 Democratization Movement Truth Commission officially acknowledged that Ch'a was the real subject of the photographed citizen soldier who had been called "Kim(-gun)," overriding Chi's allegation (Hong 2022). While this conclusion appears to refute the documentary's final hypothesis that Kim might

have been killed by the martial law troops, *Kim-Gun*'s approach to answering Chi's accusation through the belief in optical evidentiality is worthy of notice, as discussed in the following part of this article. The director of this documentary commented that what his work had found as truth was "a vacuum," not any facts about who might be the real Kim, even before Ch'a Pok-hwan turned up (C. Pae 2020: 22). Juyeon Bae (Pae Chu-yŏn) relates the self-consciousness of younger documentary makers who did not experience the violent era of the May 18 Democratization Movement to the issue of postmemory (22–23).

5 By the same token, this article does not include images from the footage *The Battle of Tengchung, China* (RG111-ADC-2417). It was one of the pieces of footage collected by the author in May and June 2017, and later that year, the research team confirmed that the footage contained images of the dead bodies of Korean "comfort women." The film footage is accessible onsite at the US National Archives II in College Park, Maryland.

6 "G-3 Daily Diary," 1944, *General Correspondence, 1943–1945*, RG493 Records of US Army Forces in the China-Burma-India Theaters of Operations, 1942–1947, Container 7, US National Archives and Records Administration.

7 "G-3 Daily Diary."

8 This, to a lesser extent, is also relevant to the previously released images of moving "comfort women." Nevertheless, this section focuses more on the direct representation of violence and violated bodies of victims.

9 Hŏ Yun (2018) historicizes the representation of "comfort women" in South Korean popular narratives. Until the 1990s, representation of the victims was rather frequently sexualized (136–39). However, since a 2004 controversy over a celebrity actress's nude photo collection that specifically used the theme of "comfort women," the media have tended to adopt desexualized representations such as that of a little girl (139–42).

10 By "counter-archive," Amad (2010: 21) means "a supplementary realm where the modern conditions of disorder, fragmentation, and contingency came to haunt the already unstable positivist utopia of order, synthesis, and totality." According to her, film has a counter-archival value and presents "multifaceted challenge to historicism" (21).

11 I use the term "camera image" here to designate both film and photography. While it is important to note the potentialities of film as a medium of the flow of life, when we think of the means by which both archival photography and film footage are accessed as historical documents—the excavation of these materials from audiovisual archives under specific national, ethnic, racial, and/or geopolitical categories; the identification and verification of information believed to be conveyed by the materials; the release and exhibition of the materials to specific or general audiences to support historical claims—the search for the defining difference between the two media comes to carry less relevance to another question whether the subject can speak, especially in the current era of digital media.

References

Agamben, Giorgio. 2000. *Means without End: Notes on Politics*. Translated by Vincenzo Binetti and Cesare Casarino. Minneapolis: University of Minnesota Press.

Amad, Paula. 2010. *Counter-archive: Film, the Everyday, and Alber Kahn's Archives de la Planète*. New York: Columbia University Press.

Chŏng, Chin-sŏng, ed. 2018. *Ilbon'gun 'wianbu' kwan'gye miguk charyo III* 일본군 '위안부' 관계 미국 자료 III (*US Documents Relating to "Comfort Women" in the Japanese Army*, vol. 3). Seoul: Sŏnin.

Chŏng, Hŭi-jin. 2019. Designated discussion at the conference "War, Women, and Violence: Remembering the 'Comfort Women' Transnationally," Sogang University, Seoul, South Korea, March 8.

Chŏng, In-yŏng. 2003. "Yi kyŏng-mo ŭi tak'yument'ŏri" 이경모의 다큐멘터리 ("Yi Kyŏng-mo's Documentary"). *Ŭmsŏng sinmun* 음성신문, October 1.

Cumings, Bruce. 2002. "War Crimes and Historical Memory: The United Nations Occupation of North Korea in 1950." In *War and Cold War in American Foreign Policy, 1942–62*, edited by Dale Carter and Robin Clifton, 156–78. New York: Palgrave Macmillan.

Denzin, Norman K., and Yvonna S. Lincoln, eds. 2005. *The Sage Handbook of Qualitative Research*. 3rd ed. Thousand Oaks, CA: SAGE.

Geertz, Clifford. 1973. *The Interpretation of Cultures*. New York: Basic Books.

Hausman, Jim, and Chŏng Il-hwa. 1995. *Hausŭman chŭngŏn: Han'guk taet'ongnyŏng ŭl umjigin migun taewi* 하우스만 증언: 한국 대통령을 움직인 미군 대위 (*Hausman's Testimony: An American Captain Who Moved South Korean Presidents*). Seoul: Han'guk munwŏn.

Hŏ, Yun [Heo, Yoon]. 2018. "Ilbon'gun 'wianbu' chaehyŏn kwa chinjŏngsŏng ŭi kon'gyŏng: Sonyŏ wa halmŏni p'yosang ŭl chungsim ŭro" 일본군 '위안부' 재현과 진정성의 곤경: 소녀와 할머니 표상을 중심으로 ("The Representation of the 'Comfort Women' of Japanese Military Sex Slavery and the Problem of Authenticity: Focusing on the Girl and Grandmother Images"). *Yŏsŏng kwa yŏksa* 여성과 역사 (*Women and History*) 29: 131–62.

Hong, Haeng-gi. 2022. "5·18 'kimgun' ŭn pukhan'gun anin ch'a pok-hwan . . . 'chi man-wŏn, myŏngye hweson sagwa hara'" 5·18 "김군"은 북한군 아닌 차복환 . . . "지만원, 명예훼손 사과하라" ("'Kim' from the May Eighteenth Movement Turns Out to Be Ch'a Pok-hwan, Not a North Korean Soldier . . . 'Chi Man-wŏn Must Make an Apology'"). *Sŏul sinmun* 서울신문, May 13, 8.

IEAS (Institute for East Asian Studies, Sungkonghoe University), ed. 2009. *Naengjŏn Asia ŭi munhwa p'unggyŏng 2* 냉전 아시아의 문화풍경 2 (*The Cultural Landscape of Cold War Asia*, vol. 2). Seoul: Hyŏnsil Munhwa.

Im, Chong-myŏng [Im, Chong Myong]. 2005. "Yŏsun sagŏn ŭi chaehyŏn kwa p'ongnyŏk" 여순사건의 재현과 폭력 ("Violence in the Representation of the Yŏsun Incident"). *Han'guk kŭnhyŏndaesa yŏn'gu* 한국 근현대사 연구 (*Journal of Korean Modern and Contemporary History*) 32: 103–32.

Im, Kyŏng-sŏk. 2002. "Ijŭl su ŏmnŭn saramdŭl—kang ta-ryŏng, chosŏn kongsandang ch'aegim pisŏ" 잊을 수 없는 사람들—강달영, 조선공산당 책임비서 ("The Unforgettable—Kang Ta-ryŏng, the Chief Secretary of the Chosŏn Communist Party"). *Yŏksa pip'yŏng* 역사비평 (*Critical Review of History*), February, 247–72.

Kang, Sung Hyun. 2019. "The U.S. Army Photography and the 'Seen Side' and 'Blind Side' of the Japanese Military Comfort Women: The Still Pictures and Motion Pictures of the Korean Comfort Girls in Myitkyina, Sungshan, and Tengchung." *Korea Journal* 59, no. 2: 144–76.

Kim, Han Sang. 2018. "Piŏnŏjŏk chiljŏk charyo: Sich'ŏnggak charyo rŭl chungsim ŭro" 비언어적 질적 자료: 시청각 자료를 중심으로 ("Nonverbal Qualitative Data: Focusing on Audio-Visual Documents"). In *Munhwa sahoehak ŭi kwanjŏm ŭro pon chiljŏk yŏn'gu pangbŏmnon* 문화사회학의 관점으로 본 질적연구방법론 (*Qualitative Research Methods from the Sociology of Culture*), edited by Ch'oe Chong-nyŏl, Kim Sŏng-gyŏng, Kim Kwi-ok, and Kim Ŭn-jŏng, 286–316. Seoul: Humanist.

Kim, Han Sang. 2020. "Palgyŏndoen p'ut'iji sok ŭi pagyŏngsim ŭn muŏt ŭl marhanŭn'ga (hogŭn marhaji mot'anŭn'ga)? Sajinjŏk saengjonja ŭi yŏnghwajŏk hyŏnjŏn kwa p'osŭt'ŭ/singmin ak'aibŭ ŭi naengjŏn chisikch'eje" 발견된 푸티지 속의 박영심은 무엇을 말하는가 (혹은 말하지 못하는가)? 사진적 생존자의 영화적 현전과 포스트/식민 아카이브의 냉전 지식체제 ("What Does Pak Yong-sim in the Excavated Footage Tell You [Or Not]? The Cinematic Presence of the Photographic Survivor and the Cold War Knowledge Regime of Post/Colonial Archives"). *Munhak kwa yŏngsang* 문학과 영상 (*Journal of Literature and Film*) 21, no. 3: 679–709.

Kim, Jihoon. 2020. "The Uses of Found Footage and the 'Archival Turn' of Recent Korean Documentary." *Third Text* 34, no. 2: 231–54.

Kim, Pong-su. 2018. "Il kŭgu seryŏk e hyŏppak tanghanŭn wianbu yŏn'gujadŭl" 일 극우 세력에 협박 당하는 위안부 연구자들 ("The 'Comfort Women' Researchers under Threat from the Japanese Far Right"). *Asia kyŏngje* 아시아경제, March 13, 10.

Kim, Sang-sin [Kim, Sang-Shin]. 2016. "Chenk'insŭn kwa swellenbŏgŭ ŭi kirokhak iron pigyoyŏn'gu" 젠킨슨과 쉘렌버그의 기록학 이론 비교연구 ("A Comparative Study of the Archival Theories of Hilary Jenkinson and Theodore R. Schellenberg"). *Kirokhak yŏn'gu* 기록학연구 (*Korean Journal of Archival Studies*) 50: 61–95.

Kim, Tae-sik. 1990. "Sŏp'yŏng: Yŏsun sagŏn kwa sajin ŭi yŏksasŏng" 서평: 여순사건과 사진의 역사성 ("Review: The Yŏsu-Sunch'ŏn Incident and the Historicity of the Photograph"). *Yŏksa pip'yŏng* 역사비평 (*Critical Review of History*), May, 350–58.

Kim, Tŭk-chung. 2001. "Yŏsun sagŏn ŭi chinsang kwa kukka t'erŏrijŭm" 여순사건의 진상과 국가테러리즘 ("The Yŏsu-Sunch'ŏn Incident and James Hausman"). *Proceedings of the Conference for the Fifty-Third Anniversary of the Yŏsu-Sunch'ŏn Incident*. Edited by the Chŏlla Chwasuyŏng Culture Institute, Yeosu National University, October 19, 3–27.

Kim, Yŏng-hŭi [Kim, Young-hee]. 2018. "5.18 ŭi kiŏk sŏsa wa yŏsŏng ŭi moksori 5.18" 의 기억 서사와 여성의 목소리 ("A Study of Women's Voice in Oral History Narratives on the Social Memory of State Violence: The May 18th Kwangju Democratic Movement"). *P'eminijŭm yŏn'gu* 페미니즘 연구 (*Issues in Feminism*) 18, no. 2: 149–206.

Kim, Yong-su. 2000. "Ilbon wianbu p'oro sajin sok yŏsŏng 1-myŏng pukhan saengjon" 일본군 위안부 포로 사진 속 여성 1명 북한 생존 ("One of the Comfort Women POWs in the Photograph Is Alive in North Korea"). *Yŏnhap nyusŭ* 연합뉴스, August 28.

Kracauer, Siegfried. 1960. *Theory of Film*. New York: Oxford University Press.

Kwŏn-kim, Hyŏn-yŏng. 2019. "Ch'immuk ŭn mari toeŏtchiman mal ŭn ŭimi ka toeŏssŭlkka? Tŭtki ŭi kongdongch'e rŭl yebihamyŏ" 침묵은 말이 되었지만 말은 의미가 되었을까? 듣기의 공동체를 예비하며 ("Silence Has Become Words, but Have Words Become a Meaning? In Preparation for a Community of Listening"). In *Chŏnjaeng, yŏsŏng, p'ongnyŏk: Ilbon'gun 'wianbu' rŭl t'ŭraensŭnaesyŏnŏl hage kiŏk hagi* 전쟁, 여성, 폭력: 일본군 '위안부'를 트랜스내셔널하게 기억하기 (*War, Women, and Violence: Remembering the "Comfort Women" Transnationally*), by Hŏ Yun, Muta Kazue, Tomiyama Ichiro, and Kwŏn-kim Hyŏn-yŏng, 64–73. Seoul: CGSI EPUB.

Morris-Suzuki, Tessa. 2005. *The Past within Us: Media, Memory, History*. New York: Verso Books.

Nichols, Bill. 2016. *Speaking Truths with Film: Evidence, Ethics, Politics in Documentary*. Berkeley: University of California Press.

Pae, Chu-yŏn [Bae, Juyeon]. 2020. "P'osŭt'ŭmemori wa 5.18: Tak'yument'ŏri yŏnghwa 'kim-gun' ŭl chungsimŭro" 포스트메모리와 5.18: 다큐멘터리 영화 '김군'을 중심으로 ("Postmemory and the Gwangju Democratization Movement: Focused on the Documentary *Kim-Gun*"). *Sŏganginmunnonch'ong* 서강인문논총 (*Humanities Journal*) 57: 5–35.

Pae, Myŏng-jae. 2019. "Yŏsun sagŏn chaesim chaep'an kongso kigak andwae" 여순사건 재심 재판 공소 기각 안돼 ("The Application for a Retrial of a Case during the Yŏsu-Sunch'ŏn Incident Avoids Dismissal"). *Kyŏnghyang sinmun* 경향신문, June 12.

Pak, To. 2017. "'1800-myŏng chuginŭn te 3-il..'. han'guk iyagiimnida" "1800명 죽이는데 3일.." 한국 이야기입니다 ("'Only Three Days to Kill 1,800 People'... It's a Story from South Korea"). *OhMyNews* 오마이뉴스, November 7.

Pak, Ŭn-ha. 2017. "'Konggam irwŏnaenŭn chinsil ŭi him'... wianbu yŏn'gut'im 3in i chŏnhanŭn yŏngsang palgul p'ulssŭt'ori" "공감 이뤄내는 진실의 힘"... .위안부 연구팀 3인이

전하는 영상 발굴 풀스토리 ("'The Power of Truth That Gains Sympathy'...a Full Story of the Comfort Women Footage Excavation Revealed by Three from the Research Team"). *Chugan kyŏnghyang* 주간경향 (*Weekly Kyŏnghyang*), July 25: 18–22.

Park, Soyang. 2005. "Silence, Subaltern Speech, and the Intellectual in South Korea: The Politics of Emergent Speech in the Case of Former Sexual Slaves." *Journal for Cultural Research* 9, no. 2: 169–206.

Raines, Rebecca Robbins. 1999. *Getting the Message Through: A Branch History of the U.S. Army Signal Corps*. Washington, DC: Center of Military History, United States Army.

Ranke, Leopold von. 1874. *Geschichten der romanischen und germanischen Völker von 1494 bis 1514*. Leipzig: Duncker und Humblot.

Sekula, Allan. 1986. "The Body and the Archive." *October*, no. 39: 3–64.

Signal: Journal of the Armed Forces Communications Association. 1953. "Please Credit U.S. Army Photograph: An Album of Signal Corps Photographs That Record History from the Civil War through Korea." May–June, 25–29.

Stapleton, Richard. 1983–84. "Jenkinson and Schellenberg: A Comparison." *Archivaria* 17: 75–84.

Struk, Janina. 2004. *Photographing the Holocaust: Interpretations of the Evidence*. London: Routledge.

Sturken, Marita, and Lisa Cartwright. 2001. *Practices of Looking: An Introduction to Visual Culture*. Oxford: Oxford University Press.

Tagg, John. 1988. *The Burden of Representation: Essays on Photographies and Histories*. New York: Palgrave Macmillan.

Yang, Ch'ang-hŭi. 2018. "Yŏsun sagŏn min'ganin haksal pujŏng kukpangbu ipchang, sajin·saryo ro panbak" 여순사건 민간인 학살 부정 국방부 입장, 사진·사료로 반박 ("The Department of Defense's Denial of the Slaughter of Civilians during the Yŏsu-Sunch'ŏn Incident Refuted by Photographs and Historical Records"). *KBS News*, May 16.

Yi, Hŏn-mi [Lee, Hunmi]. 2017. "*Cheguk ŭi wianbu* wa kiŏk ŭi chŏngch'ihak" "제국의 위안부"와 기억의 정치학 ("*Comfort Women of the Empire* and the Politics of Memory"). *Kukche chŏngch'i nonch'ong* 국제정치논총 (*Korean Journal of International Relations*) 57, no. 2: 329–66.

Yi, Kyŏng-mo. (1989) 2010. *Kyŏktonggi ŭi hyŏnjang: Yi kyŏng-mo sajinjip* 격동의 현장: 이경모 사진집 (*The Scenes of the Turbulent Era: Yi Kyŏng-mo Photo Collection*). Seoul: Nunbit.

Yi, Myŏng-hŭi. 2018. "'Ilbon'gun wianbu haksal' kirok yŏngsang ch'ŏt konggae" "일본군 위안부 학살" 기록 영상 첫 공개 ("The First Release of Moving Images Recording the 'Mass Killing of Comfort Women by the Japanese Army.'") *Kyŏnghyang sinmun* 경향신문, February 28.

Yu, Ch'ŏng-nyŏl. 1947. "Okchung ŭi kyemyŏngsŏng" 옥중의 계명성 ("The Crowing of the Cock from the Prison"). *Sinch'ŏnji* 신천지, September 1.

Zelizer, Barbie. 1998. *Remembering to Forget: Holocaust Memory through the Camera's Eye.* Chicago: University of Chicago Press.

Mnemonic Politics around the Japanese Colonial Era in Post–Cold War Taiwan: Wei Te-sheng's Colonial Trilogy and Post–New Cinema

Juyeon Bae

Introduction

Taiwan New Cinema and post–New Cinema have indulged in the recon-figuration of Taiwan's colonial history since the early 1980s. Wei Te-sheng is one of the leading figures of the trends in Taiwan. In particular, his colonial trilogy has often been studied in terms of the political, cultural, and indus-trial contexts surrounding post–New Cinema. Reflecting Taiwan's complex colonial history, which lasted for four hundred years, and its unique political situation as a "stateless" country, Wei's colonial trilogy and other films depict-ing that era go beyond filmic representation to participate in post–Cold War mnemonic politics. Referring to previous research, in this article I examine how Wei's films combine the memory of the Japanese colonial era with the current international status of Taiwan by applauding the country's remark-able diversity and modernization under the Japanese rule and not giving

positions 31:4   DOI 10.1215/10679847-10714285

attention to the influential postwar[1] powers from China and the United States. In the next two sections, I situate Wei Te-sheng's films in their industrial, historical, geopolitical and cultural contexts, since the production and reception of Wei's colonial trilogy cannot be understood without considering multiple entangled factors. Then, I investigate Wei's colonial trilogy in detail. I argue that Wei's films constitute a subimperial appropriation of the Japanese colonial era rather than its postcolonial reconfiguration.

The *Cape No. 7* Fever and the Advent of "Post–New Cinema"

In 2008, a film named *Haijiao Qi Hao* (*Cape No. 7*), Wei Te-sheng's feature debut, hit the Taiwanese box office and broke the national records for domestic cinema, recording the second-highest earnings in history, just following James Cameron's *Titanic*. The unprecedented success of *Cape No. 7* at the box office was interpreted by film critics and film practitioners as a sign of the resurrection of the Taiwan film industry. Up to then, the numbers of *guopian* (films domestically made in Taiwan) had fallen drastically since the mid-1990s, with the lowest number being nine total films produced that year and market share at 0.125 percent in 2001 (D. Lee 2018). From 1996 to 2007, one year before the release of *Cape No. 7*, the market share of domestic films was only 1 to 2 percent (S. Lim 2013: 157).

However, the situation has changed dramatically since the megahit of *Cape No. 7*. It inspired young filmmakers to enjoy commercial filmmaking within the Taiwanese film industry (Chiu et al. 2017; Berry 2017; D. Lee 2018). To distinguish these young directors from older filmmakers, the films they made during the past decade have been dubbed post–New Cinema, in reference to the Taiwan New Cinema that preceded them. Post–New Cinema directors shared the interest that Taiwan New Cinema directors had in traumatic historical events, or began their careers working with them. However, they treated those events in a lighter manner than had the previous directorial generation. Song-yong Sing (2010: 148–49) characterizes post–New Cinema as having a tendency to a "post-sadness" approach to traumatic historical subjects. This penchant also characterizes the films of the early twenty-first century. Analyzing contemporary Taiwan documentaries, Kuei-fen Chiu (2007: 25) notes that the stories set during the period of

Japanese rule that were not released under the martial law regime started to be told by Taiwan New Cinema directors and young documentarians since the late 1980s.[2] At first, they represented Taiwanese as victims of Japanese rule, the *Kuomintang* (KMT) regime and other foreign forces, but "the new imaginary seeks to reconceptualize Taiwan as a key player in the intersection of cultural flows rather than a passive victim of foreign forces" (Chiu 2007: 28).

Moreover, compared to the directors of Taiwan New Cinema such as Hou Hsiao-hsien, Edward Yang, and Tsai Ming-liang, who received much critical attention from international film festivals or art house circuits but failed to win acclaim in the domestic market, the directors of post–New Cinema were less interested in international attention than in domestic market success. When *Guangyin de gushi* (*Our Time*, dir. Tao De-chen, Edward Yang, Ke Yi- zheng, and Zhang Yi, 1982) and *Er zi de da wan ou* (*The Sandwich Man*, dir. Hou Hsiao- hsien, Zeng Zhuang-xiang and Wan Ren, 1983) were released, the films' directors marked the advent of Taiwan New Cinema. The KMT government had ideologically supervised local film productions in the early 1980s, but it supported the global distribution of these new directors' films despite their refusal to conform to the ideology of the regime. This is because of the Taiwan government's "long-term efforts to promote domestically produced films overseas as part of multiple 'screening Taiwan' projects since the Cold War" (Ma 2017: 58).

Taiwan was one of the founding members of the United Nations, but the General Assembly of the UN held in October 1970 refused to give a seat to the Republic of China (ROC, or Taiwan) because of the problem of the representation of People's Republic of China (PRC, or China) (Hickey 1997: 1031–32).[3] Following the withdrawal from the UN, more than fifty countries broke relations with Taiwan before 1978, when the United States declared that it would terminate diplomatic relations (Smith 1978), and only twenty-two countries had diplomatic ties with Taiwan by 1988 (W. Lee 1993: 43). Even worse, Taiwan was expelled from numerous international organizations such as World Bank and the International Monetary Fund (IMF) during the 1980s (Hickey 1997: 1035) and maintained official membership in only eight international bodies in 1988 (W. Lee 1993: 43). In addition to claiming the restoration of their representation in the UN during the 1970s and 80s, the KMT government made desperate efforts such as foreign aid in order to avoid diplomatic isolation during the 1980s and 1990s (Cheong 2001; Hickey 1997; W. Lee 1993).

The Taiwan government's "screening Taiwan" project was also a part of these efforts to break out of its diplomatic isolation. However, this cultural effort was unproductive because the directors of Taiwan New Cinema concentrated on festivals and arthouses, which aimed a few targeted audiences. As a matter of fact, their authorial vision, which rejected "the simplistic black-and-white storytelling methods of the past" (Berry and Lu 2005: 6), deterred audiences from the works of Taiwan New Cinema directors. To overcome the industrial crisis, they published the Taiwan New Cinema Manifesto, which called for "another cinema" in 1987 (6). As Daw-Ming Lee (2018) argues, that manifesto, though issued to promote the domestic film industry, was paradoxically a declaration of its end, for as the crisis deepened these directors started to get funds from various international entities. As a result, it became difficult to identify the national originality of their work (Ma 2017: 61).

After this long-term recession in the Taiwan film industry, Wei Te-sheng's successful debut and the emergence of a successor generation of young filmmakers was thus seen as the advent of a post–New Cinema.[4] Post–New Cinema directors including Wei Te-sheng "refused the arthouse film mode of aesthetics" that was led by Taiwan New Cinema directors (Chiu et al. 2017: 4). Also, post–New Cinema directors try to deal with weighty issues such as the Japanese colonial era or the discrimination against Aborigines in a light manner compared to their older generation. As Sing (2010) notes, Wei Te-sheng and *Cape No. 7* are considered the most prominent examples of post–New Cinema.

In 2017, Kuei-fen Chiu, Ming-yeh T. Rawnsley, and Gary D. Rawnsley published a volume entitled *Taiwan Cinema: International Reception and Social Change*, which was entirely dedicated to Wei Te-sheng. In their introduction, the editors answered the question: Why Wei Te-sheng? "This collection of essays uses Wei Te-sheng as a gateway to analyze and understand both the idea and development of Taiwan's national cinema within a social and political context that has experienced profound change" (Chiu, Rawnsley, and Rawnsley 2017a: 2). In this vein, the volume's contributors delve into Wei and his so-called colonial trilogy—*Cape No. 7* (2008), *Sai de ke ba lai* (*Warriors of the Rainbow: Seediq Bale*, 2011), and *Kano* (dir. Umin Boya, written and produced by Wei Te-sheng, 2014). Their interests are varied, but the volume's emphasis is on industrial and political issues in Taiwan and the global dimension. Other studies on Wei Te-sheng's films have also viewed them in relation to the current cultural and political scene in Taiwan. By contrast, this article situates Wei Te-sheng's films in the post–Cold War memory regime in Northeast Asia. It thus seeks to transcend the dichotomy between the national and the global, configuring the workings of an inter-Asian discursive sphere in post–Cold War Taiwan. Although this article focuses on the early twenty-first century, the discussion is not limited to that era but also extends to the period of the Cold War owing to the complex history of postwar Taiwan. Before investigating Wei's colonial trilogy, the next section briefly introduces the sphere of postcolonial memory regime in Taiwan.

Wei Te-sheng's Colonial Trilogy and the Postcolonial Memory Regime in Taiwan

Wei Te-sheng was born in 1969 and raised in a Han Chinese family in Tainan, the southern part of Taiwan. He started his film career at the studio of Edward Yang, working on Yang's *Ma jiang* (*Mahjong*, 1996) as an assistant director, and then made four short films, including *Duihua sanbu* (*Three Dialogues*, 1996) and *Liming zhi qian* (*Before Dawn*, 1997), which both received the Golden Harvest Award. Then, he made or produced the colonial trilogy. His latest film, *52Hz, I Love You*, released in 2017, is a romantic comedy set in contemporary Taipei. So far, all his feature films, including *Kano*, the film he produced, have been top-ranked at the Taiwan box office. He has been planning to make another historical trilogy (the "Taiwan trilogy") which "will look at the island's history 400 years ago from the different viewpoints of the Dutch colonizers, the ethnic Chinese migrants, and the indigenous population" (Strong 2017). His interest in Taiwan's history was not his original motivation for making films. However, after receiving critical comments from his audience, he decided to make another Taiwan historical trilogy to satisfy the audience (Rawnsley 2017: 195–96).

From this point of view, *Cape No. 7* was a kind of test bed for him to identify the commercial possibilities of a story from Taiwan's colonial history. The film primarily portrays a romance between a Taiwanese man and a Japanese woman in the present; it also summons colonial memories relating to the story of a frustrated love affair between a Taiwanese woman and a Japanese man just after Japan's defeat in World War II. Bringing young viewers who had been growing tired of Taiwanese films back to the theater, the film sparked an audience movement to watch it over and over (T. Lin 2018). Viewing the film became "a national pastime for web citizens," and audiences voluntarily adopted a "piracy ban" movement (Chang 2010: 81). After the film's success, Wei Te-sheng participated in two more films, as filmmaker, screenwriter, or producer, based on real events in the Japanese colonial period.

Of course, Wei Te-sheng's films are not the first to describe colonization in Taiwan under Japan.[5] With the lifting of martial law (1949–87), Taiwan's democratization accelerated. Simultaneously, the suppressed voices of various political parties and ethnic groups[6] began to emerge. These new currents included reexaminations of Taiwanese society and history, including the country's colonial past. Until then, textbook descriptions of the fifty-year occupation (1895–1945) by Japan had focused mostly on the anti-Japanese movement (Chou 1997: 119) since the KMT government strove to erase all traces of Japan and to sinicize Taiwan as quickly as possible. This project centered on promoting the Mandarin language through the media or education (Mamie 2014: 58). Moreover, the KMT government did not want to remind Taiwanese of the colonial history since the KMT itself was in some respects another invader on the island of Taiwan.[7] As a result, as Pei-yin Lin and Su Yun Kim (2019: 6) note in the case of Taiwan literature, unlike South Korea, where authors serving for Japanese imperialism tried to break up with their pasts right after the liberation, regrets from pro-Japanese authors in Taiwan during the colonial era came out much later, nearly in the 1990s. Chiafung Lin (2016: 6) points out that, because "colonial memories had been purposefully discontinued by the state, the younger generation's remembering not only involves overcoming social amnesia, but even more work lying in the area of reconciling with, or removing, a politically transposed memory."[8] Borrowing Marianne Hirsch's term "post-memory,"

Lin argues that these emerging post-memorial works stem from the rehisto-
ricizing efforts of youth who never experienced Japanese colonization. The
"Cape No. 7 fever" and the proliferation of other films reflecting on the Japanese ruling era during the early twenty-first century could be considered
part of such a trend.

On the other hand, the reevaluation of the colonial period since the early
1980s in Taiwan coincided with the development of the movement for
democratization. The democratization movement since the 1970s in Taiwan
finally drove the KMT government to lift martial law in 1987, and the 2000
presidential election was won by the Minzhu Jinbu Dang (Democratic Progressive Party, DPP) which advocates Taiwan's independence from Mainland China. The DPP and its supporters have tried to rewrite Taiwanese
history, resisting KMT's Sinocentric historiography,[9] and to reinvestigate the
Japanese past against KMT's structuring deletion of colonial traces (Wang
2003: 173).

Ever-changing cross-strait (Taiwan-China) relations in postwar Asia
have also influenced retrospective understandings of Japanese colonial rule.
Despite the Taiwan government's efforts to restore its international status
since the withdrawal from the UN, Taiwan has become more isolated as
China's power in world affairs has become stronger due to the mainland's
economic growth. In this process, Taiwanese nationalism emerged in the
1990s as a reaction against Chinese (Sinocentric) nationalism. In this context, Taiwan under the Japanese invaders was often compared to Taiwan
under the Mainland invaders.

Thus, both the resurgence of Taiwanese nationalism and the revisioning
of Japanese colonialism stem from the desire to redefine Taiwan's status on
the international stage in the changing geopolitics of East Asia.[10] Wei's colonial trilogy encounters this discursive sphere where two different nationalisms are competing, colonialism and postcolonialism are competing, and
nationalism and internationalism are competing. In the following three sections, this article investigates how colonial memories are negotiated in Wei's
trilogy, in formulating the concepts of "nation" and "nationalism" that lack
popular consent in Taiwan, and how the reconfiguration of the Japanese
ruling era combines with postcolonial discourse in the changing geopolitical
conditions of the post–Cold War relationship between Taiwan and China.

Go Global with Taiwanese Nationalism: *Cape No. 7*

In the opening scene of *Cape No. 7* (2008), the male protagonist Aga, becoming sick of Taipei life, leaves Taipei for his southern hometown, Heungchun. As he leaves, he smashes his guitar and shouts, "Fuck you, Taipei!" After this scene, the scenery of Taipei's landmarks appears on his back. This scene vividly declares the film's distance from the centrality of Taipei. Here, the South bears a significance with respect to the film's political nuance. Southern Taiwan was the cradle of dissent in the 1970s, as exemplified in the *Meilidao* incident of 1979 in Kaohsiung.[11] By contrast, the KMT regime and Mainland Chinese were based in Taipei. The centralization of political, economic, and cultural power in Taipei has also been regarded as a means of ethnic discrimination against the Native Taiwanese living in other cities (Wang 2003: 105–21). The economic and cultural alienation experienced by local Natives is one of the film's major conflicts.

Yu-wen Fu (2014) interprets this opening scene as an allusion to the political resistance against KMT. The year 2008, when the film was released, was a turning point for Taiwanese politics that saw a shift from the grassroots independent movement of the 1990s and early 2000s to the restoration of the KMT government as the result of KMT's triumph in the 2008 elections. Older generations that had suffered from KMT's oppression were "frustrated by the return of KMT and its Sino-centric cultural ideologies" (Fu 2014: 231). The protagonist's going to the South in the film implies such resistance to the central government.

The film mainly portrays a local band's struggle to complete their performance on the warm-up stage in one of the biggest festivals in the village. Aga's stepfather, called "Mr. Representative," organizes a local amateur band as a counterpart to the Japanese superstar band invited by a hotel owner who is an outsider. Due to the economic inequality, the villagers show a sense of defeat and loss against outsiders—that is, Mainland Chinese, like the hotel owner. Mr. Representative desperately wants to organize a Native Taiwanese band because he plans to run for mayor election and needs to collect votes from Natives who comprise an absolute majority of voters. Most of the band members seem "eccentric" (Chang 2010: 87) and hopeless at first, but they ultimately attract some attention from the local audience. Therefore their completion of their mission as a warm-up band represents a victory for the local "eccentrics"—that is, Taiwanese Natives. Fu (2014: 236) interprets this scene as the embodiment of the Taiwan nation's quest for a collective postcolonial identity, which should be multicultural and multiethnic in contrast to KMT's homogeneous Sinocentric cultural ideology. In this sense, Fu argues that the concert scene in which the band members complete their mission envisions "an inclusive and powerful notion of grassroots consciousness" (237).

While the band members are practicing for the concert, the love between Aga and Tomoko (hereafter "young Tomoko"), a band manager who is Japanese, develops as well. Throughout the film, their love story intersects with a frustrated love story from the colonial past. After Aga's return from Taipei, his stepfather has found him a job as a postal worker. Having neither interest in his job nor a sense of responsibility, Aga often hoards letters instead of delivering them. One day, he opens a returned parcel and, in it, discovers a girl's photo and love letters written by a Japanese man almost sixty years ago. Then the film flashes back to the days when the Japanese man wrote these letters to his Taiwanese lover, who was also named Tomoko (hereafter "old Tomoko"). He was a teacher in Taiwan but was returning to Japan due to Japan's defeat in World War II. His letters are full of regret and apologies for not being able to bring his lover to Japan. The two love stories intertwine as Aga and young Tomoko encounter the returned letters and try to find old Tomoko in order finally to deliver them.

The Japanese man in the past keeps apologizing to his lover but considers himself a scapegoat of the war, saying, "I have nothing to do with the war. I'm just a poor teacher." As Jie-hyun Lim (2010: 139) points out, individuals can separate themselves from the collective guilt for deeds done in their name but not by them, thereby constructing themselves as victims in collective memory, activating a sort of victimhood nationalism. The film holds Japan responsible for the war (as perpetrator), but it forgives ordinary Japanese people who did nothing directly related to the war and regards them as fellow victims of the war. In addition to the Japanese teacher's assumption of a victim identity, the film admits that Japanese could be victims like Taiwanese. The film identifies Aga in the present with the Japanese man in the past, while the Japanese woman of the present is identified with the

Taiwanese woman of the past, especially by giving both women the name Tomoko. In his sentimental attachment to Taiwan, the Japanese man in the past even expresses ambivalence about where he belongs: "I am not sure if I am going home or leaving home." It is thus difficult to distinguish victim and victimizer, especially since Aga is about to make the same mistake as the Japanese man in the past.[12]

Yet the Japanese man's exemption from war responsibility also implies the moral superiority of the Taiwanese over the Japanese in the past. During a rehearsal, young Tomoko announces that she will go back to Japan after the concert. While Aga hesitates to answer, young Tomoko gives him the current address of old Tomoko so that he can deliver the letters from the Japanese man. Having successfully delivered the Japanese man's letters to old Tomoko, Aga returns to the place of the concert just before the performance starts. He says to young Tomoko, "Do not leave, or I will go [to Japan with you]," and then starts his performance. The Taiwanese man thus avoids the mistake of the Japanese teacher; Aga displays courage and a sense of responsibility in refusing to abandon his relationship with young Tomoko.

Although the two men suffer for different reasons—Aga on the verge of losing his love due to his indecision, the Japanese teacher floundering in a historical transition that he cannot resist—the differences are less important to the film than what they have in common: the problem of whether they have the courage to preserve their love. Here, Aga, the Taiwanese, exhibits his bravery, while the Japanese teacher fails, leaving old Tomoko alone in Taiwan, probably because of their different nationalities. In addition, the film intersects the current love story with the past one, where the present is depicted in a light tone of romantic comedy while the past is seen in a rather heavy tone of melodrama. This becomes more evident through the contrast of the present scenes in vivid colors and the past scenes with low chroma. Here, the sadness and pain of the past turn into the joy of the present, and historical failure into the hope for the future.

However, Aga's courage seems to need the recognition of an external other in the film. When the amateur band finally finishes performing, a Japanese star singer, who is the same actor of the Japanese teacher in the past, is so deeply touched that he joins in during the amateur band's encore. Surprised, Aga tries to hand over his microphone, but the Japanese singer encourages Aga to continue singing. They sing together in Japanese a song named *Wild Rose*. The audience also sings along in Japanese. The little-known local amateur band thus gains recognition by moving the hearts of the famous Japanese band members. The recognition from the Japanese (former colonizer), who was supposed to have much more power or capital than the Taiwanese (former colonized), is continuously reiterated in the other two films in Wei's trilogy.

This need for recognition is related to the global geopolitics of the post–Cold War era. The film repeatedly invokes the slogan "From the local to the global." Among the characters, there is a salesman called Malasun following the new brand of Aboriginal millet wine he sells: "It's a new brand. We repackage the Aborigine's millet wine. The goal is to go international. Thousands of years of history with a new sensation." These words are echoed in the dialogue between the hotel owner and Mr. Representative. The owner of the local hotel says, "We have to go global." Then Mr. Representative responds, "What global village? You, outsiders [Mainland Chinese], build up hotels here. What about us Natives?" Therefore, the aim to go global must go with the Natives and their thousands of years of history—that is, the Taiwanese Natives' own history rather than that of the Mainland Chinese. In this sense, Taiwanese nationalism goes beyond national borders and extends to a global scale. Going south does not merely mean rebuilding Taiwanese nationalism to resist KMT's Sinocentric nationalism; rather, the film suggests that the South could become the hub for a new and robust Taiwanese nationalism on the global stage.

Claiming Land Ownership: *Seediq Bale*

Wei Te-sheng's second film, *Sai de ke ba lai* (*Warriors of the Rainbow: Seediq Bale*, 2011), deals with a real event, the Wushe incident.[13] The Wushe incident of 1930 has been reported as the last resistance of Aborigines against Japanese colonial rule. The incident started in the morning of October 27, 1930, when the Wushe village people and Japanese officers, including the colonial provincial governor, police officers, and their families, gathered in an elementary school to celebrate an annual day of athletics. Just before the event started, hundreds of armed Aboriginal men burst into the crowd and relentlessly killed almost four hundred people regardless of gender and age. The Aborigines achieved a short-lived victory until the Japanese forces brutally suppressed the rebellion by using cannons, airplanes, and poison gas. Although there is controversy about what triggered the incident, the most likely reasons were economic exploitation, suppression of Aboriginal culture, or some Japanese policeman's discriminatory behavior against Aborigines (Ching 2001: 141–43).

Seediq Bale is devoted to an epic about the rise of a national hero called Mouna Rudao. Chief of the Mehebu clan, Mouna was one of the leaders who rebelled against the Japanese colonial forces. In the opening scene of the film, young Mouna shows his bravery in hunting a huge, fierce boar. His nearly naked body and the cruel headhunting scene accentuate his heroic traits and the Aborigines' exotic way of living in the wild. The scene was filmed on a grand scale—the most expensive Taiwanese film ever made up until then—filled with various digital effects, such as the use of computer graphics for the boar's movements and underwater shooting to celebrate the birth of the hero. Although the film deals with the dark side of the colonial era, it puts entertainment elements ahead of the author's aesthetic vision by showing overwhelming spectacles and a "Western-style epic" (Yang 2012: 1115). This way of representing the past is distinguished from the serious attitude of the previous generations.

On the other hand, the hero is mythologized by being combined with ancestral spirits. When young Mouna finally succeeds in animal hunting and headhunting, his father, the chief of the Mehebu clan, declares him a hero and his villagers start to dance and drink. By hunting bravely, he becomes a "seediq bale," meaning a "true man" in Mehebu clan's language. As a symbol of manhood, his face is tattooed by his mother in a form of blood sacrifice to his ancestors' spirits. This ritual of blood sacrifice is one of the most critical elements of the myth of the birth of a hero.

Above all, this hero myth is strongly bound up with the archetypical land. When the Japanese colonial forces reach Wushe village in the film, they mercilessly slaughter the villagers while Mouna and his clans counterattack, fighting them to the death to protect the land. Through cross-editing of these two scenes, Mouna's father shouts to the Japanese: "You're not qualified to enter the heavenly home of our ancestors." The Aborigines' ownership of the land, in which ancestral spirits are enshrined, is fundamental to their existence and thus inviolable.

Chin-ching Lee claims that this strong linkage between the land and Aborigines is the filmic strategy of postcolonial politics, distinguishing the "place" of Aborigines from the "landscape" of Japan. For Lee (2013: 215), the Japanese colonial force sees the mountainous area as belonging to humans and views culture as superior to nature, whereas Aborigines dwell in the environment as one of the factors of nature; while the Japanese intruders assert their possession of nature, the Aborigines' dwelling "implies an at-homeness with place" (215). This becomes clear in a scene in which the child of a Japanese policeman asks Aboriginal clans to leave the hunting ground because he thinks that "everything here belongs to us Japanese."

Although Lee's critique of the dichotomy between nature and culture helps us to see how the Japanese colonial strategy depended on sustaining the distance between the civilized (culture) and the savage (nature) to oppress Aborigines, it is difficult to tell whether the film actually implies the postcolonial politics that Lee proposes, considering the vision of civilization that it offers. Its ambiguous view of civilization is revealed through the Hanaoka brothers, Aborigines who have become a Japanese police officer and a teacher. They knew that the Aboriginal clans would attack the Japanese on the athletics day. Rather than betray their clan or take part in the battle, they choose suicide. Before the suicide, they leave their testament on the school wall: "We, the Hanaoka brothers, are forced to leave this world. The savages are massacring the Japanese, creating an uncontrollable situation. Now we are cornered by the savages and have no other choice. It is 9 o'clock on the morning of October 27th, 1930. The savages have already occupied most of this region. The commissioner and all his subordinates have been killed in the school."

Shengfan (savage) is a term used by the Japanese to degrade Aborigines. In this sense, the Hanaoka brothers are highly Japanized Aborigines (Chou 1997: 142). The film portrays the anguish of these brothers who can be neither Japanese nor Taiwanese. One day, Mouna asks the elder Hanaoka whether he will die as a Japanese or an Aborigine. Hanaoka does not answer at that time, but in the end he chooses the Japanese way of death, wearing a kimono and performing hara-kiri (disembowelment). Their anguish is clearly stated in young Hanaoka's words: "We don't want to be savages, but no matter how hard we try to dress up like the Japanese, we will always be seen as uncivilized people." The film's empathic view of the Hanaoka brothers makes it hard to see the film as portraying opposition to civilization discourse. The director, Wei Te-sheng, also says that the film is not just about the military rebellion against the colonizers but also about the conflict and "reconciliation between culture and civilization" (*Screendaily* 2011). Here in Wei's statement, "culture" refers to ethnic cultures, which Lee calls "nature."

In this regard, the film neither completely repudiates Japanese colonialism nor accepts the Aborigines' culture without hesitation. On one hand, the film strongly criticizes the cruel actions of Aboriginal men, such as forcing the women of the clan to commit suicide so the warriors can eat during a food shortage, by photographing women's dead bodies hanging from trees in a dark tone from below. On the other hand, it portrays some positive aspects of Japanese civilization from the perspective of the Hanaoka brothers. In addition, the key reason for the Wushe incident is presented in the film as the discriminatory remarks and actions of particular vicious Japanese officials rather than structural contradictions wrought by Japanese colonial rule. In other words, the film tries to balance the negative and positive effects of the Japanese colonial rule.

What is intriguing is that mainland China is entirely absent from the film. This is related to the emergence of Taiwanese nationalism. According to Lorenzo Veracini (2012: 244), "The only way to assert a specific indigenous Taiwanese national identity without facing the issue of settler [mainland Chinese] colonialism is to narrate a story of indigenous disappearance and disavow the real settlers." As a matter of fact, Han Chinese in the film harmonize with the Aborigines and have a role in exchanging goods for the clans' survival and in mediating various clans' needs and conflicts. However, there is no room for mainland Chinese. Berry (2017: 119) points out that "any connection to China on the continent is thoroughly erased" in Wei's colonial trilogy and this should be understood as "a structuring absence," given that there were already active connections between Taiwan and China during the colonial era.

Yet I would note that, although *Seediq Bale* does not portray directly any mainland Chinese character, the film conveys a criticism of the KMT in its closing intertitle:

> Mouna Rudao's remains were found inside a cavern, somewhere deep in the mountains.... After that, his remains disappeared once again. After the second disappearance, Mouna Rudao's remains were rediscovered thirty-nine years later in the specimen room of the College of Medicine at National Taiwan University. Escorted by his offspring, after forty-three years, he finally returned to his hometown Wushe to be buried properly.

The intertitle criticizes the KMT government's incompetence and indifference by revealing that the KMT has promoted the incident extensively only as an exemplary event of the anti-Japanese movement. In reality, the KMT paid no attention to the remains of Mouna, whose body was humiliated after his death by the Japanese military. The year when Mouna's remains were rediscovered was the time when progressive voices were raised against the KMT government's dictatorship. Thus, the returning of Mouna's remains coincides with the resurrection of Taiwanese Natives' history. In this sense, Veracini (2012: 244) calls the film "a (filmic) declaration of Taiwan's (settler) independence."

It is noteworthy that Mouna's heroic life is admired by a Japanese general in the film. When the general learns that Mouna disappeared and other survivors chose suicide rather than be arrested by the Japanese, he speaks with admiration, "How can I see here the *bushido* [the morality of warriors] of samurais that died over a century ago in Japan?" Taiwanese warriors are comparable to or better than the Japanese samurai and thus prompt Japanese admiration. Through this filmic representation of respect and acknowledgment by the former colonial power, the film proposes that the Taiwanese can claim superiority in competition with Japanese colonial power.

The Dichotomy of Good Modernization versus Bad Colonization: *Kano*

In his interviews, Wei Te-sheng often complains that he is criticized by both pro-unification and pro-independence groups. *Cape No. 7* was blamed by the pro-unification side for its nostalgic portrayal of the colonial past, while *Seediq Bale* was considered "anti-Japan and pro-China" (Lin and Kim 2019:

17). If Wei appears ambivalent toward the Japanese colonial past, it might be because the attitude to the colonial past in Taiwan has ambivalent aspects. It is widely thought, for example, that the Japanese invaders only exploited the Taiwanese people before 1929 and treated them as citizens of Imperial Japan from the 1930s on (Chou 1997: 164). A complementary view is that there are both good and bad aspects of the colonial past. Here, colonization is a bad thing, while modernization is a good one (148). While the suffering of Aborigines in *Seediq Bale* could be categorized as generally bad, the Hanaoka brothers explicitly recognize some benefits of Japanese colonialism. The film *Kano* (dir. Umin Boya, 2014), in which Wei participated as a screenwriter and producer, relates to the second belief about the colonial past.

Kano is based on a true story about Taiwanese high school baseball players in an agricultural school who entered the Japanese High School Baseball Championship called Koshien in 1931.[14] Two goals of the main characters feature in the film: for baseball players to go to Koshien, and for farmers and students in the agricultural school to modernize Taiwan's agriculture. The film portrays two heroic Japanese characters in Taiwanese history: Hyotaro Kondo and Yoichi Hata. Through his professional and systematic transfer of skills and rigorous training, Kondo, the coach of a baseball team called Kano, made it possible for his students to go to Koshien. He is remembered as the person who developed Taiwanese baseball in its early stage. At a ceremony at the Hyotaro Kondo Memorial in Kondo's Japanese hometown, Matsuyama City, the president of National Chiayi University (NCYU) in Kano team's hometown expressed his gratitude to Coach Kondo, saying, "Without his persevering devotion, NCYU would not have enjoyed the enduring success or become the birthplace of baseball in Taiwan" (NCYU News 2014).

Meanwhile, another important figure, Yoichi Hata, is a civil engineer who pioneered channels to irrigate farmland. Because of his nationality, he did not appear in the Taiwanese records for a long time, but he was recently reinstated as the father of Taiwan's agricultural modernization (Tang and Fujimaki 2018: 24). In the film, Hata is portrayed as familiar and gentle to all the students who will lead Taiwan's agriculture in the future. The film shows Hata's desperate effort to build a canal. The Chianan plain in which the Kano team was based was famous for agriculture, and in fact it was in order to increase the grain supply for military purposes that the Japanese colonial authority made efforts at agricultural modernization (Y. Lee 2012: 33).[15] The film downplays this predatory intention but credits the Japanese colonial authority with the modernization of Taiwan's agriculture.

In the scene of the opening ceremony of Koshien, one of the largest and most important national sports events in Japan, a number of Japanese national baseball teams and other teams from the colonies of Chosŏn (Korea), Manchu (Manchuria), and Taiwan gather together. Shot by drone, the flags of all nations wave in the sky, and the gallery is full of spectators with a continuous roar. Reporters are rushing to cover the event. In the film, Koshien goes beyond the national scale and becomes an imperial event. Koshien should become the center of a whole universe because the sports event itself was a good means of propaganda to hide Japan's violent invasion into each colony and disseminate its "goodwill." The film celebrates this imperial event as a "transnational and transcultural" one (Liao 2017: 129) by making the Kano team ethnically diverse. It is composed of various races: Han ethnics, Taiwanese Aborigines, and Japanese. These multiple ethnicities represent the unity of multicultural, multiracial, and multiethnic people, and thus Koshien perfectly embodies transnational coprosperity in Asia, which later became the logic of Japan's war of conquest. This transnational event is celebrated in the film, in contrast to the KMT regime's suppression of multiculturalism and enforcement of a Sinocentric monoculture. Here, Japanese imperialism is used in the film almost synonymously with cosmopolitanism and evangelism.

In fact, the baseball players' destiny coincides with that of the village agriculture in the film. While the Kano team players are injured in a fight with another baseball team ahead of an important match, heavy rain simultaneously ruins the farm. These two incidents push the players and Hata to the verge of collapse. The two plot elements share celebratory moments as well. It is heard that waterways have been finally opened and thus water has directly entered the farmland when villagers gather in a welcome parade to celebrate the players who have overcome the ordeal and entered Koshien representing Taiwan. Right after the Kano team players hear the joyful news about the channel during the parade, all of them stop the parade and run to the fields. They happily jump into the water as it enters the farmhouse and enjoy that victorious moment. In this way, the film celebrates the era of Japanese colonial rule as a moment of the modernization as well as a transnational and multicultural period in Taiwan.

Intriguingly, the film's point of view belongs to Joshua Hiromi, an ace on Kano's rival team who is a Japanese high school student and star baseball player. At first, he ignores the Kano team because of his prejudice against the colonized people. However, deeply touched by their enthusiasm and skills, he begins to admire them. A few years later, the train taking Joshua to the battlefield stops for a moment in the home of the Kano team. He gets off the train and visits the playground where they practiced. He grabs a handful of dirt from the ground. Here, the land, the history of Taiwan, and the memory of the colony conjoin again. However, unlike what *Seediq Bale* shows, the land in this film is not solely the home of Aborigines; the film presents it as a space of equality where various ethnicities can coexist and symbiotically thrive. What is excluded here is the mainland Chinese. As Wei's other films show, the authority to recognize the Taiwanese belongs to a Japanese, a citizen from the former colonizer. Again, it is proposed that Taiwanese nationalism excludes mainland China but still requires the approval of imperial power.

Conclusion: Subimperialist Eyes

In Wei's colonial trilogy, there always appear Japanese characters who admire or acknowledge Taiwanese protagonists: a Japanese superstar (*Cape No. 7*), a Japanese general (*Seediq Bale*), and a Japanese baseball star player (*Kano*). Wei describes Taiwanese as ordinary, while Japanese are better endowed with power or capital in their respective spheres of entertainment, war, and sports. Chris Berry links these scenes in Wei's films with the Japan complex and the orphan complex, which appear frequently in modern Taiwanese literary works, such as Wu Zhuo-liu's novel *Orphan of Asia* (1956). Berry points out that this complex originated with Taiwan's long colonial history but is now related to its international position as a stateless country and the sense of inferiority wrought by China's growing power on the global stage, so that "the memory of colonialism is replaced with the fantasy of a benign big Other" in Wei's trilogy (Berry 2017: 120).

The fantasy of a benign big Other is often juxtaposed with the desire of recognition by external/foreign powers. This is what Kuan-Hsing Chen calls "subimperialism," which reinforces the imperialist regime. Subimperialism indicates a lower-level empire's desire for regional prominence that depends on the larger structures of imperialism (Chen 2000: 15). In post–Cold War Taiwan, especially since the early twenty-first century, Taiwanese nationalism has more actively embraced this subimperial desire to compete with Chinese nationalism and Mainland China in the stage of international geopolitics.

Wei's effort to situate Taiwan on the global stage through the representation of the Japanese colonial period and the exclusion of China from its history can thus be seen as an expression of subimperial desire rather than a manifestation of postcolonial intent. Although this article focused on Wei's colonial trilogy, the desires that make his films attractive to audiences and critics are found in other areas of Taiwanese culture. In Taiwan, an ongoing war of memory about Japanese colonial rule is exemplified in the reconstruction of Japanese structures such as shrines that were dismantled during the KMT's authoritarian regime (Amae 2011: 29). The colonial memories evoked in Wei's films engage in this mnemonic space in post–Cold War Taiwan, like other East Asian countries, which has grown over the past decades. And as we see in Wei's films, colonial memory is still competing with entangled powers from domestic and international institutions, citizens, ethnic groups, and other political actors.

Notes

This work was supported by the National Research Foundation of Korea Grant funded by the Korean government (2017S1A6A3A01079727).

1   Misawa Mamie (2014: 35) notes the difficulties in considering the period after the defeat of Japan in 1945 in Asian countries other than Japan. However, the term *postwar* is used in this article to indicate "after World War II."

2   According to Chiu (2007: 18), the 1980s' representation of the Japanese colonial rule was influenced by the 1970s' literary movement called *Xiangtu* (nativist), in which a top priority is to give a voice to the voiceless.

3   The official names of both countries are, respectively, Republic of China and People's Republic of China, but here their commonly used names, Taiwan and China, are used in this article, except in direct quotations.

4   Another representative example of post–New Cinema is *Detention* (dir. John Hsu, 2019), a film based on a popular horror video game of the same name, dealing with a tragic event in a school during Taiwan's White Terror period. By adopting the horror genre's conventions, the film achieved a great box office success, having the third-highest take at the box office gross of any domestic film in the first three days of screening at cinemas since 2011, just behind *Warriors of the Rainbow: Seediq Bale*. It also received favorable criticism from domestic and international critics.

5   In particular, Taiwan New Cinema and documentaries in the 1980s and 1990s influenced by *Xiangtu* had started to portray the Japanese colonial era from an ambivalent perspective, but films dealing with the Japanese rule in a positive manner began to be made in the early twenty-first century (Chiu 2007; Rawnsley 2014). Examples of such films include *Tiawu shidai* (*Viva Tonal: The Dance Age*, dir. Wei-Ssu Chien and Chen-Ti Kuo, 2003), *Shonenko* (dir. Lian-Ying Guo, 2006), *Wansei hui jia* (*Wansei Back Home*, dir. Ming-cheng Huang, 2015), *Wansei huajia—Tetsuomi Tateishi* (*Wansei Painter—Tetsuomi Tateishi*, dir. Liang-Yin Kuo and Shuhei Fujita, 2016), and *Hai de bi duan* (*After Spring, the Tamaki Family*, dir. Yin-Yu Huang, 2016).

6   Taiwan's population comprises four recognized ethnic groups: Mainland Chinese who immigrated to Taiwan after 1945; Hakka Han Chinese and Hoklo Han Chinese who came to Taiwan and settled down before 1945 (the distinction between Hakka and Hoklo reflects their respective hometowns); and Aboriginal Taiwanese (they are also divided into more than ten groups). In general, the category of "native Taiwanese" includes Han Chinese and aboriginal Taiwanese except Mainland Chinese.

7   Taiwan's Native people, including Chinese migrants on the island, initially welcomed the KMT soldiers when Taiwan was incorporated under the KMT regime after 1945. However, anti-KMT sentiment was provoked by the brutal suppression of the February 28 incident in 1947, a popular demonstration against KMT's discriminatory policy toward Taiwan Natives, as well as by the introduction of martial law in 1949. The White Terror against political dissidents began with the introduction of martial law and lasted for thirty-eight years. In this sense, Taiwan Natives who had lived on the island before 1945 thought of the KMT government and its soldiers as another invader and even compared the "bad" KMT invader to the "good" Japanese invader.

8   As a post-generation and those who did not experience the colonial era and other traumatic historical events such as February 28, they seem to have a collective memory about bad days of Japanese ruling era in contrast to the heyday of the KMT regime (C. Lin 2016: 6).

9   The sinicization policy imposed by the KMT government since the 1950s meant "a move away from Japanification as well as Taiwanization which favored independence" (Mamie 2014: 58), and thus KMT suppressed the Taiwanese dialect and Aboriginal history as well as the history of Taiwan's modernization under Japanese colonial rule.

10   Many Asian countries that experienced the history of Japanese colonial rule had developed

nationalism in resistance to Japan (Dissanayake 1994). Even after the war, the narrative of resistance to Japanese imperialism has been the leitmotif of nation building in many former colonies such as South Korea and China. However, colonialism and nationalism have an ever-changing relationship in different historical and geopolitical contexts. For example, nationalism combined with patriarchy suppressed the coming-out of the "comfort women" in the public sphere for a long while (Fujitani, White, and Yoneyama 2001). Yet interest in the "comfort women" issue associated with nationalism increased in the first decade of the twenty-first century when confronted with Japanese historical revisionists (Ueno 2006: 6). Therefore the relationship between nationalism and colonialism in Taiwan should be considered in these changing geopolitical contexts.

11 Also named the Kaoshung incident. *Meilidao* is a name of progressive magazine published in 1979 by political forces outside the party to promote resistance ideology and liaise among members of the organization. However, the *Meilidao* incident, in which a large number of party members were arrested, left demands for democratic reform frustrated for a while.

12 Young Tomoko shows her love to Aga before flying to Japan, but Aga hesitates to ask her to stay. This scene is intercut with scenes of the past in which old Tomoko desperately tries to find her Japanese lover, who is keeping out of sight from her at the port.

13 The incident is also known as the Musha incident.

14 The Japanese authorities had emphasized military exercises and physical education to create new body to defend the nation since the Meiji Restoration (Miller 2015: 23). High school baseball teams were introduced to several regions in Japan and its colonies, such as Taiwan and Manchuria. The Japanese colonial authorities used baseball to disseminate "the Japanese spirit that all in Taiwan would be expected to learn and live" (Morris 2011: 2). Entry to Koshien was open to residents of the Japanese colonies, such that one representative team for each colony could enter the tournament on the same basis as the regions of Imperial Japan.

15 This is clarified in the slogan deployed during the Japanese colonial rule: "Industrial Japan, Agricultural Taiwan" (Y. Lee 2012: 33).

References

Amae, Yoshihisa. 2011. "Pro-colonial or Postcolonial? Appropriation of Japanese Colonial Heritage in Present-Day Taiwan." *Journal of Current Chinese Affairs* 40, no. 1: 19–62.

Berry, Chris. 2017. "Imagine There's No China: Wei Te-sheng and Taiwan's 'Japan Complex.'" In *Taiwan Cinema: International Reception and Social Change*, edited by Kuei-fen Chiu, Ming-yeh T. Rawnsley, and Gary D. Rawnsley, 111–20. New York: Routledge.

Berry, Chris, and Feii Lu. 2005. *Island on the Edge: Taiwan New Cinema and After*. Hong Kong: Hong Kong University Press.

Chang, Ivy I-chu. 2010. "Colonial Reminiscence, Japanophilia Trend, and Taiwanese Grass-roots Imagination in *Cape No. 7*." *Concentric* 36, no. 1: 79–117.

Chen, Kuan-Hsing. 2000. "The Imperialist Eye: The Cultural Imaginary of a Subempire and a Nation-State." Translated by Yiman Wang. *positions: east asia cultures critique* 8, no. 1: 9–76.

Cheong, Ching. 2001. *Will Taiwan Break Away: The Rise of Taiwanese Nationalism*. Singapore: World Scientific.

Ching, Leo T. S. 2001. *Becoming "Japanese": Colonial Taiwan and the Politics of Identity Formation*. Berkeley: University of California Press.

Chiu, Kuei-fen. 2007. "The Vision of Taiwan New Documentary." In *Cinema Taiwan: Politics, Popularity, and the State of the Arts*, edited by Darrell William Davis and Ru-shou Robert Chen, 17–32. New York: Routledge.

Chiu, Kuei-fen, Ming-yeh T. Rawnsley, and Gary D. Rawnsley. 2017a. "From Taiwan New Cinema to Post-New Cinema: An Introduction." In Chiu, Rawnsley, and Rawnsley 2017b: 1–7.

Chiu, Kuei-fen, Ming-yeh T. Rawnsley, and Gary D. Rawnsley, eds. 2017b. *Taiwan Cinema: International Reception and Social Change*. New York: Routledge.

Chou, Wan-yao. 1997. *A New Illustrated History of Taiwan*. Translated by Carole Plackitt and Tim Casey. Taipei: SMC.

Dissanayake, Wimal. 1994. *Colonialism and Nationalism in Asian Cinema*. Bloomington: Indiana University Press.

Fu, Yu-wen. 2014. "Space and Cultural Memory: Te-sheng Wei's *Cape No. 7* (2008)." In *Postcolonial Film: History, Empire, Resistance*, edited by Rebecca Weaver-Hightower and Peter Hulme, 223–46. New York: Routledge.

Fujitani, T., Geoffrey M. White, and Lisa Yoneyama, eds. 2001. *Perilous Memories: The Asia-Pacific War(s)*. Durham, NC: Duke University Press.

Hickey, Dennis V. 1997. "U.S. Policy and Taiwan's Bid to Rejoin the United Nations." *Asian Survey* 37, no. 11: 1031–43.

Lee, Chin-ching. 2013. "Taiwanese Mountain Area as Place/Landscape Presented in *Seediq Bale*." *NCUE Journal of Humanities*, no. 7: 205–20.

Lee, Daw-Ming. 2018. "The Journey of Taiwan Cinema: From Taiwan New Cinema to Post-New Cinema." *Taiwan Insight*, October 31. https://taiwaninsight.org/2018/10/31/the-journey-of-taiwan-cinema-from-taiwan-new-cinema-to-post-new-cinema/.

Lee, Wei-Chin. 1993. "Taiwan's Foreign Aid Policy." *Asian Affairs* 20, no. 1: 43–62.

Lee, Yi-tze. 2012. "Divided Dreams on Limited Land: Cultural Experiences of Agricultural Bio-energy Project and Organic Farming Transition in Taiwan." PhD diss., University of Pittsburgh.

Liao, Ping-hui. 2017. "*Kano* and Taiwanese Baseball: Plying with Transregionality and Postcoloniality." In Chiu, Rawnsley, and Rawnsley 2017b: 122–33.

Lim, Jie-hyun. 2010. "Victimhood Nationalism in Contested Memories: National Mourning and Global Accountability." In *Memory in a Global Age: Discourses, Practices and Trajectories*, edited by Aleida Assmann and Sebastian Conrad, 138–62. Hampshire, UK: Palgrave Macmillan.

Lim, Song-hwee. 2013. "Taiwan New Cinema: Small Nation with Soft Power." In *The Oxford Handbook of Chinese Cinema*, edited by Carlos Rojas, 152–69. Oxford: Oxford University Press.

Lin, Chiafung. 2016. "Images of 'Japan' in Postcolonial Taiwan: Contested Terrain of Memory and National Identity." PhD diss., University of Tsukuba.

Lin, Pei-yin, and Su Yun Kim, eds. 2019. *East Asian Transwar Popular Culture: Literature and Film from Taiwan and Korea*. Singapore: Palgrave Macmillan.

Lin, Ting-Ying. 2018. "Ten Years after *Cape No. 7*: The Development of Cinema in Taiwan." *Taiwan Insight*, June 4. https://taiwaninsight.org/2018/06/04/10-years-after-cape-no-7-the -development-of-cinema-in-taiwan/.

Ma, Rang. 2017. "Contesting the National, Labelling the Renaissance: Exhibiting Taiwan Cinema at Film Festivals in Japan since the 1980s." In Chiu, Rawnsley, and Rawnsley 2017b: 53–68.

Mamie, Misawa. 2014. "'Colony, Empire, and De-colonization' in Taiwanese Film History." *International Journal of Korean History* 19, no. 2: 35–57.

Miller, Aaron L. 2015. "Foucauldian Theory and the Making of the Japanese Sporting Body." *Contemporary Japan* 27, no. 1: 13–31.

Morris, Andrew D. 2011. *Colonial Project, National Game: A History of Baseball in Taiwan*. Berkeley: University of California Press.

NCYU News. 2014. "NCYU President Unveils Kano Coach Kondo Memorial in Japan." October 15. https://www.ncyu.edu.tw/ncyu_eng/Subject/Detail/2319?nodeId=836.

Rawnsley, Ming-yeh T. 2014. "Film History and Public Memory in Taiwan." *Asia Dialogue*, November 20. https://theasiadialogue.com/2014/11/20/film-history-and-public-memory-in -taiwan/.

Rawnsley, Ming-yeh T. 2017. "A Conversation with Taiwanese Filmmaker Wei Te-sheng." In Chiu, Rawnsley, and Rawnsley 2017b: 53–68.

Screendaily. 2011. "Wei Te-sheng, Director of *Warrior of the Rainbow: Seediq Bale*." September 1. https://www.screendaily.com/one-on-one/wei-te-sheng-director-of-warrior-of-the-rainbow-seediq-bale/5031427.article.

Sing, Song-yong. 2010. "Qing lishi de xinling ganying: Lun Taiwan hou-xin dianying de liuti yingxiang" 輕歷史的心靈感應: 論台灣 "後-新電影" 的流體影像 ("The Telepathy in Downgrading History: On the Fluid Imaging of Taiwan's 'Post-New Cinema'"). *Film Appreciation Academic Journal* 28, no. 2: 137–56.

Smith, Terence. 1978. "Link to Taiwan Ends." *New York Times*, December 16. https://www.nytimes.com/1978/12/16/archives/link-to-taiwan-ends-carter-in-tv-speech-says-we-recognize-reality.html.

Strong, Matthew. 2017. "Movie Director Plots Taiwan Trilogy." *Taiwan News*, March 4. https://www.taiwannews.com.tw/en/news/3108481.

Tang, Shih-che, and Mitsuhiro Fujimaki. 2018. "The Unredeemed Nations: The Taiwanese Film *KANO* and Its Trans-Border Reception." *Inter-Asia Cultural Studies* 19, no. 1: 21–39.

Ueno, Chizuko. 2006. "The Place of 'Comfort Women' in the Japanese Historical Revisionism: Rise of Neo-nationalism in the Post–Cold War Era." *Sense Public*, February 28. https://www.sens-public.org/IMG/pdf/SensPublic_Chizuko_Ueno_ComfortWomen.pdf.

Veracini, Lorenzo. 2012. Review of *Warriors of the Rainbow: Seediq Bale*. *Transnational Cinemas* 3, no. 2: 243–44.

Wang, Fu-chang. 2003. *Dang dai Taiwan she hui de zu qun xiang xiang* 當代台灣社會的族群想像 (*Ethnic Imagination in Contemporary Taiwan*). Translated into Korean by Eunju Ji. Seoul: Nanam.

Yang, Che-ming. 2012. "The Postcolonial Paradox in the (Self-)Orientalization of Taiwanese History in Wei Te-Sheng's Action Saga." *Theory and Practice in Language Studies* 2, no. 6: 1114–19.

Animating the Trauma: Colonial Atrocities and the Use of New Media in Contemporary South Korean Museums

Chung-kang Kim

Introduction

In 1982, the publication in Japan of a history textbook that minimized the violence during Japan's colonial occupation of East Asia provoked great controversy in neighboring countries, including South Korea and China (Coble 2007).[1] Widely commenting on Japan's irresponsible attitude toward its colonial crimes (*Kyŏnghyang sinmun* 1982),[2] the Korean government set out a plan to rectify this "distorted history" by promoting a patriotic nationalist narrative. As part of this project, the government built Tongnip kinyŏmgwan 독립기념관 (the Independence Hall of Korea) as a space to archive, display, and commemorate the history of the Korean independence movement during the Japanese colonial occupation (1910–45). Immediately after deciding to build the Independence Hall, the government initiated a nationwide funding drive to support the endeavor; soon construction began

positions 31:4   DOI 10.1215/10679847-10714298

on the outskirts of Ch'ŏnan, hometown of famous female independence movement leader Yu Kwan-sun. Despite a setback in 1986, when a huge fire burned down a significant part of the main exhibit hall just before its completion (*Tong'a ilbo* 1986), the Independence Hall of Korea was finally ready to open in 1987. Seven immense exhibit halls, an outdoor amphitheater surrounded by a 360-degree screen and a commemoration space were constructed on an approximately 56,000-square-meter building site.

In the first month after its opening, four hundred thousand people visited the Independence Hall, including public donors, descendants of the independence movement's leaders, and students,[3] and in its first year almost a million people visited (*Kyŏnghyang sinmun* 1988). Displays within the hall conveyed the brutal nature of colonial violence through horrendous images of tortured and murdered Koreans as well as depictions of a nation proud of overcoming such trauma. The three most popular exhibits were a diorama display of *ŭibyŏng* 의병 (the righteous army); another that showed independence movement leaders being tortured by the Japanese police; and a scene involving life-size wax figures of the interim government of Korea. Although traditions of dioramas and constructed historical scenes had originated in the nineteenth-century Western culture of the spectacle (Ceram 1965), in the late twentieth century museums began to combine these old-style display technologies with electronic and digital input to increase the "sense of realism and three-dimensional" effect (Yi 2000). Exhibitions across the Independence Hall were highly distinctive, as new media technologies were used to a far greater extent than in any other historical museums in South Korea during the 1980s, and the use of computer-generated images featuring 3D and 4D elements has also been added in later renovations of the hall. This use of advanced technology was a strategic choice to attract more visitors and to enable the Independence Hall to function to authenticate the reality of colonial violence as an ever-present experience of the visitors. The historical museum, in this sense, here became "the [site] of experience" (Glassberg 2001).

This use of new visual technology to enhance a visitor's "experience" in the museum is not just limited to the case of the Independence Hall in South Korea. As Alison Landberg (2004: 33) has succinctly pointed out, these new approaches constitute global memory-making technologies and can be found in "experiential museums" like the United States Holocaust Memorial Museum and Detroit's Museum of African American History. It is indeed not uncommon to find the use of high-tech visual imagery in twenty-first-century museums. Landberg's discussion of "memory-making technologies," however, entails a far greater set of philosophical and political implications than is usually associated with the use of such visual aids, and she proposes that they can be used to facilitate the production of what she terms as "prosthetic memory." For Landsberg, prosthetic memory is a form of "mediated-memory" created through new visual techniques in museum and popular film that function to make the viewers have an emotional response to past events even though they might have no specific cultural or ethnic connection to such history. Traditionally the regime of memory was formed relative to a specific ethnic group as a means to consolidate their solidarity through a form of shared "organic memory"—for instance, through cultural traditions such as the Jewish Passover seder (26–28). Here, Landsberg draws upon Pierre Nora's (1989: 7) notion of "sites of memory" as a pivotal way to construct collective or national identity in modern times. But what Landberg argues is that "prosthetic memory" offers a form of transferable historical memory, one potentially attachable to any spectator, regardless of their own cultural identity, through the mnemonic means of capitalist mass cultural production. The significance of this mediated-memory lies in the fact that it can operate beyond the indexical or cognitive register of the historical "fact" and function to render "history into personal memories" that can powerfully influence an individual's subjectivity. Following Landberg's notion, in mediated-memory formation, it is not so important whether or not what is displayed is ontologically or factually authentic. Rather, the "reality effect" formulated through new media is of primary importance in producing the affective ramification in the viewer's mind. A similar conception has also been offered by Robert Burgoyne (2003: 223) in relation to the electronic artificial memory-making technologies used in popular film for instance, as exemplified in *JFK* (dir. Oliver Stone, 1991) by combining the real documentary footage and staged performance, in which the "immersive and affective nature" and believability of the film become more important than the historical "fact" of its narrative. In this regard, the mass-produced commodification of history within the media provides an ever-increasing range of opportunities for viewers to become engaged in the process of historical meaning-making.

While Landberg considers that mediated-memory has a more or less positive potential to support progressive political development, there are contrasting viewpoints about the commodified use of mediated-memory, especially in relation to the boom in historical museums in the twenty-first century. In tracing the changing discourses on the temporality of historical modernity in the West, which has shifted from emphasis on the "present future" enlightenment discourse to an engagement with society's "present pasts," Andreas Huyssen (2000: 25) points out that the museological land-scape of the twenty-first century has largely continued to be driven by the "marketing of memory" at a state, regional, and private level.[4] As Huyssen indicates, despite the plethora of apologetic speeches about the violence of the past made by political leaders in various mass mediatic contexts since the 1980s, the dominant historical discourse is still "national, not postnational or global" (26). While Landberg highlights the notion that "prosthetic memory" signifies the viewers' subject position, Huyssen (again in refer-ence to the Holocaust) problematizes that the vast majority of the global remembering of historical trauma actually erases a certain specific context of the violence and necessarily entails the forgetting of local and national level memory. For Huyssen, most of the memories produced within this global trend are "imagined memories." Nonetheless, he rejects an Adornian skepticism about mass cultural production and the possibility of any aban-donment of it. Instead he asserts that the boom of "marketing of memory" is unavoidable, and, in fact, it is the role of "local and national memory" to "contest" the proliferation of "cyber-capitalism and globalism" (37–38). In other words, despite the global proliferation of mediated-memory and its flattening methods of representation, it is to be expected that more and more national and local memories will emerge to produce contesting his-torical narratives. In seeking to balance the contrasting viewpoints of Huys-sen and Landberg, this article suggests that it might be useful to consider how a global populist form of mediated-memory might serve to "preserve" a nation's traumatic history through contemporary technological registers, and how the different forms of memory-making compete with each other across the national and global domains.

In this regard, here we examine the representation of colonial atrocities through the use of immersive new media technology in contemporary South Korean memorial museums. By critically examining two representative memorial museums, the Independence Hall of Korea and Sŏdaemun hyŏngmuso yŏksagwan 서대문형무소역사관 (the West Gate Prison Museum),[5] this article seeks to find an alternative cultural practice devoid of the downside of the "marketing of memory." The use of new, interactive technologies has made it easier to popularize national museums that provide stirring "edutainment." While this approach might aid in the deconstruction of the hegemonic forms of traditional museum exhibition (Song 2014) and could be seen as a positive step in dismantling the aura of authoritative curation, as Walter Benjamin (1969) argued at the turn of the twentieth century, the immersive nature of new media may also, by intensifying the realistic illusions of colonial atrocities, accelerate the antagonism between the "enemy" and the "us." The sensational display of violence through new technologies such as virtual reality (VR),[6] alongside more dramatic "theme park" elements in the museums, could engender a simplified, unitary sense of historical trauma. This use of immersive new media in museum display should also be taken more seriously if we consider that it might reduce the possibility of multiple/performative personal meanings.

Initially, the creation of these museums in South Korea could be considered in the context of a global boom in "dark tourism." The idea of dark tourism is to visit "solemn and highly sanctified places" to have individual experiences of "empathy, contemplation, and transformation" (Weaver et al. 2018). Although intended as a critical reflection on the circumstance and history of modernity (Stone 2006), it has been pointed out that this new type of museum tourism now often purposefully combines the solemnity of historical events with elements of entertainment. It is difficult to say that entertaining elements in a museum are less serious and less educational. But it might be problematic if technology itself becomes an "object of display" extraneous to the whole narrative of the museum (Isaac 2012).

The use of immersive media in museum display also entails the question of the ethics of representation. When media visualize the "pain of others," to use Susan Sontag's (2003) term, it always confronts the issue of sensationalism. In the case of the Holocaust, the ethics of visualizing trauma had long been debated among scholars and film directors. The dispute between Claude Lanzmann and Jean-Luc Godard over filmic representation of the Holocaust shows clearly two different positions: Lanzmann's *Shoah* (1985) chose to use interviews with survivors of the Holocaust, without showing any actual scenes of the Holocaust. In contrast, Godard believed that film has maximum power when it shows scenes of terror, as Alan Resnais's *Night and Fog* (1956) did for the Holocaust, while not evoking sensationalism (Saxton 2008). In a similar vein, Georges Didi-Huberman (2003) argues that even the four photographs from Auschwitz-Birkenau, what he calls "images in spite of all,"[7] function most critically as witness to the actual moment of terror.

The representation of historical atrocity within museums provokes similar questions. Among memorial museums, some choose not to directly show any scenes of atrocity, while others present brutal, graphic images as their representational strategy (Crane 2012). For example, the Independence Hall was born of a conscious postcolonial desire for a counternarrative to Japanese denial of war crimes and violence in historical textbooks; in this context, the diorama displays in the Independence Hall were an effective way to reveal the brutalities of Japan's imperial history. Nevertheless, they can also obscure the complexity of the colonial experience by portraying it as a linear story of collective national struggle toward independence. Further, as the Independence Hall has developed it has used new media technologies to create sensory and affective experiences that reenact or reactivate the colonial past in the present as a means of creating empathy within viewers. By making past events seem like palpable present experiences, what I would call "animated trauma," the museum has sought to provide moral education and provoke "personal culpability, victimhood, and responsibility" (Williams 2012)—the shared goal of many other memorial museums across the world—by carefully orchestrating anti-Japanese sentiments.

In this situation, one can wonder what psychological influence this new museological technology might have on its audiences. If the traumatic scene functions to construct collective "others" by highlighting the "pains" of the collective "us," does this cure the colonial trauma? What can one learn from watching the realistic illusion of colonial-period atrocities, created via high-tech display? What would be, then, a "proper" form of remembrance that the museum can attain within its high-tech displays, and what forms of historical consciousness could a museum seek to impart in its audiences? This last question would perhaps be the most urgent to ask, given the need for a "more nuanced understanding of common suffering and moral ambiguity" (Williams 2012) in the age of dark tourism and museum technology. In this respect, this article will first explore how this new trend of dark tourism using high-tech displays took in shape from the late 1980s, and how it has developed in contemporary South Korea, to see the way in which such immersive media technology has been aiding to create a rather more monolithic idea of nationalism and collective emotional response in South Korean museums and how this master narrative is contested through individual agency.

"Imagined" Atrocities in the Independence Hall and the West Gate Prison Museum

The film *Lost Memories 2009* 로스트메모리즈 2009 (dir. Yi Si-myŏng, 2001), produced in Korea at the turn of the twenty-first century, unfolds as an intriguing story about the imagined consequences of Japanese colonialism. The narrative centers on the assassination of the first Japanese governor general, Itō Hirobumi, who was killed by a Korean man, An Chung-gǔn, at Harbin Station in 1909. In the film's opening sequence, An Chung-gǔn's assassination attempt fails, and, as a result, the Korean nation becomes part of Japan. All Korean people speak Japanese; the Korean landscape is Japanized, and few Koreans question their ethnic identity. But ultimately, a (fictitious) descendant of An Chung-gǔn living in 2009 realizes this history is distorted and time-travels back to the year 1909 to fix the story. As soon as the protagonist helps the assassination succeed, the false history is overturned: Korea becomes an independent nation. The film's final sequence shows the Independence Hall of Korea in the year 2009, with children visiting on a school field trip. A schoolteacher shows some children photographs of the independence movement leaders, and one girl takes a close look at the photographs. She smiles at the heroes in the photographs, and the film ends with emotional music.

The film is based on a popular novel, Pok Kǒ-il's *Pimyǒng ǔl ch'ajasǒ* 비명

을 찾아서 (*Looking for Epigraphy*), written in 1987. Reflecting on the historical conditions of the late 1980s and the establishment of the Independence Hall of Korea, *Lost Memories 2009* reflects and further stimulates Korean nationalist feelings. In presenting the past, present, and the future through a back-and-forth narrative, the story suggests that the psychological trauma that Koreans feel as victims of Japanese colonialism did not end in 1945 but continues today with even greater intensity despite Korea's seventy-five years as an independent nation. As Lisa Yoneyama (1999) points out, this is partly because Japan has never taken full responsibility for its colonial aggression at the Tokyo Trial, an entirely different outcome from the Nuremberg Trials, which compelled Germany to come to terms with the legacy of Nazism. Since the 1982 textbook controversy and even up until today, the discourse of "coming to terms with the colonial past" in Asia feels instead more like a zero-sum game. The Japanese government from time to time denies certain historical facts, such as the Nanking Massacre or the widespread sanctioning of forced Korean sex workers ("comfort women"), and the Korean and Chinese governments react with strong nationalist outrage. In these exchanges, historical trauma solidifies into collective national discourse and socially (dys)functions to fuel conservative nationalism in each nation. The intermittent Japanese denial of colonialism and criminal activity makes Koreans ever more sensitively aware of the past and keeps the feeling of collective victimhood, which Jie-Hyun Lim (2012) calls "victimhood nationalism," ever present.

Under these conditions, the Independence Hall of Korea, as *Lost Memories 2009* demonstrates, becomes a holy place where the spirit of the independence movement is kept. The Independence Hall as a cultural institution under the Kukka pohunch'ŏ (Ministry of Patriots and Veterans Affairs) (Pak K. 2012)[8] therefore serves as more than a general modern museum that contains the "perpetual and indefinite accumulation of time in an immobile place" (Foucault 1984). It is the Kyŏre ŭi chip 겨레의 집 (House of the Nation), a place where celebratory national pride should be permanently represented.

When it opened in 1987 (fig. 1), the Independence Hall presented a more or less imagined world, celebrating the independence movement in a theme park style, a production staged for "dark tourists" to viscerally increase their

Figure 1 Opening Day of the Independence Hall, 1987. Courtesy of the Independence Hall of Korea.

awareness of the brutality of Japanese colonialism. Seven exhibition halls were built based on different themes in order to show a linear history of Korea overcoming foreign aggression: (1) Minjok chŏnt'ong'gwan 민족전통 관 (Hall of National Tradition); (2) Kŭndae minjok undong'gwan 근대민 족운동관 (Hall of Modern National Movement); (3) Ilche ch'imnyakgwan 일제침략관 (Hall of Japanese Aggression); (4) Tongnip chŏnjaeng'gwan 독 립전쟁관 (Hall of Independence War); (5) Imsi chŏngbugwan 임시정부관

(Hall of Interim Government): (6) Taehanminguk'gwan 대한민국관 (Hall of the Republic of Korea); and (7) Kyŏre ŭi chip 겨레의 집 (House of Nation). Outside the building, the grounds featured a huge pond, a commemoration space, cenotaphs of patriotic poems and words, the Statue of an Indomitable Korean, and Tower of the Nation. Thanks to the nationwide call for donations, 43,412 historical items were collected and exhibited at the time of opening (Tongnip kinyŏmgwan 2007: 58–59). Technologically advanced media, including "graphics, diorama displays, replicas, three-dimensional maps, slides, multi-vision, and films," were used to enhance the museum's "symbolic and commemorative presentation of the patriotic martyrs" (60).

Among all the exhibition areas, the Hall of Japanese Aggression, as the name suggests, sought to represent most vividly the atrocities of colonialism. However, this task was made difficult as there were (and are) not many actual photos or other artifacts of Japanese violence. Even bureaucratic records and secondary historical documents were limited, and thus the overall exhibition risked being monotonous and one-dimensional. To overcome this challenge, the Hall of Japanese Aggression was designed around more imaginative diorama displays than any of the other exhibition halls. It featured three primary display areas: (1) a diorama of the killing of Queen Min; (2) three dioramas of the torture of Korean independence fighters; and (3) a replica of *pyŏkkwan* 벽관 (the wall coffin), a particularly infamous interrogation tool used for the torture of independence fighters. Not surprisingly, the dioramas portraying the horrendous killing of the Korean Queen and other prominent independence movement leaders attracted the special attention of visitors. The museum added historical authority to these diorama displays by saying the scenes were based on "the testimonies of the survivors and two historical books, *Han'guk t'ongsa* 한국통사 (*The History of Korea*) and *Han'guk tongnip undongjihyŏlsa* 한국독립운동지혈사 (*The Bloody History of the Independence Movement*)." The third primary display, the wall coffin replica, explained that within this kind of tiny, coffin-like box standing up on the wall, "people were interrogated for many days and often became paralyzed" (Tongnip kinyŏmgwan 1987: 40).

The three dioramas of torture scenes (fig. 2, fig. 3, and fig. 4) were all intended to elicit a visceral response from audiences. In a particularly graphic scene from the first diorama, a naked Korean woman is tortured by two

Figure 2 Diorama display of torture scene ("twist"). Courtesy of the Independence Hall of Korea.

Japanese interrogators. The woman's bloody body sits on a chair, and her rapt facial expression sharply contrasts with those of the stern, emotionless Japanese interrogators. The second diorama captures a moment when a bloodied Korean man hangs by his arms, with two interrogators holding big sticks. The third diorama display shows a scene of *mul komun* 물고문 (water torture). Within it, a bloodied Korean man has his mouth forcibly held open while water from a kettle is poured in. All three diorama displays were labeled

Figure 3 Diorama display of torture scene ("air war"). Courtesy of the Independence Hall of Korea.

with factual explanations to further add to the terrifying atmosphere for the viewers. The aim of this display was clear: to authentically portray the torture of Korean people by their Japanese oppressors. Certainly, these life-like, three-dimensional dioramas helped convey to audiences a sense of the horrific tortures used during the colonial period; they surely also stoked emotional animosity against contemporary Japan for continuing to deny its culpability.

Figure 4 Diorama display of torture scene ("naval battle"). Courtesy of the Independence Hall of Korea.

In these displays, the wider historical context of each torture event was largely erased from the scene, and only the impression of violence remains. More problematic is that the static diorama displays not only valorize the victim but also explicitly objectify the enemy. In this sense, displays were scenes not of "reality" but of "actuality." Reality might be produced through truthful and/or photographic representation of an object, while actuality might be a "inauthentic" image that is staged as actual event. The difference can be compared to digital effects in film. On the film screen, the use of digital images is often said to threaten the realism of a film when they are recognized as unreal. However, the actuality of a digital image strategically creates verisimilitude in an attempt to resemble or impersonate reality, even if viewers are aware of its inauthenticity (Bode 2018). This "inauthentic image" produced through the three dioramas serves to politically freeze in the present a single historical moment using an emotive posthumous imagination, thus making it more intense or immersive than a real object.[9]

This method of representing colonial violence became the model for the numerous new national historical museums that would follow in the wake of the Independence Hall. During the late 1980s many new Korean museums were built in universities (*Tong'a ilbo* 1988),[10] at a national level, and across local regions (Sŏ and Yi 2009).[11] And, while the influence of the Independence Hall was profound across many different kinds of museums, it was arguably most overt in the creation of the West Gate Prison Museum. When the West Gate Prison Museum opened in 1998, even its name reflected the direction of the exhibition inside, which sought to highlight the colonial-period history of the prison rather than its use during the postliberation years of military dictatorship. A news report on the opening of the West Gate Prison Museum stated that it "restored the [colonial-period] basement, torture room, and execution ground" (*Kyŏnghyang sinmun* 1998). Although some were skeptical about preserving the prison as only a colonial structure (*Tong'a ilbo* 1987),[12] the public's desire to keep this museum as a memorial site of colonial atrocity was strong. The preservation of the historical site in this and other cases serves to intensify the factual realness of the visitor's experience, although within the museum manifold elements are carefully manipulated to create an accessible historical "illusion" of the space (Gorgas 2012).

Hence, the West Gate Prison Museum preserved the original prison building structure and restored the interior space following a thorough archaeological study of the colonial prison. Its panoptic structure fully embodies the architectural mechanism of the modern prison: the buildings of the prison have a fan shape that makes surveillance easy (Foucault 1995).[13] Inside the prison, a contemporary simulacrum of the surveillance structure contained within the edifice is revealed: visitors have a bird's-eye view of the fan-shape building from the guide map (fig. 5).[14] If the modern prison was used to dis-

Figure 5 Map of the West Gate Prison Museum.

cipline an individual's body, now, by visiting this prison museum, visitors can learn how this disciplinary mechanism was used by Japan to make the Korean state a docile subject. Meanwhile, the dioramas of graphic violence, scenes of torture and execution, create an illusion of time travel that allows visitors to experience directly the force of colonial barbarism. In this sense, entering the museum itself is a 4D experience, like walking into a theme park.

The substantial influence of the Hall of Japanese Aggression in the Independence Hall on the design of the West Gate Prison Museum is clear. When the plan for the latter museum was set out, one of the curators of the Independence Hall, Kim Wui-yŏng, advised that "what is most important . . . in restoration is to represent the most ferocious aspect of colonial oppression as explicitly as possible" (*Tong'a ilbo* 1987). Kim further advised the curators at the West Gate Museum to attempt to locate notorious places, such as the Yu Kwan-sun room (where Yu's body was allegedly torn apart and buried) and a particularly infamous torture chamber known to have existed during the colonial period. To counter concerns about the lack of extant historical materials that would help restore the prison accurately (a majority of the buildings had been restructured after the liberation), Kim argued that "orally transmitted stories" about the colonial-era prison could be the primary reference in restoration.

Kim's orientation toward restoration was greatly amplified in making the West Gate Prison Museum, and the diorama displays in the Independence Hall became the primary models for the exhibitions there. In particular, the basement torture room exhibition contains a diorama almost identical to one in the Independence Hall. In the narrative perpetuated by both museums, all Korean people during the colonial era could be classified either as independence fighters or as abused victims. Beyond the troubling reliance on sensationalism as a means to convey historical information, this orientation is even more problematic because in recreating atrocities, the curators of both the Independence Hall and the West Gate Prison Museum were compelled to depict the actuality of colonial trauma due to a lack of real historical materials and information on which to draw. This problem has only been exacerbated as museum displays have been transformed by new media museum technologies in recent years.

Animating the Trauma: Technological Transformation in the Representation of Colonial Atrocity in the Twenty-First Century

A major renovation of the Independence Hall began in the early 2000s. In preparation for the celebration of sixty years of liberation in 2005, a plan to transform the Independence Hall into a kind of theme park was established, inspired by the frequent calls for the hall to incorporate both emotionally moving and interactive displays. As other nation's museums, discarding "static" displays to make the museum more interactive was considered important to increasing its accessibility (Witcomb 2012). In particular, the implementation of new technological developments using intensified multidimensional displays was seen to be a key element.

To check and improve the overall defects of the Independence Hall and reform it as a more coherent theme park, in 2003 Korean American Nina An of the global theme park company Entertainment Design Corp was invited to help. An and her team from Lotte World, the then most recently built theme park in Korea, joined several college professors on an advisory committee. In An's opinion, the Hall was in need of redesign to accommodate a greater flow of human traffic to each of the thematically related spaces (Tongnip kinyŏmgwan 2007: 551–60). The seven exhibition halls were thematically reorganized, and each hall was colored corresponding to its theme and divided into several internally connected zones (600–1). Many new exhibitions were added to promote interaction with the visitors, such as pre-exhibition movies, three-dimensional images, graphic panels, and more diorama displays and miniatures with special effects (Kwŏn 2007). And digitized historical data about the independence movement leaders collected since 1999, including moving images such as videos of oral testimony, were accumulated to link a newly constructed cyber museum to the physical museum (Tongnip kinyŏmgwan 2007: 337–45).

It is important to remember the major roles that the theme park team played in this renovation. As Hilde Hein notes, "The constructed reality of theme parks imposes itself on and overtakes conventional understanding of reality." Theme parks provide "an atmosphere that totally encompasses visitors and lifts them out of ordinary time and space into a virtual 'free zone'" (Hein 2000: 81). This theme park effect resembles the virtual reality created through 4D technology, which fills the audience's visual field with images via a head-mounted display so that the audience is fully relocated into a virtual space. The effect of the "real thing" could be the "perceptual realism" that the visitors can feel, as Stephen Prince (1996) persuasively argued that such "perceptual realism" goes beyond an ontological or factual realism when the spectator is confronted by computer-generated effects in the digital age. Although theme parks are not electronically constructed, the virtual effect can be similar (Manovich 1998). The use of new technology in the West Gate Prison Museum and the Independence Hall, and their transformation into theme park–like experiences, were designed primarily to provide visitors a virtual experience of the colonial era. Significantly, visitors can now "walk into" colonial time and space and confront "real experience" rather than observing a "real thing" in a museum (Hein 2000).

One example of this new, virtual experience is the redesigned entrance to the Hall of Nation's Suffering. Visitors walk through a dark tunnel showing major historical atrocities during the colonial era. It is as if they are passing through a time loop and then arrive to face the torture scenes. Previous diorama displays were reoriented so that visitors can now peep into a torture room from the outside. When visitors pass by each torture room, sounds of screaming and moaning are audible. At the same time, a male narrator's very neutral explanation of the scene is projected from above. Thus, visitors are able to experience the torture scene at the same time they are made aware of the more factual background to the display. This grants visitors the unique experience of being simultaneously in the middle of an emotive and a museological space.

Perhaps the most notable change was to the diorama display of the independence movement leaders. Here a diorama is juxtaposed with a panoramic 2D animation portraying the torture scene. Information about the independence movement leaders is on display in e-books that can be viewed with accompanying aural explanations. Visitors can also now touch the replicas of the leaders of the righteous army or the enlightenment movement leaders to hear their individual stories. In the imagined battlefield where an actual-size liberation army unit was placed, visitors feel a blowing wind and hear the sounds of guns and explosions along with the voices of the soldiers in the middle of battle (fig. 6). In these displays, visitors are absorbed into a virtual reality show, exactly similar to those within a commercial theme park.

The trend toward interactive media is also seen at the West Gate Prison Museum, which deployed an expanded sensory experience as part of its renovations in 2010 (Sŏdeamun hyŏngmuso yŏksagwan, n.d.: 7). In this renovation, the overall exhibitions were divided into three categories: (1) Space for Commemoration: (2) Space for History; and (3) Space for Experience. The "Space for Commemoration" is located on the first floor, where the walls and ceiling are covered with specially produced tiles with prisoner identification cards printed on them. As an area for communion with the deceased, it creates a solemn atmosphere through the immersive display of more than five thousand such individual records. The Space for History uses digitally archived materials. As visitors touch the names of the people who were

Figure 6 4D displays of the Liberation Army's Battle.

jailed in the prison, they are shown digitized prisoner cards and information on each person. Further, interactive display is used to a great extent in the basement area. To help evoke a more gruesome emotional mood, and to supplement the diorama displays of torture, more photographic materials were added during the renovation of 2010. For example, to exemplify the traces of torture, the exhibit in the basement displays the photos of Kang Hwan-sik taken between May 1934 and December 1934 that illustrate the physical difference torture had on Kang's body, and another display shows patriot martyr Yi Kyu-ch'ang's broken finger. These photographic displays not only manifest the spectacular actuality of the horrible torture carried out by the Japanese but also serve to perpetuate its continuity in the present.

But the most theme park–inspired area is the Space for Experience, which uses interactive technology to encourage empathic responses from visitors. Visitors first enter a quiz zone that tests their historical knowledge before they move to a room that is connected to a 3D virtual figure of Yu Kwan-sun, featuring videos of oral testimonies from the surviving leaders of the independence movement. They later enter the *kongjaksil* 공작실 (operation room), where the use of interactive technology is most striking. Here, visitors can actually experience various kinds of torture, such as *sangja komun* 상자고문 (box torture), stabbing nail torture, and electric torture. The visitors put their heads inside a virtual reality cylinder while sitting on a torture rack. Then, 3D video feeds them vivid images to encourage the feeling that their bodies are being tortured. In addition, visitors can also experience being on trial. If visitors touch the sensor button, they are automatically sentenced to death. The scaffold is located right next to the trial space, and visitors can sit on the death chair, which suddenly jerks down to create the moment of hanging. This experience of animated trauma is obviously designed to be shocking. Creating such a virtually real situation in museum could provide the viewers a more "synthesizing experience" (Hein 2000). One elementary student wrote, "I was sitting on the chair, and suddenly the chair moved down. I moved just a little bit. But I could feel how afraid the people must have been who were actually bound and hanged" (Ryu 2005).

After their "real experience" in this virtual prison, many elementary school students responded with antagonism against present-day Japan. They wrote comments like, "We Koreans should develop our nation far better than Japan," or "I wish I could explode the West Gate Prison Museum, and forget about the colonial time." Other students even compared the West Gate Prison to Auschwitz and said, "It feels like this prison is worse than Auschwitz, even though . . . Auschwitz is in fact worse" (Ryu 2005). On the empty whiteboard where visitors can record their responses, most students left swear words against Japan (Pak and Ch'oe 2006). This strong antagonistic reaction might be expected given the emotive interactive method deployed by the curators at the museum.

It is conventional for many war memorials or memorial museums to rely on clear binary narratives that construct a national "us" and by extension a foreign, oppositional "them." In this respect, the Independence Hall and the West Gate Prison Museum are exactly the kind of memorial museums one would expect to be encouraged by the South Korean state's approach to its national history during the Japanese colonial period. T'ae Chi-ho (2013) pinpoints the problem this raises: the binary representation in the Independence Hall shows only national ideology and collective nationhood, not individual experiences of the colonial era.

Conclusion: New Directions in the Curative Memorial Museum

Recently, the Seoul city government announced a new remodeling and extension of the West Gate Prison Museum along with a plan for a new Interim Government Memorial in a neighboring area (*Kyŏnghyang sinmun* 2018). As part of this renovation, there is a suggestion that the museum could "restore" the currently inaccessible actual execution room using 360-degree 3D-VR images (Chŏn and Kim 2018). It seems clear that the goal of restoring the execution room in 3D-VR format would be to increase the emotive force of represented colonial trauma. At the same time, the museum is under pressure to keep adopting newer technologies lest it appear dated.

Of course, even if this obvious dichotomy is fixed within the museum display, the emotional responses of different types of tourists within any memorial museum can vary. A study by Lolitasari Ade Triana and Yun Hŭi-jŏng (2017) shows the diverse emotional responses of Korean visitors to the West Gate Prison Museum. Generally, people felt gratitude (4.47), empathy (4.33), pride (4.16), interest (3.90) and sadness (4.14), rage (4.11), shock

(3.93), and anger (3.86) the most. But the younger generations, those in their twenties, felt more pleasure and relief than older generations,[15] which suggests that young people tend to simply enjoy the entertainment elements of the exhibition rather than learn about the historical atrocities. The danger here is that "technological interactivity" in a museum could result in reducing attention to the cultural and historical explanation (Witcomb 2012), and the technology itself becomes only an "object of display" (Isaac 2012).

What this means is that the current trend of museum displays using immersive media technology (such as 4D virtual reality) could be seen as reductively functioning to both totalize the historical context and amuse the visitor, outcomes that reduce the potential for progressive politics that Landberg proposes to increase through the use of an electronic historical imagination and "prosthetic memory." Here it might be important to recall Paul Williams's comment about the social and political role of the historical museum, in the understanding that in everyday life people seldom confront the life-and-death situations referenced within the museological space. For Williams (2012: 115) the aim for a museum that displays such historical atrocities should then be to allow people "to experiment mentally with the furthest boundaries of what life can involve." In this respect, even in the context of the belligerent national relationship between Japan and Korea, a Japanese student's tour of a colonial-period memorial museum in Korea could potentially provide a positive experience of dark tourism beyond the boundaries of their normative understanding. A Japanese student named Murayama Itpei, for instance, who visited the Comfort Women Memorial Museum in 2003, eventually became a research fellow of the institution and served there for several years (*Yŏnhap nyusŭ* 2006). In this case it was not the binary narrative of colonial victimhood and oppression that moved the viewer to action but an individual encounter, her feeling the pain of an individual comfort woman as articulated within the museum. It can be said that dark tourism in this case enabled one individual to think about the self in a reflective manner, arguably even allowing her to politically reevaluate her professional life.

To that end, another approach to making the hidden history of atrocity visible may offer an alternative way. Williams demonstrates this aptly in the case of the International Peace Museum, which offers a multidirectional and transnational approach. In that museum, various material fragments and records of historical tragedies, atrocities, and destructive events—pieces of the Berlin Wall, a nuclear bomb rocket, a roof of a house from the Nagasaki atomic attack, and the soil from Auschwitz—are incorporated (Williams 2000). This transnational, fragmented exhibition is intended to make international visitors think about such horrific history in broader, interlinked terms. Although, as Huyssen comments, this approach risks reducing the ability of an exhibition to convey the specific context of historical atrocities, its laudable aim is to provoke viewers to think comparatively and reflexively about the diverse contentious history on display. Under the broad and idealistic but also undeniably positive notions of "peace" and "humanity," these types of experimental representations can be implemented to orient memorial museums toward encouraging contemplation and a broader way of reaction.

Interestingly, the most recent changes to the Independence Hall include the renaming of hall 4 (formerly the Hall of Independence War) to P'yŏnghwanuri 평화누리 (Peaceful World). This hall does not contain any specific visual material except some words of the independence movement's leaders projected in a dimly lit, almost empty space. The purpose of this space is presumably to make viewers ponder the wider meaning of "independence." On the wall, the "Declaration of Independence" of the March First movement, 1919, is exhibited. Highlighted is the third point of the declaration, which reads: "Our nation just requests our freedom for justice, guidance, survival and honor. We do not follow the exclusiveness of imperialism." This "Peace World" exhibition is an exceptional space in the Independence Hall, inasmuch as it attempts to expand the idea of the Korean independence movement to a struggle for wider humanity or human rights rather than just a national struggle between Japan and Korea.

On a different wall is also stated, "In its pursuit of liberty and peace, the Korean independence movement struck a sympathetic chord in the hearts of people around the world, inspiring them to help Koreans fight *against imperialism* and eventually secure their liberation. Korea's liberation from Japan was a hard-earned victory of the independence movement" (emphasis added). In the "Peace World" hall, the curator tried to avoid showing direct antagonism against Japan by replacing the normally standard "Japan" with the less specific "imperialism." But even this statement conforms to the narrative that the independence movement actually resulted in a final successful liberation, an approach that indicates the limits of the hall as a space for contemplation given its need to follow the official national celebratory notion of the independence movement. Within this triumphal narrative, there is no space to explore the life of normal, average Koreans in relation to colonialism, and the meaning of the grandiose statement "justice, guidance, survival and honor" is never addressed in substantive detail.

Relatedly, a special exhibition on the Nazi German death camp in collaboration with the Polish Auschwitz-Birkenau State Museum in the Independence Hall in 2014 offers an example of a wasted opportunity to expand the Independence Hall's narrow nationalist purview. Though there was potential to introduce comparisons between the Holocaust and the colonial treatment of Korea as state sponsored atrocities, unfortunately the limited approach undertaken by the curators merely suggested that the primary purpose of the collaboration was simply to equate our own historical trauma with the most infamously unspeakable terror of the Holocaust.

* * *

On a final, more positive note, perhaps it is worth highlighting the power of the public to directly transform the space of the memorial museum into a more politically active site. In 2017, in the West Gate Prison Museum, a civil demonstration was held calling for the abolition of the death penalty in South Korea (*Yŏhap nyusŭ* 2017). The myopic focus of the museum on the colonial-period history of the prison notwithstanding, the public was able to expand the symbolic meaning of the "national" "prison" museum space critically, appropriating it as a site of protest to point out that Korea is one of the few "developed" democratic countries that still maintains the death penalty. This action usefully highlights that, while it is the museum professionals who choose what to represent and how, making a political meaning out of the museum remains also in the hands of visitors.

Certainly, recent developments in museum technology can potentially increase public engagement. But when they erase the historical and cultural context or exacerbate a one-sided historical, national, or cultural position in an ongoing political dispute, they might not create as useful an interaction as intended. The memorial museum remains a significant cultural space where the politics of memory and history are created through interaction with the viewers. The year 2019 was the one-hundredth anniversary of the March First movement, and as the strained relationship between Korea and Japan continues, this would doubtless be a useful moment to rethink what it really means to be independent, have liberty, and perhaps overcome the simplistic framing of our shared histories (and futures) in order to move beyond a false binary of victim and victimizer.

Notes

1 The Chinese government also responded by starting to establish a strong resistant national historiography at this moment.

2 Among many newspapers that criticized the Japanese textbook, for instance, *Kyŏnghyang sinmun* devoted two full pages to analysis of the "distorted part" of the Japanese history textbook.

3 I myself was one of the students taken to visit the Independence Hall in 1987.

4 As Andreas Huyssen succinctly points out, the boom of the memory cultural industry over the past few decades entails the "marketing of memory," as various museums, linked to a political practice of remembrance, have developed an increasingly commercialized component. He takes many examples of 1930s–1940s Holocaust atrocities and its memorialization in the 1980s and early 1990s.

5 The West Gate Prison was the first modern prison in Korea, designed by a Japanese architect and built in 1908 just outside the west gate of Seoul as Kyŏngsŏng kyodoso 경성교도소 (Seoul Prison). Covering approximately 1,700 meters, the prison could accommodate around five hundred prisoners. After Korea was annexed by Japan in 1910, the name was changed to the West Gate Prison in 1912. Following the liberation of Korea from Japan in 1945, the space was used to imprison criminals and political prisoners until 1987. It was transformed into a museum in 1997.

6 When I talk about VR, my discussion is not limited to the virtual reality created through headset device. Rather, virtual reality here is about the "effect": how verisimilitude is constructed through various combinations of old and new media technology.

7 Didi-Huberman analyzes the four photographs taken by Sonderkommando, arguing against the scholars who characterize Auschwitz as an "unspeakable" and "unrepresentable" trauma.

8 In 1987, the Independence Hall was under the Ministry of Culture and Tourism (Munhwa kwankwangbu 문화관광부) but transferred to the Ministry of Patriots and Veterans Affairs (Kukka pohunch'ŏ 국가보훈처) in 2005.

9 Regarding the discussion of "reality effect" of the inauthentic displays such as replica and diorama, see Hein 2000.

10 *Tonga ilbo* reported the museum construction of Seoul National University, Yonsei University, Korea University, and Ehwa Women's University.

11 The significant museums that were built in the 1980s were the National Art Museum of Korea (Kungnip hyŏndae misulkwan) and the National Chŏnju Museum (Kungnip chŏnju pangmulgwan), and the National Central Museum of Korea (Kungnip chung'ang pangmulgwan) was remodeled in 1986.

12 From the beginning there were questions about the museum's perspective. One anonymous scholar said that "it is an absurd idea that only part of the history of the prison is taken out for preservation, since it was used not only during the colonial time but also during the time after the liberation" in *Tong'a ilbo* (1987). He argued for the need to preserve the prison's entire history, even parts that do not reflect well on the democratization of Korea. Unless otherwise stated, all translations are my own.

13 In *Discipline and Punish*, Foucault argues that the modern prison was designed primarily for the purpose of surveillance and bodily discipline, and not to publicly expose punishment as was so often the case up until the eighteenth century.

14 Among fifteen buildings within the prison, buildings 9 to 13, a camp for lepers, and the execution area were left for restoration.

15 The scale is from zero to five. Five indicates the strongest degree of feeling.

References

Benjamin, Walter. 1969. "The Work of Art in the Age of Reproduction." In *Illuminations*, 217–42. Berlin: Schocken Books.

Bode, Lisa. 2018. "'It's a Fake!' Early and Late Incredulous Viewers, Trick Effects, and CGI." *Film History* 30, no. 4: 1–21.

Burgoyne, Robert. 2003. "Memory, History and Digital Imagery in Contemporary Film." In *Memory and Popular Film,* edited by Paul Grainge, 220–34. Manchester: Manchester University Press.

Carbonell, Bettina Messias, ed. 2012. *Museum Studies: An Anthology of Contexts.* Maiden, MA: Wiley-Blackwell.

Ceram, C. W. 1965. *Archeology of the Cinema.* New York: Harcourt, Brace, and World.

Chŏn, Chun-hyŏn 전준현, and Kim Ki-dŏk 김기덕. 2018. "Kasang hyŏnsil ŭl hwalyong-han munhwa wŏnhyŏng kontench'ŭ kaebal" 가상현실을 활용한 문화 원형 콘텐츠 개발 ("The Development of Original Culture Content Using VR"). *Han'guk sajin chirihakhwoeji* 한국사진지리학회지 (*Korean Journal of Photo-Geography*) 28, no. 3: 31–42.

Coble, Parks M. 2007. "China's 'New Remembering' of the Anti-Japanese War of Resistance, 1937–1945." *China Quarterly*, no. 190: 394–410.

Crane, Susan. 2012. "Memory, Distortion, and History in the Museum." In Carbonell 2012: 303–16.

Didi-Huberman, Georges. 2003. *Images in Spite of All: Four Photographs from Auschwitz.* Oakland: University of California Press.

Foucault, Michel. 1986. "Of Other Spaces." *Diacritics* 16, no. 1: 22–27.

Foucault, Michel. 1995. *Discipline and Punish: The Birth of the Prison.* New York: Vintage Books.

Glassberg, David. 2001. *Sense of History: The Place of the Past in American Life.* Amherst: University of Massachusetts Press.

Gorgas, Mónica Risnicoff de. 2012. "Reality as Illusion, the Historic Houses That Become Museum." In Carbonell 2012: 324–28.

Hein, Hilde S. 2000. *The Museum in Transition: A Philosophical Perspective.* Washington, DC: Smithsonian Institution.

Huyssen, Andreas. 2000. "Present Pasts: Media, Politics, Amnesia." *Public Culture* 12, no. 1: 21–38.

Isaac, Gwyneira. 2012. "Technology Becomes the Object: The Use of Electronic Media at the National Museum of the American Indian." In Carbonell 2012: 533–46.

Kwŏn, Sun-kwan 권순관. 2007. "Tongnipkinyŏmgwan che6kwan ŭi yŏndaepyŏl chŏnsi kong'gan pyŏnhwa e kwanhan yŏn'gu" 독립기념관 제6관의 연대별 전시공간 변화에 관한 연구 ("Studies about the Transformation of the Exhibition Hall 6 in the Independence Hall"). *Digit'ŏl dijain yŏn'gu* 디지털디자인연구 (*Digital Design Studies*) 7, no. 4: 187–96.

Kyŏnghyang sinmun 경향신문. 1982. "Il kyokwasŏ hanil kwangye yŏksa waegok naeyong" 일교과서 한일관계 역사 왜곡내용 ("The Distorted Contents of Japanese Textbook about the Relationship between Korea and Japan"). August 2.

Kyŏnghyang sinmun 경향신문. 1988. "Kaewan il nyŏn tongnipkinyŏmgwan kukmin yŏksa kyoyukchang paldodum" 개관 일 년 독립기념관 국민 역사 교육장 발돋움 ("The Independence Hall Becomes the Space for National Historical Education in One Year"). August 3.

Kyŏnghyang sinmun 경향신문. 1998. "Sŏdaemun hyŏngmuso yŏksagwan onŭl kaegwan" 서대문 형무소 역사관 오늘 개관 ("The West Gate Prison Museum Opens Today"). November 5.

Kyŏnghyang sinmun 경향신문. 2018. "Imsi chŏngbu kinyŏmgwan naenyŏn e ch'ŏt sap" 임시정부 기념관 내년에 첫 삽 ("The Construction of the Interim Government Begins Next Year"). December 20.

Landberg, Alison. 2004. *Prosthetic Memory: The Transformation of American Remembrance in the Age of Mass Culture*. New York: Columbia University Press.

Lim, Jie-Hyun. 2010. "Victimhood Nationalism in Contested Memories: National Mourning and Global Accountability." In *Memory in a Global Age: Discourses, Practices, and Trajectories*, edited by Aleida Assmann and Sebastian Conrad, 138–62. London: Palgrave Macmillan.

Manovich, Lev. 1998. "Towards an Archeology of a Computer Screen." In *Cinema Futures: Cain, Abel, or Cable? The Screen Arts in the Digital Age*, edited by Thomas Elsaesser, 27–44. Amsterdam: Amsterdam University Press.

Nora, Pierre. 1989. "Between Memory and History: *Les Lieux de Mémoire*." Translated by Marc Roudebush. *Representations*, no. 26: 7–25.

Pak, Hyo-chŏng 박효정, and Ch'oe Sŭng-hun 최승훈. 2006. "P'yŏnghwa wa inkwŏn ŭi nun ŭro ponŭn sŏdaemun hyŏngmuso" 평화와 인권의 눈으로 보는 서대문형무소 ("The West Gate Prison Museum in the Perspective of Peace and Human Right"). *Chungdŭng uri kyoyuk* 중등우리교육 (*Our Middle School Education*), no. 198: 116–25.

Pak, Kyŏl-sun 박결순. 2012. "Tongnip kinyŏmgwan chŏnsi ŭi kyoch'e, powan ch'ui wa hyanghu kwaje" 독립기념관 전시의 교체, 보관 추이와 향후 과제 ("The Transformations of the Independence Hall and Its Future"). *Han'guk tongnip undong yŏn'gu* 한국독립운동연구 (*Study on Korean Independence Movement*), no. 42: 447–87.

Prince, Stephen. 1996. "True Lies: Perceptual Realism, Digital Images, and Film Theory." *Film Quarterly* 49, no. 3: 27–37.

Ryu, Hyŏn-chong. 2005. "Yŏksachŏk changso haksŭp kwa kwagŏ kiŏk ŭi munje" 역사적 장소 학습과 과거 기억의 문제 ("Learning from the Historical Site and the Problem of Memory"). *Yŏksakyoyuk yŏn'gu* 역사교육연구 (*Study of Historical Education*), no. 2: 177–219.

Saxton, Libby. 2008. *Haunted Images: Film, Ethics, Testimony, and Holocaust*. New York: Columbia University Press.

Sŏ, Sang-u 서상우, and Yi Sŏng-hun 이성훈. 2009. *Han'guk myujiŏm kŏnch'uk* 100nyŏn 한국뮤지엄 건축 100년 (*One Hundred Years of Museum Architecture in Korea*). Seoul: Kimundang 기문당.

Sŏdaemun hyŏngmuso yŏksagwan 서대문형무소역사관. n.d. *Sŏdaemun hyŏngmuso yŏksagwan* 서대문형무소역사관 (*The Western Gate Prison Museum*). Seoul: Sŏdaemun hyŏngmuso.

Song, Hanna. 2014. "Kwanramgaek ŭi ŭimi hyŏngsŏng ŭl wuihan sot'ongjŏk yŏkhal losŏ ŭi chaehyŏn kwa kwallam kyŏnghŏm e taehan yŏn'gu" 관람객의 의미 형성을 위한 소통적 역할로서의 재현과 관람 경험에 대한 연구 ("Studies on the Interactive Representation, Its Experience, and the Visitors' Meaning Making"). PhD diss., Dongdŏk Women's University.

Sontag, Susan. 2003. *Regarding the Pain of Others*. New York: Picador.

Stone, Philip. 2006. "A Dark Tourism Spectrum: Towards a Typology of Death and Macabre Related Tourist Sites, Attractions, and Exhibitions." *Tourism* 54, no. 2: 145–59.

T'ae, Chi-ho. 2013. "Tongnip kinyŏmgwan e nat'anan 'tongnip' ŭi kiŏk kwa kŭ chaehyŏn pangsik e kwanhan yŏn'gu" 독립기념관에 나타난 '독립'의 기억과 그 재현방식에 관한 연구 ("The Memory of 'Independence' and Its Representation in the Independence Hall"). *Midiŏ, Chendŏ, Munhwa* 미디어, 젠더, 문화 (*Media, Gender, and Culture*), no. 25: 145–77.

Tong'a ilbo 동아일보. 1986. "Han bŏn t'ŏjija kamchwŏjin piri p'ŏngp'ŏng" 한번 터지자 감춰진 비리 펑펑 ("Once Revealed, Hidden Corruptions Burst Out"). August 8.

Tong'a ilbo 동아일보. 1987. "Sŏnyŏl ŭi p'i' ŏllukjin yet sŏdaemun hyŏngmuso kŭg'il kinyŏmgwan' ŭro wŏnhyŏng pojŏnhaja" 선열의 피 얼룩진 옛 서대문형무소 극일기념관으로 원형 보전하자 ("The Old West Gate Prison Museum, Stained with Our Ancestor's Blood, Will Be Preserved as 'Overcoming Japan' Memorial"). April 21.

Tong'a ilbo 동아일보. 1988. "Taehakka hyŏndaesik pakmulgwan sidae" 대학가 현대식 박물관 시대 ("The Era of the Modern Museum in the Universities"). February 15.

Tongnip kinyŏmgwan 독립기념관. 1987. *Tongnip kinyŏmgwan chŏnsip'um yorok* 독립기념관 전시품 요록 (*The List of Exhibition of the Independence Hall*). Ch'ŏn'an: Tongnip kinyŏmgwan.

Tongnip kinyŏmgwan 독립기념관. 2007. *Tongnip kinyŏmgwan 20nyŏnsa (1987–2007)* 독립기념관 20년사 (1987–2007) (*History of Twenty Years of the Independence Hall, 1987–2007*). Ch'ŏn'an: Tongnip kinyŏmgwan.

Triana, Lolitasari Ade, and Yun Hŭi-jŏng. 2017. "Dakŭ tuŏrizŭm kwangwangja ŭi kamjŏng panŭng p'osishŏn'ning" 다크투어리즘 관광자의 감정 반응 포지셔닝 ("Positioning Dark Tourism Visitors' Emotional Responses"). *Kwangwang yŏn'gu* 관광연구 (*Study of Tourism*) 31, no. 5: 89–105.

Weaver, David, Chuanzhong Tang, Fangfang Shi, Ming-Feng Huang, Kevin Burns, and Ang Sheng. 2018. "Dark Tourism, Emotions, and Postexperience Visitor Effects in a Sensitive Geopolitical Context: A Chinese Case Study." *Journal of Travel Research* 57, no. 6: 824–38.

Williams, Paul. 2012. "The Memorial Museum Identity Complex: Victimhood, Culpability, and Responsibility." In Carbonell 2012: 97–115.

Witcomb, Andrea. 2012. "Interactivity in Museums: The Politics of Narrative Style." In Carbonell 2012: 580–89.

Yi, Yŏng-jin. 2000. *Pakmulgwan chŏnsi ŭi ihae* 박물관 전시의 이해 (*Understanding Museum Exhibition*). Seoul: Hangmunsa 학문사.

Yoneyama, Lisa. 1999. *Hiroshima Traces: Time, Space, and the Dialectics of Memory*. Oakland: University of California Press.

Yŏnhap nyusŭ 연합뉴스. 2006. "Ilbonin palgil iŏjin wuianbu yŏksagwan" 일본인 발길이어진 위안부 역사관 ("Japanese People Continue to Visit 'Comfort Women' History Museum"). August 13.

Yŏnhap nyusŭ 연합뉴스. 2017. "Sŏdaemun hyŏngmuso yŏksagwan e sahyŏng p'yeji chomyŏng p'ŏp'omŏnsŭ" 서대문형무소 역사관에 사형 폐지 조명 퍼포먼스 ("Light Performance of 'Abolish Death Penalty' at the West Gate Prison Museum"). November 30.

Archiving Facts and Documentary Films: Sites of Memorial Struggle for the October 6, 1976, Massacre in Thailand

Sudarat Musikawong and Malinee Khumsupa

October 6, 1976, That Which Is Kept Silent

At dawn on Wednesday, October 6, 1976, students and demonstrators at Thammasat University were beaten, shot, sexually violated, lynched, and hanged by an angry mob of state and parastate forces. There were 45 people killed (5 were state officials or paramilitary), 180 injured, and 3,037 persons arrested and many sent to nationalist reeducation, while the military took over (P. Ungpakorn 1977; Haberkorn 2008).[1] The incident on October 6, 1976, was better known as both a massacre and a state crime (Winichakul 2015; J. Ungpakorn and Yimprasert 2001). October 6 was particularly cruel in nature because it dehumanized the victim-students as treasonous criminals and foreigners (Winichakul 2020; Kongkirati 2016; Bowie 1997). Large numbers of students tried to escape but were arrested. The Kathing Daeng paramilitary poured kerosene and burned the bodies of four persons,

positions 31:4   DOI 10.1215/10679847-10714311
Copyright 2023 by Duke University Press

one of whom was still alive (P. Ungpakorn 1977: 8). The late 1970s to early 1980s also saw unprecedented political assassinations of farmers, workers, students, and Socialist Party leaders (Morell and Chai-anan 1981; Haberkorn 2011). As criminal investigations would threaten the Buddhist Sangha, military, and monarchy—all major national institutions—investigations were never pursued (Winichakul 2015: 20–21). Evidence was not found, not because it is not there, but because much was hidden or destroyed. However, traces of evidence were found in the archives.

In particular, the most significant public repository that houses evidence about the 1976 October 6 massacre is the Thammasat University Archive. The archival evidence of this brutal massacre was captured by army television cameras as well as by foreign television crews and photojournalists. There are no government archives maintained to document the event (Haberkorn 2013; Bergin 2016; Zackari 2020). Photographs and film footage of the massacre remain scattered between the Associated Press, various newspapers, and university archives (both Thai and foreign) until they were archived at Thammasat University, Cornell University, the University of Wisconsin, the Australia National Archives, and online on YouTube and on websites that assist in netizen archiving efforts. This paper discusses the tactics and constraints that activist archivists operate in while documenting past state violence in Thailand. We argue that these audiovisual archives give resonance and voice to memories that have otherwise been silenced, through alternative reproductive media such as critical documentary filmmaking and online public access archiving.

Events of past state violence have never been recognized by any official government agency and thus are not part of official Thai history books. But this does not mean that archivists neglected their duties in preserving related documents, materials, and film. *They Will Never Forget* (Utsuma 1977) and other film and video collections about the massacre are at the Thai Film Archives, which is a public organization working with the Ministry of Culture's Contemporary Art Division.[2] Its collections do not constitute any official public record. The October 6 massacre remains a past that does not fit in history that marked the attempt to eradicate the Thai political Left (Satha-Anand 2008, 2007: 188; J. Ungpakorn and Yimprasert 2001). Eiji Murashima found that since the 1970s, Thai studies was dominated by an ideological nationalism that was anti-communist (Thai Archive Association 2005: 35–38). Some argue that the massacre itself is that which cannot be remembered yet also cannot be forgotten. It is a case of *prawatisat bad-pae* ประวัติศาสตร์บาดแผล (wounded history), in which the victims, survivors, and perpetrators live with uncomfortable memories in ambivalence (Winichakul 2001, 2015). Two blanket amnesty laws were passed immediately after the October 6 massacre, implemented as state mechanisms to facilitate impunity through the juridical process. This legitimated the military coup and became a regular state technique in providing impunity for the state, military, and parastate actors to use excessive force against any political opposition (Wichinakul 2015: 22–23; Haberkorn 2015: 44–46). It would become impossible to prosecute criminals responsible for abuses, including individual state officials ordering the use of force. Documents at the National Archives, the Attorney General's Office, and diplomatic archives (US, British, etc.) play an important role in locating some of the most controversial traces of the nation's institutions' roles in orchestrating and condoning the massacre (Winichakul 2020: 37–41, 271).

Contemporary Thai political power is thus anchored in past state violence, which serves as a guarantor for continued impunity. Tyrell Haberkorn (2013) found that since the end of absolute monarchy in 1932, the Thai state has failed to be held accountable for state violence despite several instances of the use of excessive force. Those affiliated explicitly and implicitly with the state remain above the law, while ordinary people are unprotected by it (Haberkorn 2013: 110). The struggle for memory lies at the heart of any transitional justice process and memory struggles are as much about the present—and the future—as well as the past (Impunity Watch 2015).

Counter-memories that Engage Fact-Finding

Counter-memories are produced by survivors, victim families, journalists, and academics. These are collected by archivists and activists—and repurposed by filmmakers—as the raw material for truth-telling. The concept of counter-memory instructs us to read "against the grain" in the archive, while the concept of "sites of memory" contributes to the interpretation of the archive as a place of memory that generates new or reproduces previously circulated memories (Foucault 1977; Nora 1989). On the other hand, Jacques Derrida's evocation of "responsible witnessing" calls attention to how to listen to silence "found" in that which cannot be said (Sandomirskaja 2011). These three premises (reading against the grain, generating memory, and listening to what cannot be said) should be applied to analyzing counter-memories in documentary films.

There have been several feature fiction films in recent years, but few lay claims to truth-telling the way that documentary films do (Hunt 2020: 86–97). Additionally, documentary films are exhibited as part of temporary exhibitions organized commemorating the anniversary, sometimes to reveal previously unknown aspects of the massacre.[3] The documentary film is both a faithful representation and interpretation of the lived historical world, with elements of truth-telling responsibilities. This endows the documentary with particularly rich spaces for analyzing ethical and political responsibilities, as well as revealing truths (Fuhs 2014: 783). Efforts to recuperate the memory of the October 6 massacre have also benefited from digital technologies. Appadurai calls this phenomenon the technoscapes of the digital (Baumgartel 2012: 26–27; Appadurai 1996: 33–35). It is Thailand's technoscape that has archived and circulated traces of memories, facts, and lies. With little doubt, the archive can generate both truths and reproduce false memories. All the same, the technology of digital archiving and the films that use that archive both give birth to a hope for the ongoing struggle against forgetting state violence and authoritarianism.

In 2020, historian Thongchai Winichakul published his long-term work on the massacre. The "unforgetting" of the October 6 massacre is generated in the space of "active silence." During periods of continued ambivalence, the forgetting that took place (institutional covert erasure, denials, circulation of false information) unravels. And the unforgetting that occurs, even without definitive articulation or incorporation into a national narrative, begins to act as a countermovement. Such active silences exist inside and outside the archive. In some cases, active silence relies on the film archive audience or reader to be able to decipher what is not said, or even what is denied (Winichakul 2020: 131–42, 165–69). To that extent, archives aid in active silence and memory projects dedicated to unforgetting the massacre, all existing in a liminal space. Archives in themselves are, of course, not neutral in their acquisitions, restrictions, and destruction of items. And the archives become the raw materials often used in postmemory projects of various sorts, to sometimes contradictory effects and intentions.

Memory is not necessarily an individual phenomenon but can be relational in terms of social and collective memory (Halbwachs 1950). Such memories must be shared among members of a social group or community, such as the nation, in order to resonate (Bosch 2016: 4). Official histories create and maintain the unity and continuity of national consciousness by silencing alternative interpretations of historical experiences (Medina 2011: 14). The politics of memory plays out through subjugated knowledge, or, as Foucault asserts, as historical contents that have been buried or masked through functional coherence or formal systematizations. Unconventional genealogy seeks the singularity of events outside monotonous facts, in the most unpromising places, those that are "without history" (Foucault 1977: 7). The October 6 massacre is such an unpromising place, shrouded in forgetting, concealed, and never officially mentioned (Kaeosuk 1996: 88). Archival power allows local and dissident voices to be heard. The archive therefore has great potential to harness the silence and give voice to it. The archivist may create a "reading of silence" itself (Carten 2006: 220).

Traces of Evidence

Political nuances aside, there have been five major instances of state violence in Bangkok, in which the police and/or military have clashed with prodemocracy demonstrators: (1) the October 14, 1973, uprising (leading to the temporary exile of military leaders); (2) the October 6, 1976, massacre (leading to return of conservative authoritarianism in multiple forms); (3) Black May 1992 (leading to the ousting of a military government); (4) the April–May 2010 massacre against Redshirt demonstrators (eventually leading to the return of military authoritarianism); and (5) the 2020 youth demonstrations. Since the mid-1990s, the events of state violence are annually publicly commemorated at Democracy Monument or near Thammasat University and/or the October 14 Memorial (all within a one mile radius); organizers would display photographic exhibitions and street hawkers would sell reproductions of some of the most gruesome photographic evidence of state violence, in a kind of recirculation. Rosalind Morris (1998: 343, 362) asserts that photographs depicting state violence exist in a

> structural affinity [that] lies in the historically particular conceptualization of the image and power in Thailand, and especially of the relationship between absence and presence which undergirds . . . the organization of [the] country's monarchal politics in the contemporary era. [The] photographs operate in a process from which upon encounter, as a force of trauma, create the sensation of distant alienation from the real [event].

While Morris argued that reproductions alienate and perhaps desensitize viewers, we argue that the circulation of images also instigated oppositional agendas. Photographs, objects, film footage, and testimony have become the main forms of evidence housed in the digital and university archives. The massacre violence is, in a sense, reconstituted in the torn and disregarded elements of dissident material history, into established physical sites of memory-memorials, libraries/archives, exhibitions. Breaking years of silence is possible by utilizing the archive to, as Joan M. Schwartz and Terry Cook (2002: 172) suggest, read national history "against the grain" for years to come.

Before proceeding to discuss other specific cases of archiving, we want to consider first the question, What is an archive? Here we borrow directly from Diana Taylor (2003: 19–21): an archive is a collection of "supposedly enduring materials," in which its Greek etymology "arkhe" has multiple meanings: a place where records are kept, a beginning, the first place, and the government. Taylor further suggests that the "archive from the beginning, sustains power."[4] An archive's value is derived from the ability to separate time and space between the knower and the event. The archive has the capacity to shift the relevance of the original event toward particular ends. Sharing such modes of inquiry, we would like to situate archives within truth commission work and truth projects in Thailand. Archives are always curated, mediated, selected, edited, and in some cases censored. Files, documents, photos, and other material items disappear from archives. This is the case in the National Library of Thailand, which houses many partial collections of newspapers and materials from the 1970s. In 2003, during the search for much of this archival material, pages that would have referenced some of the most controversial elements were directly torn out from the National Library's physical newspaper collections. It is unclear when, why, and by whom this was done, but it was clear that the National Library did not have microfilm, nor were the collections able to replace the material, for lack of budget, capacity, or interest.[5] The archivists at both the university and national levels with whom we spoke discussed how they work within institutions that are not politically friendly to archiving controversial subjects and events, let alone state violence. In the case of one university, administrations can and do oversee the institutionalization of archives, using bureaucratic techniques to scrutinize the activities and archiving techniques. Administrative protection of state wrongdoing can ultimately undermine the collections. The archivist can become a kind of activist in their mission to acquire, catalog, preserve, and provide access to materials that are controversial (interview with archivist requested confidentiality).

Archivists who are intent in archiving state violence or Left-leaning politics have a common term by which they describe such acquisitions: *aab keb* แอบเก็บ (secret collecting). This was a term used by several of the archivists with whom we spoke to informally, despite their working at several different institutions. Out of concern that such events would be lost or disregarded by the passage of time, Thammasat University archivists found ways to acquire objects, photos, and audio recordings as well as digital sound and video footage. As political Left networks are rather small, it is known internally which archives may be responsive to housing such materials. For example, there are those who, knowingly or by recommendation, donate their personal collections when nearing retirement or death. At the Film Archives, the films acquired from individuals and government departments may contain materials about various events: royal ceremonies; the October 14, 1973, uprising; and the October 6, 1976, massacre, alike.[6] Such acquisitions are in line with their organization directive to be the nation's archive preserving film and audiovisual materials as intellectual property and heritage of the nation.[7]

Even when acquired, some items deemed too sensitive or controversial may not be cataloged, or if cataloged, their access is restricted and not curated. These represent concerted efforts to preserve but also keep hidden select archives, so that after fifty years they will be available in the public domain.[8] In this way journalists, historians, and students of national history may know of the truths that lie beneath the surface of the illustrious grand narratives that constitute the idea of the coherent, unified peaceful nation. Disruption of this narrative provides hope for real social and political change.

Listening to the Silence and the Creation of a Fact-Finding Committee

In late September 1976, Chumphorn Thummai and Vichai Ketsripongsa, two labor activists from Nakhon Pathom Province Electricity, were putting up flyers protesting the return of General Thanom Kittikajorn from exile. After his political exile, General Thanom Kittikachorn sought to return as a novice monk, essentially using Buddhism for political immunity to guarantee his return. These two activists were found hanged. While the authorities were suspected, the case was not investigated. In early October 1976, students demonstrating against the general's return reenacted this hanging. While the English daily *Bangkok Post* correctly reported the students' theater as a protest, the right-wing press *Dao Siam* claimed the students were communists enacting a hanging of the crowned prince. Both used photographs of the protest theater. This was the key case that instigated use of lèse-majesté laws against those practicing civil disobedience. And accusing the students of threatening the crowned prince led to the legitimization for the state to use violence against the demonstrators.

The civil society process of reckoning with the events began with journalists in 1996 commemorating the twentieth anniversary (Santiwutthimethi 1996). This is different from reporting on the actual events in 1976 because it was an attempt to understand that past, some twenty years later. Memories of state violence and calls for justice can be, but are not always, bound to acts of truth-telling that are reliant on photographs and testimonies. The October 6 massacre audio-video footage is an important medium of the truth-telling. While military newsreel crews were embedded, Thai and foreign journalists risked their lives "on the front line" to record the brutality that morning. Later, this footage was used for a DVD documentary film produced by the Committee for the Twentieth Anniversary of the October 6 Massacre in 1996 (J. Ungpakorn and Yimprasert 2001: 46).

Coming upon the twenty-fifth anniversary in 2001, the interest among journalists increased. In 2000 Giles Ji Ungpakorn was a political science faculty member at Chulalongkorn University who made two public accusations that became controversial.[9] The first was that he accused both *Dao Siam* and *Bangkok Post* newspapers of doctoring photographs to make the student protest theater's mock hanging resemble the then–crown prince. However, only *Dao Siam*'s reporting was inaccurate, and any evidence of doctoring of photos was not substantiated. Giles Ungpakorn's second accusation was that the then-governor of Bangkok, Samak Soonthoraveit, was involved in the October 6 massacre by instigating violence on Yan Koh, the army radio station. Subsequently, Soonthoraveit brought a libel suit against Ungpakorn. As the October 6 massacre remained unresolved, these two accusations were commonly held beliefs among the political Left. This led Ungpakorn's colleagues, academics, and journalists to begin an informal process of putting together a Truth and Fact-Finding Committee about the October 6 massacre. The committee's interview data transcripts and tapes are currently housed at the Thammasat University Archives. To commemorate the twenty-fifth anniversary of the massacre, the Truth and Fact-Finding Committee published its findings in a book entitled *State Crime in a Crisis of Change, Twenty-Five Years, October 6, 2001* and invited that generation's former student activists, media, and politicians and the victims' surviving family members to the report's launch. The findings firmly established that the October 6 massacre was an event of intentional state violence (J. Ungpakorn and Yimprasert 2001). Other, subsequent research drew similar conclusions (Streckfuss 2011: 325–27; Kongkirati 2015: 73–74).

After the release of the report, the committee did not make an effort to further lobby for any official state intervention. In this case, producing evidence of state violence in itself was a political act to:

(1) clearly establish and confirm that crimes were intentionally committed by state authorities and victims were denied justice;

(2) shift society's perception through public commemorations establishing the national significance of the events; and

(3) harness the future possibility for revisionist national history projects and generative cultural productions like narrative and documentary films, television programs, and so on.

As part of the Truth and Fact-Finding Committee, thousands of hours of interviews based on testimonies by witnesses, survivors, and perpetrators were recorded. There were also photographs, documents, and recordings, including sound footage of the militant right-wing Yan Koh radio programs. The raw audio data was donated to the Thammasat University Archives, where it was cataloged, digitized, and transcribed. However, the audio recordings remained unavailable for use due to release rights. As a matter of public domain law, under the Copyright Act 1994, materials have a fifty-year period from the moment the item was produced or from the year that the person who ceded the materials has died. In this regard materials produced fifty years ago, like those produced during the 1970s, may soon be released. There is some ambiguity as to whether oral testimony recorded in 2000 would fall under public domain once the person has died. According to the Thammsat University archivist:

> Pictures communicate more than documents and sound of voices, even more so. You can better feel intention and emotions through people's voices. . . . We had a release process for the documents and audio archives for the *Sarakadee Magazine* interviews that were submitted to us. We have different levels for the right to release—archives audio release, transcripts, edited transcripts, or not at all. After fifty years, unreleased archival materials can be made public after the death of said person . . . i.e., General Sutsai Hatsaidin [who was a known leader of the Red Gaurs (Krathing Daeng) paramilitary group] did not allow for an audio release but allowed for an edited transcript. Now his family has the rights until the fifty-year period from which the recording was produced [in 1996].[10]

The editors from *Sarakadee Magazine* donated their recordings of both survivors and perpetrators of the 1976 massacre to the Thammasat University Archives. In addition, the archives also acquired the Truth and Fact-Finding Committee interviews about the October 6 massacre. These audio collections captured the sound of voices of persons who were either witnesses, victim/survivors, or perpetrators of the massacre. The voice carries resonance, an emotion that cannot be captured in transcripts. While materials available legally in the public domain may offer some possibilities, much also depends on the country's regime, political climate, and the degree of continued use of libel cases and/or blanket amnesty laws absolving wrongdoing. If not for the archives, such testimonies would have been unavailable to researchers, journalists, and filmmakers in Thailand or to anyone who has an interest in the matter.

While the libel suit against Ungpakorn was later dropped, there was still a degree of libel case fearmongering used to threaten anyone who sought to publicly name individual state officials and officers who played a role in the October 6, 1976, massacre. While no court case has succeeded to date, cases like Ungpakorn's case with the politician Samak Soonthoraveit normalized impunity, leading to a chilling effect. Many are careful not to name individuals. The ease with which libel cases are brought to Thailand's courts continues to be an impediment to restorative justice projects that seek individual accountability and guarantees individuals guilty of state violence a great degree of impunity.

Archives as the Place of Witnessing: The National versus University Archives

In Thailand, the archive is the bearer of tradition, power, and knowledge. At each transformative juncture of the modern Thai state, archives and materials are arranged and recategorized in accordance with the new regime. The National Library constructs modern knowledge of "Thailand" not only as a Buddhist nation but also a monarchal constitutional country. According to Patrick Jory (2000: 372–73), the National Library was to be the center of the preservation of knowledge after the overthrow of the absolute monarchy in 1932. The Wachirayan State Library was officially renamed the National Library. The National Library's mandate was also the preservation of important publications (i.e., books, magazines, and newspapers). While initially the Archive Department was part of the National Library, in 1952 the National Archives became a single, autonomous unit, outside of the National Library. As such, the National Archives maintain the core values of the Thai state. It is a well-known fact that, on occasion, researchers were denied access to both the National Archives and the National Library by collections recategorized as "out of service." Additionally, denying access to foreigners who have no researcher permit or denying access for reasons of "national security" were other common practices (Harberkorn 2013: 111–12). The National Library requires official authorization for use. Therefore, to effectively gain access, users tend to request broad topics such as "human rights." The archive user must first find where the targeted sources are housed. Sometimes such sources exist in atypical places with no archival organization, no organized topics (Jory 2000; Haberkorn 2013). Hence, for some of the most controversial topics, the National Library and National Archives would be limited repositories for state violence and leftist histories.

Thammasat University has become one of the major strategic venues to exhibit and hold events about Thailand's contentious politics and history. It is much like a living museum, because the university became the stage for student activism and national protests. Prajak Kongkirati notes that the political agendas of university students leading up to the 1970s were shaped during their exposure to lectures in the university. Such radicalization contributed to an alternative history based on a people's history (Kongkirati 2005: 11–13). There were protest posters, books, pamphlets, and large-scale street billboards produced by various student groups or clubs. Student activist publications items evaded censorship because they were categorized as "publications" and were depoliticized by the strategic use of the university administrators' photographs onto the front pages (429–31). The materials (posters, journals, student publications) are now housed at the university archives. Currently, the government does not enforce censorship with the university archives per regulation, but self-censorship in archival practices may occur through acquisition decisions. Oversight by university administrators may deem what materials are worthy of archival importance, disposal, or omission.

The Thammasat University Archives, when officiated in 1991, were to be a repository of the university's long history tied to the nation's history. But they also became the first public site of a definitive collection of leftist materials, including the collections of the October 6 massacre. Thongchai Winichakul helped to initiate Thammasat University to pursue an institutional archive in the early 1990s, at first as a home for leftist dissident materials. The historian Suthachai Yimprasert donated large portions of his personal Communist Party of Thailand (CPT) archives. They jokingly called this activity *keb* เก็บ (storing away or preserving) the Communist

Party into a museum. The archive was institutionalized by others, including the historian Chanvit Kasetsiri, when he was rector of the university (Winichakul 2011–12: 8–25). In the meantime, after the twentieth commemoration of October 6, the archive also significantly extended the collections in evidence-based materials such as photographs, media recordings, and recorded interviews. The archives began with relative autonomy under the office of the president. And due to the politicized space of Thammasat University and the faculty involved, it became one of the only places in the country to archive radical left-wing documents (Kongkirati 2015: 73–74; Winichakul 2011–12).[11]

Online Documentation/Archiving/Circulation

By the time of the thirty-fifth anniversary of the massacre, the commemorative committee itself also played an active role in organizing donations of personal collections to the university archives. When the committee to organize the October 6 commemorations publicly called to collect new photos from anonymous sources, many new stories about ex-students who lost their lives during the massacre or communist conflict emerged. These were uploaded into circulation online on several websites including http://119.59.99.174/~net2519/?page_id=1006 and https://doct6.com/ (Tangwisutijit and Bhumiprabhas 2002).[12]

The 2519.net website was the first step toward establishing an open-source comprehensive online hub particularly for information about the October 6, 1976, massacre, including articles, short digital film clips, photos, chronologies, testimonials, and lists of relevant materials from the Thammasat University Archive and even the National Archives. The administrators for the website were former student activists from that generation and their family, but digital websites organized by private individuals are often not permanent. The activists from this generation's political left are known as the October generation and have become important in Thailand's current politics as established journalists, academics, politicians, and corporate leaders (Lertchoosakul 2012, 2013).

By the 2010s, digital online archives converged with digital independent filmmaking. In 2016 Chulalongkorn University political scientist Puangthong Pawakapan and historian Thongchai Winichakul formed a committee to develop a project titled "Documentation of October 6," an online archive of the October 6 massacre.[13] With key former student activists providing financial support and documentary producer Patporn Phoothong, this online archive continues to produce films, curated collections, and merchandising focused on the October 6 massacre and public events engaged in truth-telling.

Specifically, Pawakapan's academic background is in truth and reconciliation processes as well as in peace studies. And through her work with the People's Information Center, the volunteer fact-finding committee archiving the case of the crackdown against the Redshirts in 2010, Pawakapan was well qualified for the work. The project organizers sought new truths about the 1976 massacre and worked with a team to archive documents and exhibitions, both on Facebook and on other websites. While some of the physical materials were housed at the Thammasat University Archives, the digital images were housed on the "Documentation of October 6" website (Doct6.com). Phoothong, who joined the project to document October 6 was tasked with acquisitions and conducting interviews for documentary productions available on the website. What were once pieces of evidence previously scattered in personal archives were now curated in a user-friendly, well cataloged, and open-sourced online site (Thongsinwatee 2019: 89–92). As a result, after the fortieth anniversary of the massacre in 2016, the online archives were set up in 2017 and relaunched in 2018.[14] By the end of December 2021, the Facebook page had 87,797 followers.[15] Additionally, ongoing documentation of this digital archive used the interviews of massacre survivors in the format of digital videos to chronicle the memories of those who survived the massacre. With strategic convergence of open-access online digital platforms, these oral histories were uploaded onto the website using the YouTube platform. There are six video interviews thus far.[16] Alone, each may be comparatively small in numbers of views but still cumulatively significant, with over 186,000 views (as of March 7, 2022). The project also sponsored short documentary digital films with higher production value (discussed below), which increased the overall cumulative viewership. Doct6.com is not the only independent digital archive about the October 6, 1976, massacre.[17] Another notable site is 2519.net, which was launched in 2002 and, at the time of writing, is accessible at http://119.59.99.174/~net2519/. This website also sought to provide further accurate information and generate discussion about the massacre (Tangwisutijit and Bhumiprabhas 2002).[18] Memories of state violence and calls for justice can be, but are not always, bound to acts of truth-telling that are reliant on photographs and testimonies. The October 6 massacre audio-video footage has become an important medium in truth-telling practices.

Documentary Films: Participatory Documentary to Truth-Telling

While since the launch of the website Doct6.com there have been several documentary films, we would like to highlight Phoothong's first film as producer, *Silenced Memories* (2012), in order to reveal the significance of the voice in capturing and transferring the sound of emotions—from speaker/witness to audience/witness. Along with Phoothong, Saowanee Sangkara directed and edited the documentary film *Kwahm song jum rai siang* (*Silenced Memories*) (Phoothong and Sangkara 2012). The film is subtitled in English, making it accessible to international audiences. The film's eighteen months of research began in the Thammasat University Archives and the National Library. The researchers faced two problems: how to present private memories of parental loss to the public, and how to represent the violence of the October 6 massacre without reproducing the brutality. Sangkara and cinematographer Saowanit Keetasangkha watched hours of footage and edited the film several times, but they decided not to use any of the archival footage that depicted real violence. Instead, they focused on the victim's parents (Phoothong 2012: 5–14, 26).

With pain in her voice, Mother Lek, who was also first featured in the previously discussed *Sarakadee Magazine* in 1996, retells how her son Manu Wittayaporn was shot and died from a single bullet wound. She searched all the hospital and temple morgues to find her son's body in order to provide him with proper burial rites. Delivering the keynote speech addressed at the thirty-ninth commemoration, Mother Lek continued her with participation in the commemorative activities at Thammasat University for over forty years. The documentary gives literal voice to her traumatic memories without interruption. Her voice pauses, cracks, and explodes with deep sadness and anger as she recalls when Manu was alive as an activist before he was killed and how he was found and then posthumously accused of communism. Neighbors refused to acknowledge his humanity. While the voice remains the most powerful element of the documentary's truth-telling technique, visuals remind audiences of Manu's face through old photographs and his student identity card.

Jarupong Thongsin was a second-year student at Thammasat University in 1976. While a photo confirmed that Jarupong was killed, his family was never properly contacted by any morgue. His father still searched for him for ten years, until friends contacted the family. Jarupong's parents, having never found their son's body, lived with hope that he was possibly alive and had gone underground (Winichakul 2016). Jinda Thongsin lived with parental traumatic memory privately for almost twenty years before conveying it to a public audience for the first time at the twentieth-anniversary commemoration in 1996 (interviewed in the widely circulated *Sarakadee Magazine*), and then once more in the 2011 documentary film. The documentary film utilizes the visuals and sounds of the train tracks in Jarupong's hometown laid over Father Jinda's own words—which has a resonance of personal pain punctuated into the timbre of his voice. The audience listens to his recollections through his reading of his own diary about the family's despair. He recounts his confusion, traveling countless times via train from Surat Thani province to the capital in search of, but never finding, Jarupong's body. Ten years after the 1976 massacre, he received a letter informing him that his son's body was dragged by rope by the neck in the football field at Thammasat University. Understandably, it shocked him. As a father, he denied the legitimacy of the photograph, for a long time, not believing that it was true. Years after the documentary, he passed away in 2016.

In *Silenced Memories* (2012), Lek Wittayaporn, the mother of Manu, and Jinda Thongsin, father of Jarupong, are portrayed as the living victims of the October 6 massacre. Learning about their experience of loss by watching the documentary, the potential for "responsible witnessing" for audiences arises as a key subtext. Revisiting the past through loss creates a moment of opportunity for audiences in a future time to critically question the dominant narratives about national unity. Listening to the sorrow of their voices retelling the last time they saw their sons alive, to descriptions of the time spent searching for or identifying their sons at the morgue, deeply moves audiences. Viewers are compelled "to believe" the human aspect of loss (Sandomirskaja 2011: 252). *Silenced Memories* was uploaded to YouTube for recirculation (Phoothong 2016–17). However, even a documentary focused on parental loss could be subject to censorship under Thailand's culture of fear. The online public platform YouTube was the most obvious choice, but uploading it necessitated an unlisted foreign account outside of Thailand to evade any government restrictions.[19]

Returning to the October 6 digital archive, *Silenced Memories* became the foundation for Pawakapan and Phoothong to coproduce a second film featured on the archives' website. *Respectfully Yours* (2016) features interviews with the elderly parents of the students who were killed (Pawakapan 2019: 341). This film presents those killed and their living victim-family members as individuals. A third film related to the October 6 digital archives is *Two Brothers* (2017), directed by award-winning director-cinematographer Teerawat Rujintham. The film interviewed the elder brothers of the two labor activists Chumphorn Thummai and Vichai Ketsripongsa (previously discussed). An interesting commonality is that all three intimate documentaries focus on the experience of the loss that a family suffers. This enables those unconnected to the massacre to relate through empathy. Recall, these were the activists who were murdered and hanged when putting up protest posters against the return of General Thanom in September 1976. Close to four decades later, we may not relate to the politics of the 1970s student movement, but we relate to the mourning of a loved one. Once an outsider can connect to the sentiment of loss, there is the potential to want to know more: What, how, why did this happen? Then, what can I do? For Pooja Rangan (2017), the "participatory documentary," especially the ethics of immediation, is coded in the audio visual. That means that the camera is the third voice that produces an urgent response for the viewer to "act now" based on a sense of ethical obligation. Herein its power is found in the question, What can I do? The documentary is the potential open-ended space to initiate support for a humanitarian response to crisis (Rangan 2017: 9–12).

Part of transformative politics necessitates a change of heart. Chumphorn's and Vichai's lynching in the 1970s inspired the student guerrilla theater to reenact the gruesome event, gathering thousands to the campus to protest against the return of dictatorship. This play was falsely charged as a mock hanging of the crown prince by *Dao Siam*, a right-wing newspaper. This incited the ultranationalist royalist anti-student factions to violence. Being largely absent from Thai schoolbooks, Chumphorn's and Vichai's killings had been erased from official history but revisited in documentary film.

Aside from the films' link within the digital archives, they, along with over forty-eight other videos, are also viewable on YouTube.[20] Even the *Sarakadee Magazine* audio interviews have been rereleased in January 2022 onto this open-source archive curated by Doct6.com. Synergies, convergence, and recirculation on open-access platforms are key to spreading the knowledge about the October 6 massacre. On YouTube (as of March 7, 2022), *Respectfully Yours* had 12,794 views and *Two Brothers* had 52,484 views.[21] While the count may include repeat viewing, we can still approximate that in March 2022 there could have been close to 685,000 views total between all of the October 6 digital archived YouTube videos.

Autonomous archives refer to the act of archiving to publicize marginalized histories, usually for the purpose of developing a counterpublic justice agenda (Moore and Pell 2010: 257). The efforts to archive the October 6 massacre function similarly to this sense of an autonomous archive. And much like the concept of "autonomous archives," film production processes also became techniques that illicit truth-telling. In the process of documentary filmmaking, directors, and producers conduct research and seek factual details through testimonial interviews (Pawakapan 2019: 342–43). The most recent documentary about the massacre used select filmic archives accompanied with new interviews, new photographs. *The Dawn of a New Day* (2021) was launched on the Doct6.com site, again linking to YouTube with 26,245 views (as of March 7, 2022).[22]

Conclusion

Memories of the October 6 massacre, despite being threatened by obliteration, could not be "rescued" by any state-initiated fact-finding committee or official processes for justice due to the blanket amnesty law. However, with the continued production of autonomous archives, innovations in archival exhibition practices, social media sharing, and some YouTube documentary films, there are ways for truth-telling to occur.

And yet all memory is partial. It is made from fragments of truth, longing, and even falsities. The voice can carry an emotional impact in its delivery of the telling—sometimes beyond death, imbued with contradiction—fabrication, fragmentation, and truth, as is the case with Father Jinda's and Mother Lek's interviews. Telling previously disallowed truths as "speech activity" becomes incredibly important when recorded (Rajala 2017: 8). While the reproduction of testimonies remains in safe keeping in the archives of the news agencies, film archives, and universities' collections, the online civil society communities are less patient. They might not always wait for the laws of public domain. The open-source access to digitized archives reconfigures the postmemory landscape. Open-access digital archives push the limits of truth acknowledgment in Thailand, but not yet in the direction of archival utilization for justice agendas for state responsibility or war crime tribunals. Such overt uses are still circumvented by the political use of libel law and the statute of limitations. Perhaps it is just a matter of time before future generations activate the archives toward justice agendas.

As Rangan (2017) suggests, a once-singular massacre depicted in documentaries supposedly affecting few dissident others can become a collective call to humanitarian intervention, in what is called "immediation." In Thailand, the following are already in operation: autonomous archive practices of secretly keeping, moments of opportunity in which new digital online technologies are aligned in convergence, and the call to responsible witnessing for past state crimes. Together when participatory documentation instigates immediation, there can be a new political possibility. Participatory documentation resists and rejects authoritarian state violence. Participatory documentation marks a third voice—neither victim-survivor nor perpetrator, but a perhaps new generation of witnesses years after. In resonance with the victims and survivors of the October 6, 1976, massacre, this new generation demands truth and justice after decades of military rule, in the aftermath of the 2010 Redshirt massacre and the 2020 uprisings. We believe that documenting the October 6, 1976, massacre became a humanitarian ethic, immediation in action. There is hope that these engaged forms of spectatorship, witnessing, recirculation, and digital archiving have become the new dissident politics challenging the recurrence of state violence that is reemerging in Thailand. Let us all be free to document, while responsibly bearing witness.

Notes

This research was made possible with the support of the Scholarship Fund, Chiang Mai University. We would like to especially thank the editors Sandeep Ray and Han Sang Kim, Thongchai Winichakul, Puangthong Pawakapan, Chalida Uabumrungjit, tammy ko Robinson, Patporn Phoothong, and Tara Needham, as well as the blind reviewers who provided commentary. Last, we thank the many archivists who were so generous with their time and committed to making the archive a public service. Special thanks to Film Archives of Thailand. This research project is based on previous data collection from Sudarat Musikawong's dissertation (IRB Approval HS-366, University of California, Santa Cruz, 2002), secondary and archival online research, and observations at public events from 2014 to 2017.

1   There is variation among reports and research because there are no official documents. Three years after the 1973 uprising Field Marshall Thanom Kittikachorn, then exiled prime minister, sought social immunity. He returned to ordain as a novice monk. Four or five thousand congregated to protest his return at Thammasat University. One pivotal event at the university was the reenactment of a murder case in which two electric workers who were labor activists in Nakhom Pathom were hanged while posting anti-Thanom posters. These events were shrouded with doubt, police mishandling, and collusion. *Dao Siam*, a right-wing newspaper, falsely reported that the mock hanging was staged by the students to represent the Crowned Prince with intent to destroy the monarchy. See J. Ungpakorn and Yimprasert 2001; Bowie 1997.

2   *They Will Never Forget* can be viewed at Salaya Thailand หอภาพยนตร์ (Film Archive Thailand), YouTube, https://www.youtube.com/watch?v=X_mqbEpxv_A (accessed July 8, 2023).

3   See also Kaewmala 2020. Here in this tweet one can follow and see the thread discussion on the October 6 massacre augmented reality exhibition produced by younger generations in their twenties through forties. Most chats are in Thai, but Thai_Talk is one in English. Twitter synergizes the coverage of the physical exhibition *Kwan* แขวน (*Lynched*) (2020) at Thammasat University with online social media, expanding its audiences.

4   While repertoire (performance and intentionally curated events referencing past events) enacts embodied memory, repertoire is ephemeral, nonreproducible knowledge that requires the presence of being there as part of its transmission.

5   These observations were made during Sudarat Musikawong's archival research 2014.

6   Pers. comm. (conversation with an archivist who wishes to remain anonymous), Bangkok, October 17, 2016.

7   Film Archive, https://www.fapot.or.th/main/about/vision (accessed March 9, 2022).

8   Office of the Council of State, Phrarachbạnyut Likhsit 2537 พระราชบัญญัติ ลิขสิทธิ์ ๒๕๓๗ (Copyright Act 1994), Section 4, Article 19, 1994, http://web.krisdika.go.th/data/law/law2/%C506/%C506-20-9999-update.pdf (accessed November 20, 2022).

9   Giles Ji Ungpakorn is son of the rector Puey Ungpakorn, who went into exile due to the October 6 massacre, who himself is currently in exile due to lèse-majesté.

10 Pers. comm. (conversation with an archivist who wishes to remain anonymous), Bangkok, October 17, 2016.

11 See Thammasat University Archives (หอจดหมายเหตุมหาวิทยาลัยธรรมศาสตร์), http://archives.library .tu.ac.th/ (accessed March 9, 2022). The website archives the Thammasat University Archive Bulletins since 1996 up to 2022. After 2022, only the physical services are available at the Thammasat University Rangsit Suburb Campus.

12 The Tula-Dharm ตุลาธรรม (Justice) website was originally accessible at https://www.2519 .net from 2002–2019 and is now accessible at http://119.59.99.174/~net2519/ (accessed August 23, 2023). Older renditions of the website are archived on the Internet Archive Wayback Machine at https://web.archive.org/web/2021*/http://www.2519.net (accessed July 9, 2022).

13 See "Banthuek Hok Tula" บันทึก 6 ตุลา ("Documentation of October 6"), https://doct6.com/ (accessed July 9, 2023). The main originators of the "Documentation of October 6" web archive were survivors of the massacre and historian Thongchai Winichakul; the archive's manager is political scientist Puangthong Pawakapan; and the technical team and curators for accompanying digital as well as in-person exhibitions is the team from the publishers Fa Diew Kan (Same Sky Press).

14 The websites mentioned the "Documentation of October 6" and development of the website and Facebook page online. See Sunthornchatwarawat and Photisan 2020.

15 See the "Documentation of October 6" Facebook page, https://www.facebook.com/6tula2519/ (accessed July 8, 2023).

16 These video clips belong to the "Documentation of October 6" website, which interviewed persons related to the massacre victims. These clips were uploaded and stored on YouTube. See "Banthuek Hok Tula" บันทึก 6 ตุลา ("Documentation of October 6"), YouTube, https:// www.youtube.com/channel/UCAkq-Z3kRRSUc8Mvmgzlu3Q/videos (accessed July 8, 2023).

17 "Banthuek Hok Tula" บันทึก 6 ตุลา ("Documentation of October 6"), https://doct6.com/ (accessed July, 8, 2023).

18 See Princess Maha Chakri Sirindhorn Anthropology Center (Public Organization), SAC catalog online, http://202.29.72.53/record_page1.php?id=21263 (accessed March 9, 2019). The new website may be accessed at http://119.59.99.174/~net2519/ (accessed August 23, 2023).

19 See Phoothong and Sangkara 2012. However, the YouTube account was hacked in 2021 and is now temporarily housed at https://drive.google.com/file/d/1EJOONyfmhJbPNolQUpyyet KOKv7xfM2W/view?usp=sharing (granted access by permission of filmmakers).

20 See Banthuek Hok Tula บันทึก 6 ตุลา, YouTube video, uploaded by @user-jf6xt5il3v, 2017, https://www.youtube.com/channel/UCAkq-Z3kRRSUc8Mvmgzlu3Q/videos.

21 See "DuaiKhwam Napthue" ด้วยความนับถือ ("Respecfully Yours"), YouTube video, 23:35, uploaded by Banthuek Hok Tula, 2018, https://www.youtube.com/watch?v=ig2DCytG8_Y; "SongPhinong" สองพี่น้อง ("The Two Brothers"), YouTube video, 20:21, uploaded by Banthuek Hok Tula, 2018, https://www.youtube.com/watch?v=KbQ9817ZZlI.

22 See "Kon Fa Sang" ก่อนฟ้าสาง ("Dawn of the New Day"), YouTube video, 30:52, uploaded by Banthuek Hok Tula, 2022, https://www.youtube.com/watch?v=ocrHyePnqXc.

References

Appadurai, Arjun. 1996. *Modernity At Large: Cultural Dimensions of Globalization*. Minneapolis: University of Minnesota Press.

Baumgartel, Tilman. 2012. "Imagined Communities, Imagined Worlds: Independent Film from Southeast Asia in the Global Mediascape." In *Southeast Asian Independent Cinema*, edited by Tilman Baumgartel, 21–31. Hong Kong: Hong Kong University Press.

Bergin, Bob. 2016. "Defeating an Insurgency—the Thai Effort against the Communist Party of Thailand, 1965–ca. 1982." *Studies in Intelligence* 60, no. 2: 44–68. https://doct6.com/wp-content/uploads/2019/10/Bergin-Defeating-Insurgency.pdf.

Bosch, Tanja E. 2016. "Memory Studies: A Brief Concept Paper." Working paper, Media, Conflict, and DEMocratisation, University of Leeds, January.

Bowie, Katherine. 1997. *Rituals of National Loyalty: An Anthropology of the State and Village Scout Movement in Thailand*. New York: Columbia University Press.

Carten, Rodney G. S. 2006. "Of Things Said and Unsaid: Power, Archival Silences, and Power in Silence." *Archivaria*, no. 61: 215–33.

Foucault, Michel. 1977. *Language, Counter-memory, Practice*. Edited by Donald F. Bouchard. Ithaca, NY: Cornell University Press.

Fuhs, Kristen. 2014. "The Legal Trial and/in Documentary Film." *Cultural Studies* 28, no. 5–6: 781–808.

Haberkorn, Tyrell. 2008. "Notes toward Marginal, Unrealized, and Incomplete Histories." *Stance: The Thai Feminist Review*, no. 2: 188–96.

Haberkorn, Tyrell. 2011. *Revolution Interrupted Farmers, Students, Law, and Violence in Northern Thailand*. Madison: University of Wisconsin Press.

Haberkorn, Tyrell. 2013. "Tracing an Uneven History: Notes on Sources and Trajectories of Thai State Violence." *Asian Journal of Peacebuilding* 1, no. 1: 109–16.

Haberkorn, Tyrell. 2015. "The Hidden Transcript of Amnesty: The 6 October 1976 Massacre and Coup in Thailand." *Critical Asian Studies* 47, no. 1: 44–68.

Halbwachs, Maurice. 1950. *The Collective Memory*. Translated by Francis J. Ditter Jr. and Vida Yazdi Ditter. New York: Harper.

Hunt, Mathew. 2020. *Thai Cinema Uncensored*. Thailand: Silkworm Books.

Impunity Watch. "Asia Exchange Report: 'Memory for Change': Memorialisation as a Tool for Transitional Justice." Utretcht, Netherlands: Impunity Watch, 2015. https://www.impunity watch.org/wp-content/uploads/2022/08/Report_Memory_for_Change_Memorialisation _Tool_2015_eng-1.pdf.

Jory, Patrick. 2000. "Books and the Nation: The Making of Thailand's National Library." *Journal of Southeast Asian Studies* 31, no. 2: 351–73.

Kaeosuk, Suwapha. 1996. "Botrian chak prawattisat thi lai khon yak luem" บทเรียนจากประ วัติศาสตร์ที่หลายคนอยากลืม ("Lessons from History Which Many Want to Forget"). *Sarakadee Magazine* 12, no. 140: 86–112.

kaewmala (@Thai_Talk). 2020. "There's an exhibition entitled #แขวน ('Hanging') at Thammasat Thaprachan campus." Twitter, October 6, 11:22 a.m. https://mobile.twitter.com/Thai _Talk/status/1313333848038465537.

Kongkirati, Prajak. 2005. *Lae laew khwam-khluean-wai ko prakot: Kan-mueang watthanatham khong nak-sueksa lae panyachon khon sip si tula* และแล้วความเคลื่อนไหวก็ปรากฏ: การเมือง วัฒนธรรมของนักศึกษาและปัญญาชนก่อน*14*ตุลา (*And Then There Were Movements: Cultural Politics of Students and Intellectuals before October 14, 1973*). Bangkok: Thammasat University Press.

Kongkirati, Prajak. 2015. *Kan mueang watthanatham Thai wa duew: Khamsongcham/watha-karm/amnat* การเมืองวัฒนธรรมไทยว่าด้วยความทรงจ/วาทกรรม/อำนาจ (*Thai Cultural Politics: Memory/ Discourse/Power*). Nonthaburi, Thailand: Fa Diew Kan (Same Sky Press).

Kongkirati, Prajak. 2016: "Kan lot thon khwam pen manut phuenthi thang sinlatham lae khwamrunraeng: Chak 'kha khommionit mai bap' thueng 'kamchat siannamphaendin'" การลดทอนความเป็นมนุษย์พื้นที่ทางศีลธรรมและความรุนแรงจาก "ฆ่าคอมมิวนิสต์ไม่บาป" ถึง "กำจัดเสี้ยนหนาม แผ่นดิน" ("Dehumanization and Moral and Violence Space: From 'Killing Communist Is No Sin' to 'Get Rid of Enemy of State'"). *FaDiewKan (Same Sky)* 14, no. 2: 39–76.

Lertchoosakul, Kanokrat. 2012. "The Rise of the Octobrists: Power and Conflict among Former Left-Wing Student Activists in Contemporary Thai Politics." PhD diss., London School of Economics and Political Science.

Lertchoosakul, Kanokrat. 2013. "Kan ruefuen lae kankorang sangtua khong khwam pen khon duean tula: Chak nak sueksa faisai phu phaipae su khon duean tula-nak tosu phuea prachathippatai haeng thotsawat 2510" การรื้อ ฟื้นและการก่อร่างสร้างตัวของความเป็น "คนเดือน ตุลา":จากนักศึกษาฝ่ายซ้ายผู้พ่ายแพ้สู่คนเดือนตุลานักต่อสู้เพื่อประชาธิปไตยแห่งทศวรรษ 2510 ("Restoration and Rebuilding of Being an 'October Person': From Lost Leftist Students to October Democracy Fighters of the Decade 1967–77"). *FaDiewKan (Same Sky)* 11, no. 2: 133–77.

Medina, José. 2011. "Toward a Foucaultian Epistemology of Resistance: Counter-memory, Epistemic Friction, and Guerrilla Pluralism." *Foucault Studies*, no. 12: 9–35.

Morell, David, and Samudavanija Chai-anan. 1981. *Political Conflict in Thailand: Reform, Reaction, Revolution*. Cambridge, MA: Oelgeschlager, Gunn, and Hain.

Morris, Rosalind. 1998. "Surviving Pleasure at the Periphery: Chiangmai and the Photographies of Political Trauma in Thailand, 1976–1992." *Public Culture* 10, no. 2: 341–70.

Nora, Pierre. 1989. "Between Memory and History: Les lieux de mémoire." *Representations*, no. 26: 7–24.

Pawakapan, Paungthong. 2019. "Bot rien jak krongkarn banteuk pawattisat hok tula" บทเรียนจากโครงการบันทึกประวัติศาสตร์ 6ตุลา ("Lessons from the Documentation of October 6, 1976 Project"). In *Ra-wang pritsana lae Satha Chaiwat Satha-Anan kapkarn mueng-manud-nai-sadtawad-thi-yi-sip-aed* ระหว่างปริศนาและศรัทธา ชัยวัฒน์ สถาอานันท์กับกาเมืองมนุษย์ในศตวรรษที่ *21* (*Between Enigma and Faith: Chaiwat Satha-Anan and Politics in the Twenty-First Century*), edited by Janjira Sombatpoonsiri and Prajak Kongkirati, 337–56. Bangkok: SayamPraritat.

Phoothong, Patporn. 2012. "The Work of 2011/2012 A.P.I. Fellows: Towards Peace and Reconciliation: Case Studies of Peace Museums in Japan and the Philippines." In *Engage! Public International Transforming Society*, 20–31. Nippon Foundation Fellowships for Asian Public Intellectuals.

Phoothong, Patporn. 2016–17. "Beong lang klamsongcham rai seang: Khamsongcham (tuk) tamhai ngeab klong pooh lae mae hatekarn hok tulaklom 2519" เบื้องหลังความทรงจำไร้เสียง:ความทรงจำ(ถูก)ทำให้เงียบของพ่อและแม่เหตุการณ์ 6 ตุลาคม 2519 ("Behind the Scenes: Suppressive Memories Silence of the October 6, 1976, Massacre"). *Thammasat University Archives*, no. 20: 5–14.

Phoothong, Patporn, and Saowanee Sangkara, dirs. 2012. *Silenced Memories*. YouTube video, 25:59. Uploaded by Nguyen Dong Thi, October 13, 2014. https://www.youtube.com/watch?v=JAbgvsDvkT4.

Rajala, Anne Lill. 2017. "Documentary Film, Truth, and Beyond: On the Problems of Documentary Film as Truth-Telling." BA thesis, Arcada University.

Rangan, Pooja. 2017. *Immediations: The Humanitarian Impulse in Documentary*. Durham, NC: Duke University Press.

Sandomirskaja, Irina. 2011. "Derrida on the Poetics and Politics of Witnessing." In *Rethinking Time: Essays on History, Memory and Representation*, edited by Hans Ruin and Andrus Ers, 247–55. Huddinge, Sweden: Södertörn University.

Santiwutthimethi, Wandi. 1996. "Kham haikan khong khon run 6 tula 19" คำให้การของคนรุ่น 6 ตุลา 19 ("Statement of the October 6, 1976, Generation"). *Sarakadee Magazine*, 86–112.

Satha-Anand, Chaiwat. 2007. "Reflections on October 6, 1976: Time and Violence." *Crossroads: An Interdisciplinary Journal of Southeast Asian Studies* 19, no. 1: 185–97.

Satha-Anand, Chaiwat. 2008. "The Trauma of October 6, 1976: Collective Amnesia, a Disowning of Guilt." *Bangkok Post*, February 26.

Schwartz, Joan M., and Terry Cook. 2002. "Archives, Records, and Power: From (Post Modern) Theory to (Archive) Performance." *Archival Science* 2: 171–85.

Streckfuss, David. 2011. *Truth on Trial in Thailand: Defamation, Treason, and Lèse-Majesté*. London: Routledge.

Sunthornchatwarawat, Wirapong, and Kowit Photisan. 2020. "Chak Paungthong Pawaka-pan Thengthongchai Winit Chakun: Hok tula khutkhaui nitirat" จากพวงทอง ภวัครพันธุ์ถึงธงชัย วินิจจะกูล: 6ตุลาฯ การขุดคุ้ยนิติรัฐ ("From Paungthong Pawakapan to Thongchai Winichakul: October 6 Excavating Jurisprudence"). *Way Magazine*, February 24. https://waymagazine .org/from-puangthong-to-thongchai/.

Tangwisutijit, Nantiya, and Subhatra Bhumiprabhas. 2002. "Website Sheds Light on Oct 6 Massacre." *Nation*, September 7. Archived at https://db.sac.or.th/clipping/th/news/read /254519627 (accessed 9 July 2023).

Taylor, Diana. 2003. *The Archive and the Repertoire: Performing Cultural Memory in the Americas*. Durham, NC: Duke University Press.

Thai Archive Association. 2005. "Sampat phiset Eji Murashima 'Ekkasan jotmaihet Thaidee kwa yeepun'" สัมภาษณ์พิเศษ เออิจิ มูราชิมา "เอกสารจดหมายเหตุไทยดีกว่าญี่ปุ่น ("Special Inter-view with Eiji Murashima: Thai Archival Documents Are Better than Japan"). *Thai Archive Newsletter* 2, no. 1: 34–38. https://www.thaiarchives.org/wp-content/uploads/2017/05/02.pdf.

Thongsinwatee, Premyuda. 2019. "Kan cheungching pheunthee haeng khwam songcham Goraneesuksa phap tai haet karn hok tulakom songhanunggao" การช่วงชิงพื้นที่แห่งความทรงจำ กรณีศึกษาภาพถ่ายเหตุการณ์ 6 ตุลาคม 2519 ("The Contention for Memorial Spaces in Memory of the October 6, 1976, Massacre: A Case Study in Photography"). Bachelor's degree independent study, Silpakorn University. http://www.sure.su.ac.th/xmlui/handle/123456789/15270.

Ungpakorn, Puey. 1977. "Violence and Military Coup in Thailand." *Bulletin of Concerned Asian Scholars* 9, no. 3: 4–64.

Ungpakorn, Ji, and Suthachai Yimprasert. 2001. *Achayakam rat nai wikrittakan plianplaeng, 25 pi 6 Tulakhom 2544* อาชญากรรมรัฐ ในวิกฤตการเปลี่ยนแปลง (*State Crime in a Crisis of Change, Twenty-Five Years, October 6, 2001*). Bangkok: Khanakammakan Rap Khawmoon Læ Seup Phayan Heitkan 6 Tulakom 2519 คณะกรรมการรับข้อมูลและสืบพยานเหตุการณ์ 6 ตุลาคม 2519 (October 6, 1976, Fact-Finding and Witness Interviewing Committee).

Utsuma, Sema. 1977. *They Will Never Forget*. Tokyo: Pacific Asia Resource Center. 35mm, 35 min.

Winichakul, Thongchai. 2001. "We Do Not Forget the Sixth of October: The 1996 Com-memoration of the October 1976 Massacre in Bangkok." Paper presented at the workshop "Imagining the Past, Remembering the Future," Cebu, Philippines, March 8–10.

Winichakul, Thongchai. 2011–12. "Kamnoet ho jot Maihet Thammasat kap phak Khommionit Haeng prathet Thai" กำเนิดหอจดหมายเหตุธรรมศาสตร์กับพรรคคอมมิวนิสต์แห่งประเทศไทย ("The Birth of the Thammasat University Archive and Communist Party in Thailand"). *Thammasat University Archives Bulletin* 5: 8–25.

Winichakul, Thongchai. 2015. *Hok tula luem mai dai cham mai long* 6 ตุลา ลืมไม่ได้ จำไม่ลง (*October 6, Cannot Forget, Cannot Remember*). Nonthaburi, Thailand: Fa Diew Kan (Same Sky Press).

Winichakul, Thongchai. 2016. *Tam ha luk chotcham lae wang duai khwam ngiap* ตามหาลูก จดจำและหวังด้วยความเงียบ (*Finding Memories of the Child and Hoping with Silence*). Forty Years of Memory of the October 6, 1976 Massacre. *Matichon Weekly*, September 18. https://www.matichonweekly.com/column/article_8096 (accessed July 7, 2023).

Winichakul, Thongchai. 2020. *Moments of Silence: The Unforgetting of the October 6, 1976, Massacre in Bangkok*. Honolulu: University of Hawai'i Press.

Zackari, Karin Hongsaton. 2020. "Framing the Subjects: Human Rights and Photography in Contemporary Thai History." PhD diss., Lund University.

Contributors

Juyeon Bae is a research associate professor at the Critical Global Studies Institutes, Sogang University, South Korea. She is also an executive committee member at Seoul International Women's Film Festival. She earned her doctoral degree from the Department of Culture, Film, and Media Studies at the University of Nottingham. Her PhD thesis examined the representation of Asian migrants such as the Korean diaspora, North Korean defectors, and labor/marriage migrants in contemporary Korean cinema. Her research interests include women's memory writing, migration within Asia, genocide in postcolonial Asia, nationalism, and transnationalism in East Asian cinema.

Peter J. Bloom is professor of film and media studies at the University of California, Santa Barbara. His work focuses on French and British media from a postcolonial and global perspective, with an emphasis on West Africa and Southeast Asia. Most recently, his work has addressed the contemporary effects of colonial history, with an emphasis on digital media formats and contexts. Media archaeology, radio studies, African media studies, and the politics of media culture are themes that he addresses through archival and ethnographic

positions 31:4   DOI 10.1215/10679847-10714324

research. He has taught graduate courses on semiotics, textual analysis, international radio studies, and cultural studies. Currently, he is completing a coedited volume entitled *Inadequacies of Perception* and a book length manuscript entitled *Radio-Cinema Modernity: The Catoptrics of Empire, Counterinsurgency, and Pan Africanism*. More information about his work can be found at https://www.filmandmedia.ucsb.edu/person/peter-bloom/.

Malinee Khumsupa is an assistant professor and head of the School of Politics and Government, Faculty of Political Science and Public Administration, Chiang Mai University, Thailand. She is the author of a book titled *The Hidden Meaning of the Democracy Monument of Thailand* (2006). She obtained a PhD in Thai Studies from Chulalongkorn University in 2011. Her research focuses on postcolonialism in Southeast Asia, cultural studies, film studies, and politics in the virtual sphere, including youth politics and K-pop fan culture. She is the author of "Divided Virtual Politics: Micro-Counter Transcripts" (2018) and "The Lens of Micro Counter-Public in Authoritarian Thailand, 2006–2016" (2021). She is the coauthor, along with Sudarat Musikawong, of the following articles: "Counter-Memory: Replaying Political Violence in Thai Digital Cinema" (2016), "Notes on Camp Films in Authoritarian Thailand" (2019), and "Film Is Dangerous: Ten Years of Censorship in Thailand's Cinema, 2010–2020" (2022).

Chung-kang Kim is an associate professor in the Department of Theater and Film at Hanyang University. She completed her PhD at the University of Illinois, Urbana-Champaign, in 2010 with a focus on Korean popular film, culture, and history. She is editor of *ReFocus: The Films of Kim Ki-young* (2023) and is working on a book manuscript entitled *Attractive Nation: Politics of Popular Culture in Trans-War Korea (1937–1971)*. She is coauthor of *Rediscovery of Korean Cinema* (2019) and *Queer Korea* (2020). Her published articles include "Skin-Deep? The Politics of Black Korean Identity in Post-1945 Korean Literature and Film," in the *Journal of Literature and Film* (2014); "Nation, Subculture, and Queer Representation: The Film Male Kisaeng and the Politics of Gender and Sexuality in 1960s South Korea," in the *Journal of the History of Sexuality* (2015); and "Monstrous Science: *The Great Monster Yong'gari* (1967) and Cold War Science in 1960s South Korea," in the *Journal of Korean Studies* (2018).

Han Sang Kim is associate professor and chair of the Department of Sociology at Ajou University, Suwon, South Korea. His teaching interests include visual sociology, qualitative methods, and the sociology of film and media. He has conducted research and written on the themes of film archives, the ethics of photographic representation, post/colonial visual culture, and mobilities. His most recent book is *Cine-Mobility: Twentieth-Century Transformations in Korea's Film and Transportation* (2022), which traces the association between cinematic visuality and modern transportation mobility in forming a modern subjectivity in twentieth-century Korea. He has been concurrently working on his second book project based on his doctoral dissertation on US film propaganda activities toward South Korea from 1945 through 1972, putting on a self-reflexive critique of information-oriented archival approaches to film materials and expanding the project onto a methodological exploration. He has published essays in the *Journal of Asian Studies*, *Journal of Korean Studies*, *Inter-Asian Cultural Studies*, and several other journals in Korean. He was the inaugural programmer of the Cinematheque KOFA at the Korean Film Archive in Seoul. He taught at the University of California, San Diego; Boston University; and Rice University during his postdoctoral years.

Sudarat Musikawong is an associate professor at the Institute for Population and Social Research at Mahidol University in Thailand. She received her PhD in sociology from the University of California, Santa Cruz, and her BA in interdisciplinary studies from the University of California, Santa Barbara. She positions her investigations within cultural-political sociology and ethnographic research. Her publications include "Notes on Camp Films in Authoritarian Thailand" (with Malinee Khumsupa), in the *Southeast Asia Research Journal* (2019), as well as "Gendered Casualties: Thai Memoirs in Activism," in *Meridians: feminism, race, transnationalism* (2013); "Mourning State Celebrations: Amnesic Iterations of Political Violence in Thailand," in *Identities: Global Studies in Culture and Power* (2010); "Between Celebration and Mourning," in *Toward a Sociology of the Trace* (2010); and "Art for October Thai Cold War State Violence in Trauma Art," in *positions: east asia critique* (2010).

Sandeep Ray is a writer, visual artist, and historian. He is associate professor and head of the School of Media Languages and Cultures at the University of Nottingham Malaysia. Sandeep received his BA from Hampshire College, his MA from the University of Michigan, and his PhD from the National University of Singapore. He taught at the University of Wisconsin, Rice University, and the Singapore University of Technology and Design prior to his current position. Sandeep's research emphasizes connections between media and history. He has related interests in nonfiction or "documentary" film, the novel, memoirs, newsreels, old media, global refugee crises, and transnational approaches to Asian studies. His 2021 monograph *Celluloid Colony* explores ethnography in Dutch propagandistic film in colonial Indonesia and was a finalist for the EuroSEAS 2022 Social Science Book Prize. Sandeep's documentary films have been reviewed in the *American Anthropologist* and in *Visual Anthropology* and have screened at many festivals and film forums, including the Flaherty Seminar, the Margaret Mead Festival, the Whitney and Getty Museums, and the Films Division of India.

Keep up to date on new scholarship

Issue alerts are a great way to stay current on all the cutting-edge scholarship from your favorite Duke University Press journals. This free service delivers tables of contents directly to your inbox, informing you of the latest groundbreaking work as soon as it is published.

To sign up for issue alerts:

1. Visit **dukeu.press/register** and register for an account. You do not need to provide a customer number.

2. After registering, visit **dukeu.press/alerts**.

3. Go to "Latest Issue Alerts" and click on "Add Alerts."

4. Select as many publications as you would like from the pop-up window and click "Add Alerts."

read.dukeupress.edu/journals